Westfield Memorial Library
Westfield, New Jersey

W9-CJC-919

APACHE DAWN

ALSO BY DAMIEN LEWIS

Operation Certain Death

Desert Claw

Bloody Heroes

Cobra Gold

Westfield Memorial Library
Westfield, New Jersey

APACHE DAWN

ALWAYS OUTNUMBERED, NEVER OUTGUNNED

Damien Lewis

St. Martin's Press ⚏ New York

APACHE DAWN. Copyright © 2008 by Damien Lewis. All rights reserved. Printed in the United States of America. For information, address St. Martin's Press, 175 Fifth Avenue, New York, N.Y. 10010.

www.stmartins.com

Library of Congress Cataloging-in-Publication Data

Lewis, Damien.
    Apache dawn : always outnumbered, never outgunned / Damien Lewis. — 1st U.S. ed.
        p. cm.
    Originally published: London : Sphere. 2008.
    ISBN 978-0-312-59301-8
    1. Afghan War, 2001- —Aerial operations, British. 2. Apache (Attack helicopter) 3. Great Britain. Army. Air Corps. I. Title.
DS371.412.L49 2009
958.104'7—dc22

                                                      2009024026

First published in Great Britain by Sphere, an imprint of
Little, Brown Book Group

First U.S. Edition: December 2009

10 9 8 7 6 5 4 3 2 1

In memory of Vince Hussell, gone but not forgotten

Once an Apache pilot, always an Apache pilot

'Nothing is impossible'

> The motto of the Second World War Glider Pilots
> Regiment, the forerunner of the Army Air Corps

'They have earned their spurs in the heat, dust and fire of combat, in the face of challenging and complex operations and often in the face of great danger'

> Air Chief Marshal Sir Jock Stirrup, on the
> Apache operations in Afghanistan, 2007

'Never in the field of human conflict has so much been fired at so many by so few'

> Apache pilot Steve James, commenting on
> Operation Chakush

'Woe to he who is seen'

> Motto of 664 Squadron, Army Air Corps

UZBEKISTAN

KYRGYZSTAN

CHINA

TAJIKISTAN

TURKMENISTAN

■ Dushanbe

JOWZJAN   BALKH   KONDUZ   Taloqan   ● Feyzabad
Sheberghan ●   Mazar-e   Konduz
               Sharif●   TAKHAR   BADAKHSHAN
IRAN   Sar-e Pol ●   Samangan ● Baghlan ●
           Meymaneh ● SAR-E   SAMANGAN   BAGHLAN
              FARYAB   POL   Mahmud-e   2
        BADGHIS   Raq
              ● Qal'eh-ye Now   BAMIAN   Charika ● 9 Mehtarlam Asadabad
        Herat   Bamian ● 7 8 1
                                         6   Islamabad
HERAT   GHOWR   Chaghcharan ●   Kowt-e ● 5 ●Kabul   ■ INDIA
                                  Ashrow 3 Jalalabad
              ORUZGAN   ● Baraki
                      Ghazni ● ● Gardeyz
                      GHAZNI   Zareh   4
              Tarin   Sharan
              Kowt
Farah ● FARAH   Qalat
                  ZABOL
        Lashkar   PAKTIKA
        Gah ●   Kandahar ●
Zaranj ●
NIMRUZ   KANDAHAR   1. LAGHMAN
                                 2. KONAR
        HELMAND   3. NANGARHAR
                                 4. PAKTIA
                    PAKISTAN   5. LOWGAR
                                 6. VARDAK
                                 7. PARVAN
                                 8. KABUL
                                 9. KAPIGA
IRAN   ■ National capital
                                 ● Provincial capital

                                 200 kms
                                 100 miles

Afghanistan

Contents

Acknowledgements

In keeping with the traditions of the Army Air Corps, who value teamwork and *esprit de corps* so highly, this book has truly been a team effort and I extend my gratitude to all those who have helped make it possible. Very special thanks are due to the soldiers of the Corps who freely gave up their time to be interviewed or to discuss with me, or otherwise communicate with me, about this book. This includes, but is not limited to, Steve, Barry, Tim, Alex, Colin, Jamie, Ben and Dean. Special thanks also to Lieutenant Colonel Jon Bryant, Commanding Officer of 3 Regiment, Army Air Corps, for pulling out all the stops to help make this book possible. Thanks are due to the ground troops who helped me with the writing of this book, and who are named in the body of the book itself, and in particular Sergeant Paul 'Bommer' Grahame of the Light Dragoons. I extend my thanks to Lieutenant Colonel Justin Holt, Royal Marines, for assisting me with the story. Thanks also to Major Keith W. Scott, RMP, and David Beamont, for help in making this book come to fruition.

Thanks to Alan 'Traff' Trafford, a devourer of manuscripts – your comments were hugely useful. Thanks, too, to Steve 'Farmer' Clarke for the beer and the comments on the early drafts. Thanks in particular to N. P. O'Hern for the excellent comments early on. And special thanks, as ever, to my father David Lewis for the comments on early drafts.

Special thanks also to Adam Strange, Zoë Gullen, Kirsteen Astor and all at Little, Brown, who from the very first saw the potential in this book and of the Apache Attack Regiment's story as a whole, and shared in my belief, and that of the soldiers, that it needed to be told.

Finally, special thanks to Eva and the lads, as ever, for the patience.

A Note of Thanks from the Apache Aircrews, 662 Squadron, Army Air Corps

The Apache aircrew whose stories feature in this book would like to pay special tribute to the services of the men and women who kept their machines flying during their one-hundred day tour in Afghanistan, and to the men and women who support the combat operations of the Apache attack squadrons in so many different ways.

This includes, but is not limited to: the men of the Royal Electrical Mechanical Engineers who kept the Apaches serviceable while in theatre, working all hours and providing a service second to none; the ground crews of the Apache attack squadrons, whose tireless work refuelling and re-arming the Apaches during the intense heat of combat won battles and saved lives; the medical staff of the Camp Bastion Field Hospital, who laboured tirelessly and with consummate courage to save the lives of injured soldiers air-lifted out of the field of battle; and the RAF aircrew of the Chinooks who flew into battle time after time alongside the Apaches, in order to evacuate wounded British and Allied troops. Special thanks also to Aviation Training International (ATIL), who design, operate and constantly strive to improve the Apache flight simulators, without which the Apache training programmes would be so much the poorer.

Very special thanks also to the unsung heroes – the wives, partners and families who sacrifice so much in so many different ways to support us in what we do: often just being there and lending an ear is worth more than words can ever express. To us this is priceless. And finally, thanks to the charity Help for Heroes for all the work they do in assisting wounded comrades and raising the profile of our armed forces.

A percentage of the royalties earned from this book will be donated to Help for Heroes.

Author's Note

This is the story of one flight of two Apache attack helicopters in action in Afghanistan during their baptism of fire in the summer of 2007. It tells of the actions of the four men who flew those Apaches during a tour that lasted one hundred days. I am grateful to two pilots in particular, Baz and Steve, for sharing their stories from that tour. I am also grateful to their younger front-seaters, Tim and Alex, who were happy for their stories to be told alongside those of their more experienced co-pilots. This book is their story, and it is told as far as is possible in their own words.

What each of the Apache pilots would stress is that theirs is an archetypal tale, one that illustrates the wider heroism and valour, and the shared challenges that all Army Air Corps Apache pilots experienced during their first months of combat operations in Afghanistan. The year 2007 was the Golden Jubilee of the Army Air Corps, in which the Corps celebrated a long and distinguished combat history stretching back to the D-Day landings and before. The record of the Apache regiments in 2007 did much to further that tradition, and this book could arguably have been written about any of the Apache aircrew who served, their stories equally replete with drama and daring.

The actions depicted in the Prologue of this book, during the Jugroom Fort rescue mission, were carried out by the men of 656 Squadron, Army Air Corps. The four men of the flight featured in the main body of this book are from 662 Squadron, Army Air Corps. I have included the Jugroom story because it is a high profile tale of the heroics demonstrated by the Apache attack helicopter pilots during their first months in combat, and because the men of the Apache Attack Regiments as a whole wanted that story to be told. It is a tale of extraordinary daring beyond the call of duty, but it is by no means unique – as I hope the entirety of this book demonstrates.

Wherever possible, the British Apache attack helicopter regiments maintain a policy akin to that of UK Special Forces and do not make public the names of their aircrews. This is to minimise the danger of reprisals against Apache pilots or their families in the UK or elsewhere. Accordingly, I have used pseudonyms for the Apache pilots portrayed, unless their names have already appeared in the press or the pilots themselves asked me to do otherwise. The faces of the Apache pilots in the photos used in this book have been redacted for the same reasons.

All other aspects of this story remain unchanged. Accounts of the actions that took place are based upon interviews with the soldiers and airmen. Conversations between soldiers have been recreated from the memories of those involved and from diaries written by those soldiers at the time of their deployment. I have endeavoured to report accurately and truthfully the events portrayed. However, inquests have not yet been held into some of the deaths reported in these pages. Any insult or injury to any of the parties described or quoted herein, or to their families, is unintentional. I will be happy to correct any inaccuracies in later editions.

The Ministry of Defence requested that a number of points of operational security sensitivity were not published in this book. Some units of British and Allied soldiers have not been identified, again at the request of the MOD. In addition, any contributions or statements of a political nature herein are those of the author and the author alone and they do not represent or reflect those of the Secretary of State for Defence.

The 1st Battalion Worcestershire and Sherwood Foresters was renamed 2nd Battalion The Mercian Regiment (Worcesters and Foresters) in August 2007, as 662 Squadron's deployment was drawing to a close. *Ugly* was the call-sign for all four Apache attack helicopter flights of 662 Squadron during their summer 2007 Afghan deployment. The official name of the flight featured in this book was Five Flight.

Prologue
WILDMAN

15 January 2007, Helmand Province, Afghanistan

They called themselves the wildmen. The lead Apache of the flight was call-sign *Wildman Five Zero*, its wing aircraft *Wildman Five One*. Their credo was simple: to do whatever it took to get the job done. Their job was to fly their ugly, killer aircraft in support of British ground troops, and to kill the enemy wherever they found them. And, like true wildmen, they would do whatever it took to get the job done.

That morning's attack had started with a briefing by torchlight in the dead hours of darkness, out in the empty wastes of the Afghan desert. The tough yet softly spoken soldiers of the Royal Marines, Zulu Company, 45 Commando, had gathered around their maps, their head-torches casting a soft halo of light as they conferred in whispers.

The assault on the enemy stronghold of the Jugroom Fort had been long in the planning, and for weeks the Brigade's Recce Force had kept eyes on the enemy position, gathering vital intelligence in preparation for the attack. H-hour was 0600 hours, barely thirty minutes away. Then they would hit them hard.

The aptly named Operation Glacier was the last thing that the enemy would be expecting. It was the bitter cold of an Afghan winter, the January skies threatening snow. There were unwritten rules as to how the fighting went here, or at least there had been. The spring and summer were the shooting season, the winter months too cold and miserable for any soldier to be out and about spoiling for a fight.

But the men of 45 Commando were about to bust those rules wide open. They were attacking during the closed season, so as to prevent the enemy from rearming and regrouping during the winter months. And they were doing so against a target that the enemy had presumed was an impregnable stronghold, and so off limits to such a threat.

Jugroom Fort – a high-walled fortress ringed by watchtowers – is situated in Garmsir, to the extreme south of Helmand Province. This was the enemy's true heartland, and they thought their forces invincible here. The Commando's aim was to take the enemy by complete and utter surprise, the shock of the assault giving them a much-needed advantage.

In Garmsir, enemy territory consists of some twenty square kilometres – land that at one time would have been densely populated. Now it is a series of bombed-out, cratered buildings connected by a maze of tunnels, ditches and caves. The enemy have near-total freedom of movement within this area, being able to move fighters into firing positions without being spotted.

British forces are so familiar with the area that every ruined building, footpath, ditch and tree has a nickname or an objective name. Three Walls, Snowdon, Taunton, Euro Disney – the names had evolved through a mixture of simple observation of a shape or a feature, and the ever-present British squaddies' humour.

The enemy were known to have heavy machine guns and multi-barrelled anti-aircraft weapons positioned in the Garmsir Box, as the entire territory is called.

Going into Garmsir was like going into the lion's den. But to the men of Zulu Company, 45 Commando, this was just another mission. Some forty-eight hours earlier, their ground convoy of Viking armoured vehicles had headed out of Camp Bastion, driving up via the vast and empty desert to the west. In so doing, they aimed to avoid detection by the enemy until the last possible moment before the attack.

That night they had lain up in start lines in the desert, on the opposite side of the Helmand River to the Jugroom Fort. With its massive mud-walled defences, the enemy were known to feel secure in there. This night would be no different, especially as the nearest British forces were some five kilometres away and on the far bank of the river.

At Garmsir the Helmand River is a kilometre or more across, its waters a mass of swirling currents and lurking sand banks. Crossing it poses a real obstacle to most military operations. But not to Operation Glacier. The Viking is a tracked, amphibious vehicle, and the attack was to be launched in the hours of darkness directly across the river.

At 0600 hours dead the Vikings' massive diesel engines coughed into life, and the convoy lurched forwards. Some two hundred crack Royal Marines crouched in the vehicles' rear compartments, as the two-compartment armoured vehicles churned through the open desert, each turn of their tracks bringing them closer to the coming battle.

The Vikings hit the river south-west of the target and barely slowed as they did so, their armoured hulks cleaving the icy waters and throwing out muddy waves of a coffee-like consistency. The convoy ploughed onwards, churning through the mud, sand and scrub of a series of flooded islands.

As the vehicles neared the far bank, the first salvos from the British guns sailed overhead and smashed into the enemy positions. Bang on schedule, mortar teams from 42 Commando had unleashed their 81mm rounds as a sharp wake-up call for the enemy.

The crump of the shells exploding in and around the mud-walled fortress sent shockwaves across the water, shattering the stillness of the barely nascent Afghan dawn. Reaching the far side of the Helmand River, the Vikings reared up, tilted over the river-bank and pulled away towards the fort walls, some five hundred metres up ahead.

The Vikings closed with the fort, an armoured wave sweeping forwards. For now, at least, their steel skins kept the soldiers crouched inside safe from the enemy guns. As they neared the target, each soldier checked his weapon one last time, making sure he had a round chambered and the safety flicked to 'off'. They had every reason to believe that the second they were out of those vehicles they would be under intense enemy fire.

Muzzle flashes sparked on the walls up ahead, as the enemy gathered their forces to repel the ground assault. From the Vikings' open turrets the gunners on the .50-calibre heavy machine guns answered fire with fire, the soldiers feeling the reassuring roar-growl of the heavy-calibre weapons reverberating through the armoured hulls of the vehicles. The .50-cal Browning was the weapon the enemy were said to fear most, and for good reason: its rounds can punch through both armour and walls as thick as those of the fort.

Just to the north of the fort there was a series of blinding flashes, as rocket-propelled grenades (RPGs) were fired from enemy positions hidden in thick woodland. The dirty brown smoke trails looped towards the advancing British forces, which were well within the RPG gunner's three-hundred-metre effective range.

Though armoured, the Viking is not invulnerable to a direct hit by an RPG, which has a high-explosive anti-tank (HEAT) warhead, designed to burn through all but the thickest armour.

That first grenade round barrelled in at its maximum velocity of 295 metres per second, smashing into the desert in front of the lead Viking, the explosion plastering it with dirt and shrapnel. A second and a third RPG bracketed the column of vehicles with fire, as the RPG gunners found their range and their aim.

The assault force needed to take those RPG gunners out, and fast. The Joint Terminal Attack Controller (JTAC) embedded with the assault force had been assigned a 'Widow' call-sign, just like every other JTAC in the Afghan theatre. His job was to liaise with the air power and artillery support, calling in fire onto enemy positions.

It was time to radio the pair of Apache helicopter gunships that were inbound overhead.

'Wildman Five Zero, this is Widow Seven Nine,' the JTAC yelled into his radio. 'Wildman Five Zero, Widow Seven Nine – do you copy?'

'Widow Seven Nine, this is Wildman. Go ahead,' came back Apache flight leader Captain Tom Owen's reply.

'*Wildman, Widow Seven Nine.* You are clear into the overhead. My locstat the column of Vikings; enemy forces with RPGs two hundred metres north-east of my position, in tree line. Call ready for talk on.'

'Visual your locstat, visual tree line. Ready for talk on.'

'Roger, the enemy are all up that dense woodland with RPGs. I need immediate suppressing fire now.'

'Roger. Will be attacking on a heading of 190 with 30mm, ten-round burst initially.'

'Happy with that. Call engaging.'

Rolling his Apache attack helicopter in to the attack, Tom flipped up the metal guard on his left-hand pistol grip control column, and pulled the trigger. Beneath the cockpit there was the familiar chunter of the cannon on the Apache's chin turret as it roared into life, spewing out a ten-round burst of 30mm high-explosive shells.

Seconds later the burst hit the tree line, bright flashes among the shadowed foliage showing where the 30mm rounds were blasting the position apart. Splintered branches flew in all directions as the pair of Apaches fired repeated twenty-round bursts. With the cannon fire pounding the wood land, there were a series of sharp secondary explosions as the enemy fighters' RPG rounds were ignited by the 30mm rounds.

Below the hunting Apaches the column of Vikings rolled to a halt. The men of 45 Commando bomb-burst out of the rear doors and charged for the massive slab of the fort's mud-built walls. Slapping a string of bar mines, detonation wire and fuses to the base of the structure, the men took cover and blocked their ears.

Seconds later each bar mine exploded with a deafening blast, and a series of man-sized breach holes were blown through the thick outer wall of the fort – the Royal Marines' entry points into the enemy's lair. But the British forces were taking murderous fire, which seemed to be coming from every patch of cover imaginable.

There were weapons aimed at them from the fort walls, from the wood line to the north and even from the bush and scrub in the direction from which the convoy had come. The men of 45 Commando were caught in a 360 degree box of enemy fire, and were being targeted by small arms, machineguns and more RPGs.

Under the relentless pounding of the enemy guns the Royal Marines suffered their first casualty. All of a sudden there were cries of 'Medic! Medic!' This was to be the first of several wounded soldiers rushed to the safety of the Vikings and evacuated from the battlefield during the first hour of Op Glacier.

The battle degenerated into a brutal, close-quarter firefight as young Royal Marines with fixed bayonets tried to force their way into the labyrinth of the fort. The enemy were giving no quarter. Using underground tunnels and rat-runs, their fighters were emerging to attack from all sides, including the rear, and the Marines were taking ferocious Taliban fire.

Widow Seven Nine, 45 Commando's JTAC, put an urgent call through to the British headquarters at Camp Bastion, requesting a casevac to pick up the wounded. Two men had gone down in the first minutes of the battle, and he feared they were going to take more casualties.

At the first ring of the field telephone at their Camp Bastion base, pilots and aircrew of the incident reaction team sprinted for the Ops Room, vaulting over the Hesco walling as they did so. Within minutes the Chinook aircrew were on the flight line and spinning up the aircraft's rotors, with a pair of Apache attack helicopters doing likewise.

Garmsir was a twenty-five minute flight south of Bastion. That should provide ample time for the ground forces to extract the wounded in the Vikings and establish a landing zone (LZ) where the casevac Chinook could put down in relative safety.

Once the Chinook and two Apache escorts were airborne, they headed low and fast away from Camp Bastion. The three aircraft hugged the contours of the empty desert so as to fox any 'dickers' – spies that might be watching their departure, and preparing to call ahead with their mobile phone to issue a warning to the enemy.

At a safe distance out, they power climbed to five thousand feet and set a course for Garmsir. *Garmsir.* It was a unique operating environment for the Apache aircrews, and one that almost always meant heavy action whenever they were deployed there.

The four Apache pilots knew that there was no 'normal' life on the ground in enemy territory, so the risk of hitting civilians was next to zero. And with every feature having its own objective name, the 'talk-on' to target was beautifully simple and quick.

From three miles out the scene from the Apache cockpits was unbelievable. Two massive plumes of black smoke were barrelling into the pale Afghan sky, marking out the location of the battle. There was tracer spewing forth from all sides, slamming into the desert and the fort walls, and ricocheting violently into the sky.

There were the flash and smoke plumes of RPGs firing from the enemy positions. There were fierce fires burning in the interior of the Jugroom Fort itself, fires that had been started by a 105mm artillery barrage during the initial assault. And across the river the British support weapons were pouring in fiery arcs of tracer, looping high above the water.

The radio traffic was hectic over the battlespace. On the ground, *Widow Seven Nine* was coordinating close air support from the two Apache attack helicopters, plus fire from the 105mm howitzers of the Royal Artillery and the Scimitar tanks of the Light Dragoons firing their 30mm cannons.

The pilot in the lead inbound Apache waited for the radio traffic to go quiet for a second, then jumped in.

'*Widow Seven Nine*, this is *Wildman Five Three*. Do you read me?'

'*Wildman Five Three*, *Widow Seven Nine*. You are loud and clear.'

'*Widow Seven Nine*, *Wildman*. Inbound flight of one Chinook casevac, two Apaches. ETA ten minutes. Standard loads; ninety minutes' playtime. Do you have LZ?'

'*Wildman*, *Widow Seven Nine*. Nearest hostiles – muzzle flashes from the eastern riverbank and fort. All friendlies are inside known locations. Affirm you need LZ, coordinates to follow.'

'Roger, happy friendlies. Awaiting confirmation LZ, plus ETA for the casualties.'

'Roger. Wait out.'

The aircrew waited to hear when the wounded soldiers were expected at the landing zone. It would take some time to extract them from the chaos of the battlefield, and get them to a location where the soldiers could clear a safe area for the casevac Chinook to land. The first responsibility of the Apache aircrew was to get the Chinook in and out with the wounded and safely en route for Camp Bastion.

Several seconds after the *Widow*'s 'wait out', the radio burst into life again. There was a rush of muffled voices off-mike, and then the *Widow* was talking. He was breathing hard. He'd clearly been running.

'*Wildman, Widow Seven Nine*. ETA at LZ twenty mins casevac.'

'Roger. Confirm, twenty mins at LZ.'

'There are now four wounded. Repeat, four wounded requiring casevac.'

The *Widow* paused for a second to catch his breath. As he did so, the deep rumbling of a .50-cal heavy machine gun could be heard in the background, amid the whine of incoming rounds.

'We have one T1 casualty . . .'

The *Widow* proceeded to list the status of the wounded: a T1 would have life-threatening injuries; a T3 was the least serious. A T4 meant dead, which took second priority after getting the wounded off the battlefield.

The pair of Apaches escorted the Chinook on to the makeshift LZ, one staying high to keep eyes on the enemy, one going in low to provide close support. The big twin-rotor helicopter descended in a storm of rotor-blown dust, its ramp coming down to collect the wounded.

The instant the rear wheels touched down, the marines rushed their wounded comrades into the aircraft's cavernous hold. After barely a minute on the ground the Chinook lifted off and set a course for Camp Bastion, flying low and fast away from the battlefield.

Some three hours into the ferocious firefight, the Vikings pulled back from the smoking walls of the Jugroom Fort under heavy fire. The soldiers of 45 Commando began to fall back towards the river.

Enemy resistance had been fearsome, yet the men of the Commando believed they had hit the enemy hard and given them a bloody nose.

It was only when the Vikings reached their original start lines, regrouping in the desert to the west of the Helmand River, that they realised that one of their number was unaccounted for. The radios went haywire as all units checked for any knowledge of the whereabouts of the missing man, Royal Marine Lance Corporal Mathew Ford.

'All call-signs, this is *Widow Seven Nine*. All call-signs: we have one man unaccounted for. I say again, we have an MIA, an MIA. MIA was last seen in the area of the front wall of the fort . . .'

All responses were negative and the horrible reality started to sink in that one of their number was missing in action (MIA). Lance Corporal Mathew Ford had led his section at the vanguard of the assault. He had last been seen in close-quarter combat at a breach in the main wall of the fort.

It is a given of British military operations that no man shall be left behind. In the chaos and red mist of battle, 45 Commando had broken that cardinal rule. There was no debate to be had: they were going back in to retrieve their missing comrade. Dead or alive, captured or still at liberty, they were not leaving their soldier behind.

The Commando's Regimental Sergeant Major, Colin Hearn, and the overall commander of Operation Glacier, Lieutenant Colonel Rob MaGowan, took charge of the situation. They asked for volunteers to remount the Vikings and return to the battlefield to retrieve the missing soldier. There was no shortage of men willing to do so.

Meanwhile, an unmanned aerial vehicle (UAV) – a pilotless drone – had been orbiting at ten thousand feet above Jugroom Fort, searching for any sign of Lance Corporal Ford. Using powerful infrared scanners, the RAF pilot remotely flying the UAV had spotted an unusual heat blob lying just outside the fort's walls.

Zooming in his daylight camera to maximum magnification, the distinctive uniform, helmet and body armour clearly showed him to be the Royal Marine. The coordinates of the figure, plus a description of his location, were radioed to all British air and ground units in the battlespace.

As the volunteer force reloaded their weapons in preparation for the coming rescue mission, there was a radio call from Tom Owen, pilot of the lead Apache orbiting above. Getting the Vikings back across the river and into battle would take time, he argued, time that the Lance Corporal could ill afford – if he was still alive.

Tom suggested an alternative rescue plan. It was far better to use the Apaches to fly a rescue force into the fort. The Apache was a robust and heavily armoured, yet agile, aircraft and they could be in and out of there within five minutes, all being well.

There was only one drawback: the Apache barely has room for the two pilots – a front- and a rear-seater – to squeeze into the cockpit, and certainly no space for passengers. The soldiers making up the rescue force would have to strap themselves onto the outside of the aircraft, perching perilously on its small stub wings.

Four men were chosen out of the host of volunteers for the maverick airborne mission. The mission was led by Captain Dave Rigg, a commando-trained Royal Engineer seconded to 45 Commando.

Despite thinking he was about to be thrown into a deliberate enemy ambush, Captain Rigg volunteered immediately to take part in the rescue. He knew he would be returning to face an aggressive and determined enemy, who were already alert to the company's presence and were very likely to anticipate their return to find Lance Corporal Ford.

He was joined by three other volunteers: Marine Gary Robinson, Marine Chris Fraser-Perry and the RSM himself, Colin Hearn, a man who believed in leading by example.

Moments after the pair of Apaches had touched down, the four men ran over to the aircraft, ducking low and shielding their faces from the sandstorm kicked up by the rotors. The Apaches powered down, and the aircrew hurriedly explained to the four soldiers exactly what they had in mind.

Each aircraft would carry one soldier perched on each of its stub wings as they flew back in to rescue the Royal Marine. As the two aircraft headed into the fort, a third Apache, recently released from the casevac mission, would provide top cover, putting fire on to enemy positions wherever it was required.

With the element of surprise, plus the confusion, Tom reckoned they could be in and out in a matter of minutes with the missing soldier strapped to one of the helicopter's stub wings alongside the soldier-passenger. At least, that was the theory.

The Apache aircrew had learned about this strap-on rescue method during training in the UK. It was an emergency procedure for rescuing downed airmen. But it had never been tested for real by British Apaches, and certainly not in a combat situation.

U-shaped steel bars are fitted to the Apache's sides, providing grab-handles to help aircrew move in and out of the cockpit. Once the Royal Marines had clambered on to the stub wings, each hooked himself on to the grab-handles using a couple of climbing karabiners and a strop – a tough cargo-strength strap – to do so.

The Apaches spun up to power, kicking a blinding dust storm into the eyes of their strapped-on passengers. The four soldiers sat facing forwards, each carrying with him an assault rifle, webbing kit, spare magazines for his weapon, and grenades. Each was positioned more-or-less opposite the Apache's rear cockpit, with his head bang in front of the gaping air intake of the screaming Rolls-Royce turbine. The noise was deafening.

It was 1115 hours – more than five hours after Op Glacier had begun – when the pair of Apaches lifted off from the desert, straining to get airborne with the extra load. Buffeted by the downwash of the rotors, the four soldiers felt the Apaches climbing gently, as the pilots eased their aircraft to a hundred feet of altitude.

Setting a course eastwards for the river and Jugroom Fort, the two Apaches nosed ahead at forty knots airspeed. Any faster and the wind-chill factor would freeze the passengers on the stub wings.

Captain Tom Owen's Apache, *Wildman Five Zero*, led the airborne assault, carrying RSM Colin Hearn and Marine Garry Robinson strapped to his machine's stub wings. His wing aircraft, *Wildman Five One*, piloted by Staff Sergeant Karl Bruce, carried

Captain Dave Rigg and Marine Chris Fraser-Perry back into battle.

At first the flight was like the rollercoaster ride from hell. The two aircraft swooped down to hug the smooth contours of the river, their rotors whipping up a storm of spray as they did so. By sticking to the cover of the watercourse, the aircraft sought to hide their approach from the enemy guns for as long as possible.

But as the pair of Apaches thundered up over the far riverbank, things got worse. There were muzzle flashes sparking out of the smoke-clouded fort, and bullets cutting the air all around the aircraft. While the Apache aircrew were cocooned in a cockpit shell lined by Kevlar armour, their four passengers had no such protection.

None had ever felt so exposed, or so vulnerable.

Scanning the terrain below, Tom saw the entire fort shrouded in thick smoke from burning buildings. The terrain around the fallen Marine was rough, and there was only space for one aircraft to land. And with enemy fighters positioned some fifty metres or less from where that aircraft would have to put down, some kind of diversion was needed.

Putting his aircraft into a shallow dive Tom made the decision to land inside the fort's very walls. By doing so he aimed to sow confusion among its occupiers, and to buy his wing aircraft time to effect the rescue. He flipped low over the outer wall, the Apache being met by a hail of bullets as it did so, and went down in a storm of rotor-blown dust in to the very centre of the fort.

Behind him, in the second Apache, Karl Bruce descended in a cloud of dust to a point just outside the fort's wall, in close proximity to the British soldier. It was an extraordinary piece of flying by both pilots, especially as the last few seconds had been completed in the blind brown-out of a rotor-blown dust storm, when they had been flying on instruments only.

Tom kept the rotors spinning, the downwash kicking up dust, which mixed with the smoke of the burning buildings to form a thick cloud. It billowed outwards from the stationary aircraft, forming a choking wave of brown-black opaqueness that quickly engulfed the interior of the fort.

The rolling dust cloud was both a blessing and a curse. While it helped to shield the aircraft from the enemy, little was visible inside the fort. As the soldiers unstrapped themselves from the lead Apache, they realised that they had become disorientated: they were unsure of where their comrade lay.

In the blind-out of the dust storm, and with enemy forces loosing off wild bursts of fire, they had lost all sense of which was the direction in which to find him. The soldiers' confusion was clearly audible to the Apache aircrew over the radio net, and Tom's co-pilot, Staff Sergeant Keith Arthur, decided to help.

From the vantage point of the Apache's cockpit he'd got a good fix on the Royal Marine's position as the aircraft had gone in to land. Folding back the slabs of side armour so he could exit the aircraft, he grabbed his SA80-2K carbine, which was jammed into the space beside his seat, and vaulted out of the cockpit to lead the way.

Tom's Apache had been on the ground for barely a minute, although it seemed like an age. Suddenly, accurate rounds started whining through the air all around the vulnerable aircraft. Sharp muzzle flashes pierced the muddy light as the lone Apache was targeted by enemy machineguns firing out of a mud-walled building to its right.

The Apache has an automatic system that disables the 30mm cannon as soon as the aircraft touches down. There is good reason for this: the aircraft doesn't have sufficient clearance to aim and fire the cannon properly while on the ground.

Tom could kick the big gun on the aircraft's chin turret into life by overriding the cut-out system. Mounted on a pivot, the 30mm cannon can hit a target ninety degrees to either side of the aircraft. But if he did try to swing the big gun around to engage the enemy, it was more than likely to plough into the packed earth of the courtyard.

But while his Apache, *Wildman Five Zero*, couldn't return fire, there was an Apache circling above him that could. Tom radioed *Wildman Five Three*, the Apache piloted by Captain Nick Born, and did a rapid talk-on to target.

An instant later the incoming Apache spat a tongue of white fire from the cannon on its chin turret, unleashing a twenty-round burst of 30mm high-explosive rounds. They tore into the enemy position, the heavy calibre rounds chewing up the thick mud walls and blasting chunks of masonry into the air.

With the orbiting Apache putting down a barrage of covering fire, the commandos and the airman dashed across the fort, dodging enemy tracer as they did so. At the fort's outer wall they linked up with their fellow soldiers from the second Apache. Grabbing the prone form of Lance Corporal Ford from where he was lying at the base of the wall, they hoisted him between them and made a mad dash for the rescue helicopter.

They emerged from the shadow of the fort wall silhouetted against the storm of swirling dust. The waiting Apache aircrew spotted them, and pilot Karl Bruce and Warrant Officer Mark Rawlings jumped out of their seats. Reaching down, they began to help drag the fallen soldier up the eight feet or so that the Apache's stub wings stand off the ground.

Once they had lain him across the grey-green metal of the stub wing, they began to strap the Royal Marine to the steel grab-handles. All the while they were taking enemy fire, the crack of weapons and the whine of rounds cutting the air to either side of the stationary aircraft. It was high time they got the hell out of there.

Captain Rigg and Marine Fraser-Perry checked the fixings on the Lance Corporal one last time, while the pilots lowered themselves into the cockpit. With no time to strap themselves on, the two soldiers clung to the grab-handles as the rotors slapped at the air above, straining to get airborne.

Moments later, Apache *Wildman Five One* thundered into the air. It power-climbed to sixty feet altitude, the machine dropping its nose and gaining airspeed as it did so, and then it headed away from the fort towards the river and safety.

Meanwhile, the two soldiers and one airman from *Wildman Five Zero* sprinted back through the chaos of the fort to rejoin co-pilot Tom at the waiting Apache. Just as soon as they were all aboard, Tom got the 'Go! Go! Go!'

He pulled full power on the collective lever and the aircraft's screaming turbines thrust the Apache into the air. It went low and fast, skimming over the outer wall of the fort, following in the wake of *Wildman Five One* towards the river.

The pair of battered Apaches headed away from the enemy guns, making for the safety of the open desert, each being chased by hungry fingers of tracer. At such close quarters as the engagement in the fort, even small arms fire – 7.62mm rounds from the enemy's AK-47s – could have done serious damage to the aircraft's aluminium fuselage.

The aircrew set a course north-east for Camp Bastion, neither pilot having any idea how badly damaged his aircraft might be. Either way, it was both a miracle and a testament to the Apache's awesome engineering, that the machines had got them in and out of there alive.

Their priority now was to get Lance Corporal Ford back to headquarters. No one knew how badly injured he was, but they hoped and prayed that they might be able to help the soldier by getting him to the Camp Bastion Field Hospital alive.

As the dull thud of the helicopter rotor blades faded away to nothing on the cold desert wind, the battle for Jugroom Fort was finally over. But for the Apache pilots, their work in Afghanistan was only just beginning.

1

KUSH DRAGON

15 January 2007, Salisbury Plain, Wiltshire

As the storm of rotor-blown dust settled over Jugroom Fort and a pall of ink-grey smoke drifted into the steel blue of the winter sky, the enemy emerged to gather up their wounded and count their dead. It was barely 1145 hours Afghanistan time, 0630 hours back in the UK, where, on an airfield on Salisbury Plain, a second Apache aircrew stirred.

It was day one of Exercise Kush Dragon, and the four pilots of flight *Ugly* were about to learn the tough lessons of that morning's actions at Jugroom Fort. The lithe forms of eight Apache attack helicopters of 662 Squadron, Army Air Corps (AAC), squatted on the runway at Netheravon Airfield, barely visible in the pre-dawn murk, with their rotors sagging earthwards.

Netheravon sits on the eastern border of Salisbury Plain, the largest military range and training area in the UK. Over ninety-four thousand acres of heath and forest provide ground troops and airborne forces with a massive expanse upon which to undertake exercises. Every acre would be needed for Kush Dragon, a brigade-level rehearsal for the forthcoming deployment to Afghanistan.

Along with the Apaches of 662 Squadron, key elements of 12th Mechanised Brigade (12 Mech) had assembled on Salisbury Plain that morning. Come May, the Brigade would be headed for Afghanistan to relieve the battle-fatigued Royal Marines, and the Apache aircrews of 664 and 656 Squadron. After the bitter Afghan winter the enemy would be gearing up for a spring offensive, and the coming May–August deployment was expected to be a far from quiet one.

Kush Dragon was the culmination of months of preparation, and there was a buzz of excitement among the drab green Army vehicles sheathed in camouflage netting, the soldiers billeted under canvas and the Apache aircrew quartered at Netheravon. Prior to setting foot in the war-torn badlands of Helmand, this was the nearest these men would get to testing their mettle, and that of their complex military machines, in battle.

Over the coming week, ground forces of the Royal Anglians (The Vikings), the Worcesters and Foresters, and armoured units of the Light Dragoons would rehearse full-on battle scenarios among the rolling hills of Salisbury Plain. They would pit themselves against an enemy played by TA soldiers wearing typical Taliban dress and using the type of hit-and-run tactics so common in the Afghan deserts and mountains.

The war in Afghanistan traces its roots back to the 9/11 terror attacks on America. Terrorists used hijacked airliners to target the Twin Towers and the Pentagon; the driving force behind those attacks was identified as a shadowy organisation based in Afghanistan. For years, Osama bin Laden's al-Qaeda network had been sheltered and nurtured by the Taliban, who provided a safe haven from which to plan, and prosecute, their attacks.

In the months following 9/11, Operation Enduring Freedom had been launched, a coalition war to rid Afghanistan of the Taliban – and al-Qaeda with it. Since then, the Taliban had been routed and a democratic government voted into power in Afghanistan. Yet the Taliban's malignant force had endured and a string of al-Qaeda terror attacks had followed in Indonesia, Spain and – in July 2005 – London.

The ongoing war in southern Afghanistan was to drive the Taliban out of their principal refuge, Helmand Province. British forces spearheaded the Helmand campaign as part of a NATO-led coalition that worked to bring peace and security across the wider

region. Elsewhere US troops concentrated on hunting down al-
Qaeda. Exercise Kush Dragon was but one piece in a larger jigsaw
of a coalition of nations at war.

On Salisbury Plain that morning, Lynx and Chinook helicopters
were preparing to deliver airmobile troops into battle, while
Apache and Harrier ground attack aircraft pounded the 'enemy'
from the air. At Larkhill and Westdown live firing ranges, ground
forces would contribute barrages of 81mm mortars and 105mm
shells – adding to the nine million large-calibre rounds fired on the
Plain since its 1897 inception as a military range.

With Kush Dragon continuing day and night for six days, it
promised to be a noisy week for the inhabitants of the villages scattered around the Plain. This was a prospect the local populace
seemed to greet with remarkable cheer. Among notices regarding
church cleaning and flower arranging rotas, the *Chitterne Parish
Newsletter* contained a small announcement entitled 'Up on the
Plain'.

This gave daily schedules for Kush Dragon, including parachut-
ing, aircraft trials, fast jet activity, live firing and helicopter night
flying. Otherwise, the newsletter concluded of Kush Dragon, 'it
should cause little disturbance'.

As Captain Barry 'Baz' Hunter headed for his 7.30 a.m. briefing
on day one of Kush Dragon, he passed by the ground crews readying the Apache attack helicopters for action. He'd spent many a
year doing the same job himself. It is a tradition of the Army Air
Corps ('the Corps') that any soldier, regardless of rank, can aspire
to be a Corps pilot, the elite of whom undoubtedly fly the
Apaches.

Baz Hunter was a typical Corps recruit. He'd left school at sixteen with only the barest of qualifications and spent a short period
working in a factory. Joining the Army was his route out of that
humdrum existence. Accepted into a Junior Leaders regiment, he
had raised merry hell and spent more time in the gaol than out of
it. At first, there were doubts that he would make the grade as an
adult soldier.

'The gaol had been my second home. Then I got into the Corps and quickly began to grow up and calm down. While I was still a ground crewman, this guy took me on a flight up to Leeds. By the time we landed I knew that I wanted to be a pilot. But when I went for selection I was told I was too fat, plus I failed my maths test.

'The interviewing officer told me that if I lost the weight, then they'd put me onto a crewman's course – the first step to becoming a pilot. After three months of living on tomatoes and grapefruit juice, I failed maths again but was thin enough to scrape in, and they said they would take me "on risk". I ended up as an air observer in Gazelles, doing navigation, and then I became a TOW missile operator on the Lynx. Joining the Army was a decision I would never regret.'

Some thirty years later, Baz was the Regimental Qualified Helicopter Instructor for 3 Regiment, Army Air Corps, and one of the most experienced Apache pilots in the Corps.

As he walked past the main hangar at Netheravon, Baz called out a greeting to the ground crews, hailing those he knew by nickname. Formalities are dispensed with wherever possible, in order to forge the closeness between ground crew and aircrew that is the backbone of the Corps.

He approached the Ops Room and fell into step alongside Steve James, one of his closest mates in the Corps. Steve was a Warrant Officer, and he and Baz had flown together in many theatres of war. Steve was also scheduled to be Baz's wingman on the coming Afghan posting.

The eight Apaches of 662 Squadron would be deployed to Afghanistan as four flights of two aircraft. Baz would pilot one Apache; Steve the sister aircraft, and that would make up one flight, whose call-sign would be *Ugly*.

Baz liked to think that their flight had been named after Steve, who, with his squat, bulky form and receding hairline, was certainly no oil painting. A famously light sleeper, Steve looked pasty-faced and knackered whether on active operations or not, with dark panda rings around his eyes. This morning was no exception, and Steve was hardly the archetypal image of what a top-gun Apache pilot was supposed to look like.

Like Baz, Steve was a northerner and a 'ranker' – someone who had come up from the junior ranks. He'd joined the Army after doing passably at school, but getting in to 'more than a bit of trouble.' For a while he'd tried to handle working in an office, before realising there had to be more to life than that.

He'd decided to try the Army, with the aim of becoming a tank driver. But, two months into his training, he'd seen the Corps's Blue Eagles display team flying Lynx and Gazelle helicopters during an air day. At that very moment he'd realised that this was his dream job.

Now, some twenty years later, Steve was an ace shot on the Apache and the Gunnery Instructor on 662 Squadron. Word was that he'd be applying for his officer commission any day soon. He was an excellent pilot, having seen action in many of the same theatres as Baz, and often flying alongside his senior Army Air Corps pilot buddy.

'You've got guys from council estates who left school with no qualifications now flying Apaches,' remarks Steve. 'And that's exactly how it should be. The Army is better than society in that it doesn't write people off – it gives them every chance and allows their qualities to shine. It lends a hand to those who fell foul of the school system, and equally takes graduates from Eton and Cambridge. How many of those guys who went off the rails at school ever thought they'd get a chance to try to be an Apache pilot – let alone achieve it?'

Steve was a self-effacing kind of bloke, with a quiet, grey-man persona. But this belied his innate courage, and the fact that he had a razor-edged sense of humour. He had been awarded the Queen's Commendation for Bravery, having single-handedly rescued two aircrew from a burning Lynx that had crashed in the Omani desert.

'The Lynx had taken off, didn't pull up properly and hit the deck hard. It rolled over and ended up under my aircraft in flames. I climbed up the Lynx that was now lying on its side, jumped down and pulled the two guys out. Dunno quite how, as I'm a small bloke. I guess it must've been the adrenalin.'

Steve was rarely lost for words, especially with Baz, who was forever trying to wind him up. As they entered the Netheravon Ops Room, Baz couldn't resist having a dig: 'Morning, mate. You look like the walking dead. Slept well again, did you?'

'How could I, with an old man like you in the next bunk?' Steve retorted. 'You were up and down for a piss half the night, Slack Bladder!'

In spite of his quiet-man persona, Steve had always been a hit with the girls. He put it down to his ability to make them laugh. Do that, and most women would quickly forget that you were as ugly as sin. But then he'd met and fallen for Tracey, a northern lass with sparkling eyes and a shock of blonde hair, plus a sense of humour as sharp as his own. Recently engaged, he'd put his days of womanising behind him.

As much as Baz argued that flight *Ugly* was named after Steve, Steve maintained the reverse was true. Outside of the Corps, people seemed to have an image of what an Apache pilot should look like: a muscular and square-jawed young warrior-Adonis. When they met the reality in the form of Baz Hunter – pushing fifty, hair flecked with grey and a slight beer gut to contend with – they were often more than a little surprised.

On the rare occasions that Baz made it to a nightclub or a bar and got chatting to a woman, he could pretty much predict how things would turn out. He had a mischievous glint in his eye and an open countenance that promised fun, and he was easy to talk to. But as soon as a pretty woman asked him what he did for a living, and he told her that he was an Apache pilot, that was generally the end of the conversation.

'You try to convince her you really *are* an Apache pilot and the reaction is "yeah, whatever". She's expecting some blond, blue-eyed twenty-something with a square jaw and muscles like iron – not someone old enough to be her dad, with a double chin and a paunch. What she doesn't know is that the cockpit is so cramped that if you did have any stature, or pumped muscles, you'd never squeeze yourself in there in the first place, let alone get out again in a hurry if your aircraft went down.'

Most women couldn't abide a bullshitter. Invariably, the pretty woman would return to her friends, leaving Baz to shrug philosophically and to console himself with his pint and his mates. He didn't really give a damn. He was happily married to Tracy, his wife of two decades standing. They had a feisty daughter, Jenny, who was just about to head off to university. He was far too content with life to worry about his chances of getting hit on by the ladies.

'Funnily enough, every girl seems to have a boyfriend or a brother who's an Apache pilot,' Baz remarks. 'The Apache fraternity must consist of several thousand pilots if you believe everyone you speak to. In fact, there are only about 120 of us. Which makes it even more amusing when someone refuses to believe you.'

Baz was one of the old and the bold. During thirty years' service he'd flown more helicopter hours than just about any other Corps pilot. He'd done hundreds of hours in the Gazelle and the Lynx over Northern Ireland during the Troubles, flying missions that were often bordering on the insane. And he'd gone on to pilot the Lynx during the Balkans conflict, in a ground attack and troop transport role.

He'd ended up in Bosnia, flying search-and-snatch operations, hunting down Serbian war criminals. At one time he and his aircrew had been captured and held by the Serbs, which, Baz reckoned, was about as hairy as things could get. More recently, he had been one of only twelve British pilots sent to the US to train on the Apache, and he'd completed the first UK training programme. But somehow, Baz just knew that the coming Afghan deployment was going to eclipse all of that.

Since taking delivery of the first of sixty-seven Apache attack helicopters in 2000, the British Army had been unable to use them due to a dearth of trained aircrew. That situation had now been turned around, and the Apache Attack Regiment's Afghan deployment marked their combat debut. It was high time the Apache programme proved that it could deliver bang for its bucks.

Baz and Steve took their places at the rear of the Netheravon briefing room, a couple of old hands among the young guns of the

Squadron. Some of the new boys making up the aircrews were young enough to be the son that Baz had never had. At times, he felt something of a protective, fatherly instinct towards the twenty-somethings fresh out of Sandhurst. For them, Afghanistan was truly going to be a trial by fire.

To make up crewing shortages, pilots who had only just passed out from the Army Pilots Course, and straight after Sandhurst officer training, were being trained on the Apache. At first this had concerned some of the old and the bold, who worried that their lack of experience might be a handicap in combat. How misplaced such concern would prove: one of those new boys, Nick Born, would return from Afghanistan having won the Distinguished Flying Cross.

The Apache is a two-seater machine, with the front-seater concentrating on engaging the weaponry and 'fighting' the aircraft, while the rear-seater concentrates on flying the aircraft and navigating to target. To make things easier on the young guns, each was teamed up with one of the older, more experienced pilots.

Baz's front-seater, Captain Timothy Porter, certainly had something of the archetypal Apache 'look' about him. A youthful twenty-nine-year-old, Tim had a shock of unruly blonde hair, piercing blue eyes and boyish good looks. From officer training at Sandhurst, Tim had graduated onto the Army Air Corps pilot course, flown the Gazelle for a short period, and then done his Apache training.

Afghanistan was going to be Tim's first operational tour. With a wife and children back home in England, Baz figured that it was going to be tough on the young officer. But he reckoned that Tim would do okay. While he was quiet and somewhat shy, the little Baz knew of him pegged him as a competent and brave pilot; one not afraid of a fight.

'Tim and I had established a firm, respectful friendship over the past year or so. We had flown together and socialised together . . . Like me, Tim has a competitive streak and can quickly turn from nice guy to full-on aggression when required. I knew we would be good in combat together.'

Baz had first run into Tim when he had failed one of the Apache training modules, and Baz had been tasked to get him through it. From that experience alone he knew that Tim hated failure.

Baz had captained many a flight in his time, and he little needed the experience of doing so again. Instead, the Corps had decided to place Tim on a horribly steep learning curve by making him the commander of flight *Ugly*. In that way the young guns would learn from the old hands, and vice versa, strengthening the fighting capabilities of the entire squadron.

Baz advised the squadron commander on the crew resourcing side of things: 'As an Apache pilot, you don't get to choose who you'll be partnered with. I try to look at who will get along together. But we don't put best mates with best mates. Instead, we try and have a rank balance, teaming up high experience with low experience. This is an important side of how we operate: the last thing you need in an Apache is crew conflict . . . Afghanistan was going to be like nothing the squadron had ever experienced before, and a true test of the pilot's training.'

The Army Air Corps has a culture of openness and honesty, and if any pilot makes a mistake he is encouraged to put up his hand and declare that he's messed up.

'We're more or less alone in the Army in being so open,' Baz remarks. 'We're a tiny, close-knit team, especially in the Apache squadrons. Like Special Forces, we value merit as much as rank. But in Afghanistan Tim was going to be commanding a senior pilot, one who had actually instructed him: me. It took big bollocks to do that.'

Steve James's front-seater was Captain Alexander Wagner, a twenty-five-year-old fresh from Sandhurst. Alex's fellow aircrew ribbed him that he was the spitting image of Will Young, the cheesy Pop Idol star. Alex had acquired the reputation in 662 Squadron of being a 'totally pleasant bloke'. Nothing was too much for him, and the Will Young jibes were like water off a duck's back.

Alex was fit, smart and educated, and big on outdoor pursuits, especially sailing and mountain biking. He had no combat experience, having only just graduated from Apache training.

As Steve had been on a previous Afghan tour, he brought a wealth of combat experience to the flight. He had volunteered to join 662 Squadron's deployment, so as to pass on that experience to those who were untested in battle. He knew Alex to be a good listener and someone who took criticism well. The two men planned to rotate command of their flight, swapping over every other sortie.

'Alex was competent, forwards looking and loyal. I knew he'd share the load with me, and that we'd work decisions through. I also knew him to be a sound bloke, who just gets daft and smiles a lot whenever we were out on the beers. He was level-headed and I knew Alex would do all right out there.'

In candid moments, Steve and Baz admitted that the young guns did have one advantage over the old boys. The array of digital, computerised systems facing an Apache pilot in the cockpit is truly mind-numbing. A younger generation brought up on PlayStations, iPods and video games generally found the digital interface more natural and user friendly.

As for how the aircrews would perform on Salisbury Plain, their every waking hour would be consumed by Kush Dragon. This was the most realistic and testing military exercise that Baz had ever experienced: 'From Netheravon we conducted duties entirely as if we were in theatre. Salisbury Plain had been cleverly divided and mapped to represent an area not dissimilar to Helmand. The enemy were created with soldiers dressed as Afghans who followed scripts. Those scripts included turning up at *shuras* [traditional village meetings], rioting and acting as Taliban taking on our forces and testing them to the full.

During that first day ground troops got to taste the reality of combat up close and personal, while fighting their way through the purpose-built village on Copehill Down. There, they learned the tactics of fighting in built-up areas. Giant twin-rotor Chinooks of 27 Squadron RAF practised casualty evacuations under fire as they responded to call outs from units hit by improvised explosive devices set by the enemy on the roadside, and detonated remotely using mobile phone signals.

Like sheepdogs protecting a vulnerable flock, the Apaches

escorted the bulbous, slab-sided Chinooks in to their 'hot' landing zones, ready to pound the enemy with a potent array of weaponry should they show themselves. The Taliban had pledged to shoot down an Allied helicopter in Helmand as a prize, and the big Chinooks were the most likely target. The Apaches were supposed to find and kill the hostile forces before they could bring a helicopter down.

This alone was a daunting responsibility. At the same time as acting as Chinook escorts, the Apaches were tasked with finding, fixing and killing any enemy that might be hitting ground troops. That was the *raison d'être* of the close air support provided by the Harrier jets and Apaches, the key air assets available to British troops in the Afghan theatre.

As the Apache aircrews were painfully aware, much was expected of their forthcoming baptism of fire. Kush Dragon gave them a vital feel for the realities of combat.

'In Kush Dragon we operated exactly as we would in Afghanistan,' Steve remarks. 'They had Afghans down there posing as translators, and we had kit that simulated a missile firing or locking on, which set the alarms screaming on the Apaches. They even had UAVs flying overhead, providing live video feeds of the battlefield.'

'Nothing gets closer than an Apache' is one of the favourite sayings of the Corps. It was a theory that was amply demonstrated during day one of simulated battle on Salisbury Plain.

'At one stage we were proving so efficient at finding and "killing" the enemy that we were requested to back off,' remarks Baz. 'We were politely asked to go back to Netheravon as ground troops were not getting to complete the battle exercises that were expected of them.'

But in practice, the aircrew knew that Taliban would lurk among the civilian population, using Afghan women and children as human shields. And in reality, no British Apache had ever fired a shot in anger prior to Afghanistan. For both aircraft and aircrew alike, Afghanistan would be the place where all would get blooded.

On the evening of the first day of Kush Dragon, word of the

epic battle for Jugroom Fort began to filter into the Ops Room at Netheravon. There were confused reports of a downed Apache aircrew, and of a last-ditch rescue mission. Every Apache pilot dreaded the prospect of their aircraft going down, and having to fight and survive for several days in hostile territory.

While the Apache's cockpit is horribly cramped, it is the role of every pilot to rescue his fellow aircrew, and in theory the grab-handles on either sides of the aircraft can be used to strap on a downed airman. But most pilots believed their armoured aircraft – a 'flying tank' as Steve described it – was all but indestructible. Rarely had any of them practised the strap-on extraction method that 656 Squadron had used that morning in Jugroom Fort.

As more reports came in of Apaches evacuating casualties, no one seemed sure who had been wounded: was it aircrew or ground troops? Either way, the harsh realities of war-fighting in the Afghan theatre began to sink in. British forces were up against a battle-hardened and fanatical enemy, with tried and tested weaponry at their disposal. It was all well and good war-gaming for battle, but anything was possible out there in a real war.

As day two dawned the Apache aircrews attended a briefing with the Operations Officer, Sam Haldon, who presented all the latest available information from Jugroom. This was to ensure that they could better shape their training in reaction to real combat scenarios – both during Kush Dragon, and after, in the Apache flight simulators back at the regiment's headquarters, at Wattisham Airfield in Suffolk.

There was a shared sadness in the Netheravon Ops Room when news came in that the wounded Royal Marine, Lance Corporal Ford, had failed to survive the flight back to Camp Bastion. But tragic though his death might be, it detracted little from the almost insane courage demonstrated by the Apache aircrews and their strapped-on soldier passengers. As far as Steve was concerned, such maverick daring was the defining tradition of the Corps.

'We were gripped by the story of Jugroom. The fact that they had managed to strap the Royal Marine to the aircraft and get him home was amazing. We had discussed crew extraction in the past, but until this point we'd barely paid lip service to it, thinking it so wacky. All of a sudden it had taken on massive importance, with all of us discussing what we would do if we were to find ourselves shot down in Helmand.'

662 Squadron's plans for Kush Dragon were quickly redrawn to include live rehearsals for extraction of downed aircrew or injured ground troops. Using a specially-designed strop and a karabiner attached to the flight harness, a downed pilot could clip onto the Apache's grab-handles and be lifted clear of the danger zone.

'We practised for all different scenarios,' Baz remarks. 'What if you were on your own – could you lift a downed pilot onto the side of the aircraft, or would you simply rope him to one of the wheels? Better a broken limb than to be left behind . . . We talked through all the options, while secretly hoping that we'd never have to put any of them into practice on the ground in Afghanistan.'

Pilots began to work out how they would stow the combat, escape and evasion equipment they might need should they go down in Helmand. Each had to fit in to his cramped cockpit an SA80-2K carbine – a shortened version of the standard SA80 assault rifle designed specifically for use by tank and Apache crew. Additionally, they had to carry enough water to survive in the Afghan desert, emergency food rations, cold weather gear, a Browning pistol, and the magazines of 5.56mm ammunition for the carbine.

On day three of Kush Dragon the story of the Jugroom rescue mission exploded in the media. It was all over the morning papers and the TV news bulletins. 'Helicopter in dramatic rescue bid for Marine,' declared the BBC. 'Strapped to Apaches and dodging fire – how troops recovered fallen comrade' was the *Guardian*'s headline. 'Marines launch rescue by strapping themselves to Apache,' ran the story in *The Times*.

The Apache aircrew of 656 Squadron were hailed as true heroes. As for the pilots of 662 Squadron, they were thrilled to see the Apache programme finally getting some positive press, and they concentrated on learning the lessons of the Jugroom incident well. Baz reckoned it had injected some hard reality into the aircrew's training and mission preparations, making Kush Dragon a doubly realistic and rigorous exercise: 'We incorporated the lessons of Jugroom into Kush Dragon, and came away feeling more than ready. We gelled as crews and as a flight. This was the start of our bonding as a tight team.'

Yet at the same time Baz knew that the future was another country – Afghanistan.

'I'd trained all my life for this mission, and dreamed of flying an aircraft such as this one in combat. Yet still it was daunting. Those who'd never been in combat worried if they would perform to the high standards expected. Would they be any good in deliberate ops against an experienced and fanatical enemy? Would the Apache be the right aircraft for the job even? And every time we went into combat we knew we'd have to justify the cost of the aircraft.'

Kush Dragon had hardened the men for the trials that lay ahead. As for the Jugroom incident, each of the pilots of 662 Squadron hoped that he would have done the same thing in that fort, if faced with the same circumstances. To leave no man behind – that was the credo of the Corps.

And every man of 662 Squadron hoped that the same would be done for him, should his aircraft go down over the harsh mountains or lonely desert plains of Afghanistan.

2

NO DANCING AT GILA BEND

In a sense, it was only fair that so much was being expected of the Apache in its debut combat role. At an overall project cost of some £4.2 billion, the introduction of the Apache was one of the British Army's most expensive gambits. Critics of the programme argued that the money could have been better spent on personal kit, weaponry and more armoured vehicles for the ground troops fighting in Iraq and Afghanistan.

The Apache was intended to revolutionise the way that British troops were fighting the war on the Taliban's home turf in Helmand Province, a remote and rugged region half the size of England. Until now, the Helmand deployment had been largely characterised by static war fighting based around 'platoon houses'.

Commonly, these were fortified district centres positioned in the main towns. By virtue of their occupation of platoon houses, the Afghan government was able to claim that the coalition – the British, American, Danish, Dutch, Czech and allied Afghan troops – were holding territory and controlling Helmand.

But in reality British troops were taking the brunt of the fighting, and they were in static positions that were vulnerable 24/7. Because the Taliban knew exactly where the British soldiers were situated, they could opt for a time and line of attack of their own choosing. The platoon houses were also next to impossible to re-supply – whether by land convoy or by air – because their supply routes were predictable and therefore vulnerable to ambush.

In 2007 all that was set to change. The static platoon house strategy was going to evolve. Highly mobile airborne and land forces would take the fight to the enemy, striking quickly and with massive force deep into their heartland, and would maintain a presence in areas they had cleared. The aim was to drive the enemy out of their comfort zone and to force them on to the defensive. Demoralised and in disarray, having lost their bases and taken casualties, the enemy would give up the fight.

That, in turn, would enable British forces to concentrate on the second plank of their strategy: 'hearts and minds' operations. During past conflicts – Malaya, Borneo, Northern Ireland, Iraq – the British Army had learned that fighting alone rarely won the day. Without bringing the local people on side – those who sheltered and nurtured the enemy – the war would never truly be over. Such was the case in Helmand, where an effective hearts and minds campaign was crucial to vanquishing a resurgent Taliban.

The presence of the Apache attack squadrons in theatre was key to enabling a more mobile form of soldiering. Unlike other forms of air cover, the Apache was able to spend extended 'loiter time' over target. This meant that it could devote serious amounts of time to working with the ground troops, hunting out enemy forces. With its unrivalled array of target acquisition systems, enemy forces had few places to hide, day or night. And with its ability to unleash its weapons with pinpoint accuracy, the Apache constituted a devastating fire platform.

'Apaches are crewed by soldiers, the majority of whom have experience soldiering on the ground,' comments Lieutenant Colonel Jon Bryant, the Commanding Officer of 3 Regiment, Army Air Corps. 'During planning of deliberate operations the Apache crews and commanders are intimately involved, and so they have an excellent awareness of what the ground commander is trying to achieve and how.'

Air Chief Marshal Sir Jock Stirrup, the head of Britain's Armed Forces, would say the following about the Apache's impact in Afghanistan: 'We always knew the Apache was a potent weapons system and that the people who operate and support it were brave and professional. They have demonstrated those qualities – and more – in the most demanding circumstances.'

What was it that made the Apache such a formidable weapons platform, one with the potential to transform battlefield operations? According to the Ministry of Defence, the Apache is 'the most advanced and significant weapons system to enter service with the British Army'. The aircraft provides a completely new capability, allowing the Army to punch above its weight.

In May 2000 the first of sixty-seven Apaches had been delivered to the British Army by the US company Boeing. The Apache was already a well-proven machine, with an exemplary track record. The AH-64D Apache Longbow first entered service in 1998. The original US Army specification called for an attack helicopter that could engage, and defeat, massed ranks of Soviet armour, while evading their anti-aircraft weaponry. The aircraft design was to embody weapons punch, survivability and agility.

The US military demanded a machine that could operate in any theatre of combat, day or night, in fair weather or foul. It had to have a higher level of survivability – the ability to take hits and keep flying – than ever achieved before. It had to carry a greater load of weaponry than any predecessor, while its performance, which goes hand-in-hand with agility, had to be unbeatable. And, once deployed, it had to require a minimum of maintenance to keep it flying.

The US Army called for an aircraft that could carry eight anti-tank missiles, 320 rounds of 30mm ammunition, and enough fuel for a two-hour mission, while still achieving a rate of climb of 450 feet per minute.

The Apache Longbow achieved all of this and more. Its cruise speed is 258 kilometres per hour, but it can also fly sideways and rearwards at 83 kph. Its manoeuvrability is truly awe-inspiring, with the helicopter able to perform very rapid changes in flight path, and even loop-the-loop and fly upside down. And its rate of climb is a staggering 2460 feet per minute – more than five times the original US Army specification.

On standard fuel tanks, the Apache has an endurance of over two hours, giving it ample scope to reach the battlefield and loiter over target. It is capable of carrying 2948 kilograms of ordnance, a feat unsurpassed by any previous attack helicopter. The aircraft's speed and agility allow it to conduct high-speed nap-of-the-earth – flying at low altitude, maximising stealth and surprise and reducing exposure to enemy weapons.

In terms of survivability, 99 per cent of the Apache's Kevlar armour plating is used for protecting crew, fuel and the rotor drive systems. Eschewing heavy armour elsewhere, every component is engineered to keep the Apache flying in the face of heavy fire. The Apache's mechanics are designed so that the aircraft can take and survive a hit by a 23mm shell, keeping it airborne long enough to get back to base. This is achieved by isolating sensitive equipment, via built in redundancy (the ability to dispense with using damaged components), and the use of shatterproof materials.

The Apache has twin engines, mounted one on either side of the fuselage. Should one engine fail, the aircraft can remain flying on the other. Hot gases streaming from an aircraft's turbines can provide an ideal heat signature for infrared guided missiles to lock onto. With the Apache, the engines are wrapped in a Black Hole system, which sucks in cold air, circulates it around the engine and mixes it with the exhaust gases. This lowers temperatures to a level at which exhausts are largely invisible to heat-seeking missiles.

The standard 1423 litres of fuel are stored in two tanks, into which nitrogen gas is pumped to occupy any free space. An inert gas blanket lies over the fuel, so preventing fire. The tanks are engineered to take a hit from an armour-piercing round, but if a bullet should blast a hole in either tank they self-seal with a specially designed foam. The tanks seal sufficiently well to retain enough fuel for the aircraft to get back to base.

On most helicopters, the rotor drivers are highly vulnerable to enemy fire. With the lubrication system punctured, the oil supply drains away and components overheat, seize and shatter. On the Apache, all drive systems have a 'run-dry' function, or are grease-lubricated, allowing the aircraft to keep flying should the oil supply have drained dry.

Crashworthiness, the last plank of survivability, is at a premium. The turret-mounted 30mm cannon is collapsible, which prevents the heavy weapon smashing in to the front-seater should the aircraft go down. The Apache's seats are energy-absorbing, collapsing into the aircraft and cushioning any blow. The two front and one rear wheel are designed to crumple, again taking much of the impact of a crash. Even with the wheels collapsed inwards from an emergency landing, the Apache is able to take to the air again and make its way back to base.

Overall fuselage design ensures that the crew would survive – and possibly walk away from – a vertical impact at a velocity of forty-two feet per second. In the unlikely event of losing both engines, the Apache is designed to autorotate: the rotors are driven by the up-rush of air as the aircraft falls, slowing the descent and enabling an emergency landing.

But ultimately, the effectiveness of any warplane depends upon the accuracy and potency of the firepower it can unleash on target. And herein lies the greatest strength of the Apache. The aircraft has three main weapons systems.

First, the Hellfire AGM-114, a forty-six kilogram laser-guided missile. Eight of these can be carried on each of the aircraft's stub wings. Each Hellfire is fitted with a nine-kilogram conical warhead designed to burn through the heaviest armour.

Second, the CRV7 2.75-inch folding-fin rockets, which can carry either armour-piercing high-explosive incendiary semi-armour piercing (HEISAP), or flechette warheads. Nineteen rockets are carried in each weapons pod, making a total of seventy-six if the Apache is fully rocket-armed. The CRV7 weapons system is generally used against light armour, vehicles and troops positions.

And third, the M230 30mm Chain Gun, mounted in the remotely controlled chin turret. The cannon fires some six-hundred high-explosive rounds per minute, from a 1200-round magazine. It is capable of destroying targets from more than four thousand metres' distance. It utilises a highly reliable, electrically-driven chain mechanism to load rounds, and the gun turret can swivel through ninety degrees to either side of the aircraft.

The Apache's weapons are operated via a series of fire control systems, central to which is the target acquisition and designation sight (TADS), mounted in a pod on the nose of the aircraft. Alongside that is a pilot night vision sensor (PNVS), which transforms total darkness into the fluorescent green glow of infrared daylight, in which the contours of hills, trees, buildings and vehicles are visible. This allows the aircraft to operate at night, or in fog and rain, or when the battlefield is obscured by smoke or dust.

Three target acquisition systems are embedded in the nose pod: a 127-times magnification video lens, a 39-times magnification forward-looking infrared unit and a 12-times magnification optical telescope, akin to a pair of powerful binoculars. The aircrew view the nose pod's imagery on screens the size of a portable television in each cockpit, while data is punched in to the fire-control computer using a palm-sized keyboard.

The Apache's weapons are aimed by the aircraft's targeting systems. The Hellfire follows a laser guidance beam into its point of impact, but the rocket pods and the 30mm cannon are aimed conventionally, using a crosshair sight.

Yet perhaps most extraordinary of all is the Apache's manual firing system. At the flick of a switch either pilot can select manual, at which point the weapons systems will automatically slave to his line of sight.

The pilot's helmet has a clip-on arm that drops a monocle-like screen in front of his right eye. This is the helmet-mounted display (HMD). In each corner of the cockpit are sensors that detect exactly where the right eye is looking, locking the weapons systems to the pilot's eye-line.

At the centre of the HMD is a crosshair sight, akin to that on a sniper's scope. As the pilot's eye moves, so, for example, the 30mm cannon swivels in direct relation to where he is looking. Select the range and weapon, look at the target and pull the trigger – that is exactly where the rounds will land.

The British version of the Apache is designated the WAH Mk1.

The standard US Apache Longbow is modified at the Westland helicopter factory in Yeovil, Somerset. Here, the aircraft is fitted with a state-of-the-art radio system, which enables aircrew to communicate with individual soldiers on the ground, other aircraft and headquarters command and control. The British Apache is also fitted with a pair of more powerful Rolls-Royce engines for extra lift and speed.

The real strength of the British Apache, however, lies in its radar system and defensive capabilities. It has a state-of-the-art helicopter integrated defensive aids suite (HIDAS), which enables it to evade enemy ground fire and missiles. HIDAS is produced by BAE Systems and it is possibly the best such system in the world.

The British Apache also has a saucer-shaped radar dome, fitted directly above the main rotor – an invaluable extra tool for locating and killing the enemy. This fire control radar can sweep the battlefield and identify targets, locking-on weapons systems as it tracks them.

Despite the British variant's differences from its American forebear, the Apache pilots feel a close affinity with the US Army's Longbow heritage. At the annual Apache pilot's dinner, an original Apache longbow is passed from airman to airman in a tradition that was started the year the British Apache regiments were formed. There are the inevitable comments about this being; 'the first time the longbow has been used in anger by the British since the Battle of Agincourt'. That ceremony takes place before the serious drinking commences and the night descends into mayhem.

Nothing like the Apache attack helicopter had been designed or built before. The way it operates is very different from dropping a laser-guided bomb from twenty thousand feet on to pre-identified coordinates, as most warplanes do. The Apache is unique, and it has a unique relationship with the troops on the ground. It is a ferocious hunter-killer, seeking out its targets at low level, up close and personal, and it has all the refined senses of a top predator – including night vision to find, track and kill its prey.

For Steve and Baz, who had flown just about every aircraft

available to the Army Air Corps, there was no other machine that they would have felt more comfortable, or more capable, of taking to war in Afghanistan.

'As far as we were concerned, the Apache was *designed* for Helmand,' remarks Steve. 'We couldn't wait to get out there.'

But before they could do so there was one more mission-critical exercise for the men of 662 Squadron. The one deficiency of Salisbury Plain as a military training area is that it doesn't allow for live aerial firing. In fact, there is nowhere in the UK large enough to accommodate the full array of weaponry carried by the Apache.

And so, three weeks prior to their Afghan deployment, the men and machines of the Squadron set out for the wilds of Arizona. With their main rotors removed, two Apaches were loaded on each of four RAF C-17 Globemaster transport aircraft for the long flight to Gila Bend, part of the Barry M. Goldwater Range.

Gila Bend provides an area for aerial gunnery, rocketry, electronic warfare, and high-hazard testing for some of the most advanced elements of the US armed forces. It had taken twenty hours to reach Gila Bend, and upon arrival the Apache aircrews were relieved to discover that it offered them the perfect ground upon which to unleash their virgin weaponry, in particular the Hellfires.

As with most things in life, they did it far bigger in the USA. At 2,664,423 acres, Gila Bend dwarfs Salisbury Plain. Its vast swathes of desert and mountain are topped off by 57,000 cubic miles of air-space. It has three theatre-specific range areas, representing Europe, the Middle East and Asia. It has nine air-to-ground ranges, with range control officers situated in watchtowers to score the accuracy of airstrikes.

Realism is provided by targets such as old tanks, trucks and armoured vehicles, with full-scale mock-ups of enemy weapons systems scattered among them, including surface-to-air missiles and anti-aircraft guns. Urban areas are created using steel shipping containers, stacked three or more high to imitate streets, houses and military complexes. There are trains running on railway tracks, and even an enemy airbase complete with aircraft.

Most importantly for 662 Squadron, the temperature, altitude and terrain at Gila Bend were very much like the conditions the Apaches would face in Afghanistan. With the summer approaching, flying conditions would be 'hot and high' – high temperature, plus high air density – which would noticeably reduce the aircraft's performance.

Repeated strafing runs against shipping-container buildings proved the range, accuracy and devastating firepower of the Apache's Chain Guns. Somehow, the Apache aircrew just knew that this was going to prove the weapon of choice in Afghanistan. The live firing exercises also produced valuable lessons that the simulations on Salisbury Plain had been unable to deliver.

'In Arizona we saw the guys opening up with their .50-calibre tracers on the ground, telling us to watch their tracer to identify the location of an enemy target,' Steve remarks. 'Trouble was that ground forces would sometimes talk in colours, and what we see on our screens is in black and white, or green and black if it's at night. Part of the training was to explain what we could or couldn't do, and our limitations.'

The live firing of Hellfires came into its own during the night exercises. On one of these an Apache pilot asked the soldier on the ground to illuminate a target with his hand-held laser. The pilot loaded the code of the ground laser into his flight computer so he could lock the Hellfire on to it. Then he called for 'spot on' – meaning fire your laser at the target. But the soldier misheard him and went for 'spot off' instead, just as the pilot squeezed his trigger. The laser lock was lost the moment the missile left the weapons rail.

'We think that Hellfire ended up in Mexico, as it was never heard of again,' remarks Baz. 'The pilot got a hell of a lot of stick for it, and had to buy us a hell of a lot of beer as a result.'

That evening in the bar aircrews relaxed and revisited that rogue Hellfire strike. With the rogue operator stumping up the beers, the good cheer began to flow, and the British pilots got chatting to their American counterparts. 'The great thing about the British Army is that soldiers learn to drink and still keep control,' remarks

Baz. 'We seemed to spend most of the night fighting off these butch cowboy types who wanted to dance with us. Not that that's a bad thing – but we drew the line at dancing to country and western, no matter how good-looking the blokes might be. At one point we wondered if we'd wandered onto the set of *Brokeback Mountain*.'

As the Afghan deployment drew closer the ghosts of the Jugroom Fort rescue mission haunted 662 Squadron. In an effort to lay them once and for all, each pilot was put through a Survival, Evasion, Resistance and Escape (SERE) training course – just in case their Apache went down and the aircrew had to go on the run in Afghanistan.

SERE is a discipline developed by American and British Special Forces, and it is a gruelling physical and psychological trial. SERE training aims to prepare aircrew at high risk of capture to survive under any conditions – desert, mountain, jungle or arctic – in combat or captivity. Skills taught include wilderness living, emergency first aid, land navigation, camouflage techniques and communications. For the Resistance and Escape phase, training focuses on enabling a captured soldier to resist an aggressive interrogation.

In addition to teaching physical and psychological skills, a code of conduct is central to SERE. First, that a soldier will never surrender of his or her own free will. Second, that a soldier will continue to resist and try to escape, if captured. Third, that a soldier keeps faith with fellow prisoners in every way. Fourth, that a soldier will give out only that information required of a prisoner of war and will avoid answering further questions. Last, that a soldier will make no statement disloyal to his or her country or its cause.

In the British military the Resistance and Escape phase of SERE is more commonly called Conduct after Capture training. Interrogators use any means possible to break down a soldier and force them to betray their fellow men. The aim is to demonstrate in as realistic a way as possible the treatment a soldier should expect if captured. Most sessions are videotaped so that interrogators can better illustrate a soldier's strong points and also where mistakes may have been made.

During Steve James's Conduct after Capture session, he gave his interrogators the Big Three, the only information the enemy is entitled to ask of a prisoner of war: name, rank and number. Further questions were fired at Steve in a bewildering succession, but to each he gave the standard reply: 'I cannot answer that question, Sir.' If he broke down and talked, he knew he'd fail his SERE training and face a re-run of the nightmare that he was being put through.

Finally, one of his tormentors told him to crouch down like a bunny rabbit.

'I'm sorry, I cannot answer that question,' Steve replied, speaking like an automaton.

'Its not a question – it's a bloody order!' the interrogator snapped. 'Now do it.'

Steve got down on the floor, doing his best impression of a rabbit.

'Right, now put these straws up your nostrils.'

He took the proffered drinking straws and did as he was ordered.

'Right, prance around the room like a bloody bunny.'

Steve proceeded to hop around the room with a couple of straws inserted in his nostrils, while the interrogators tried their hardest not to laugh at the balding bunny rabbit bouncing around them.

Steve eventually completed his SERE training, having done passably well. 'But then came the bad news: Baz is also a part-time interrogator, and as bad luck would have it he was present at the centre and witnessed my humiliation during the bunny rabbit incident. Predictably, he's never let me forget it!'

Despite the piss-taking, Baz knew that SERE had real importance, as it steeled the pilots for the worst that might lie ahead.

'The Jugroom Fort incident had brought home the reality of what SERE was for. It was deadly serious. It was in case an Apache went down in Helmand and the aircrews were in danger of capture by the enemy.'

After Kush Dragon, Gila Bend and SERE, the Apache pilots were finally ready.

'We had trained for nearly a year and a half, and felt we were probably the best prepared and most battle-ready squadron to hit Afghanistan,' remarks Baz. 'This was due in part to the reports that had come back from theatre, which had in turn shaped our training – training that had been refined from brigade level down.'

On returning to their Wattisham headquarters from Gila Bend, the Apache aircrews had two weeks' leave before deployment. Most wanted the waiting to be over, and to finally prove themselves in combat. Each pilot would be heading for battle with the aim of upholding the long and distinguished tradition of the Corps.

The Army Air Corps traces its roots back to 1878, when gas-filled tethered observation balloons first took soldiers into the air. By 1912 rudimentary warplanes were in operation, and on 13 May 1912 the Royal Flying Corps was born. Six years later the Royal Air Force was formed, and at a stroke the Army lost all of its flying capabilities to the RAF. Ever since then there has been a healthy rivalry between the RAF and the Corps.

In 1941 Winston Churchill realised that he needed an airborne division to get Allied troops back into mainland Europe. Factories were flat-out manufacturing warplanes, tanks and battleships, so Churchill ordered the furniture industry to start building wooden assault gliders that could be towed into battle. Soldiers were trained to fly the gliders as part of the newly formed Glider Pilot Regiment (GPR), one of the main forebears of the Corps. The GPR played a major role in the Second World War, from Normandy to North Africa, and from Burma to Sicily.

Two of its most famous missions were Operation Overlord, the D-Day landings, and Operation Market Garden, the attempt to capture bridges over the Rhine. After the war, the Glider Pilot Regiment was reduced to one paltry squadron. But as the pre-eminent role of the helicopter emerged during the Vietnam and Korean conflicts, the GPR was hurriedly reformed as the Army Air Corps. Since then the Corps has played a role in major conflicts including Northern Ireland, the Falklands, the Balkans conflicts and in Iraq.

The rivalry with the RAF has continued, and more often than not the Corps has found itself overshadowed by the RAF's higher-profile air assets. With the arrival of the Apache attack helicopter, the Corps sensed that all that was about to change.

For the pilots of 662 Squadron their coming baptism of fire would coincide with the Golden Jubilee of the Corps. In May 2007, as 662 Squadron deployed to Afghanistan, soldiers of the Corps, led by the Regimental Sergeant Major, Darren Corby, would be mounting a series of ceremonial guard duties in London.

As the final countdown to the Afghan deployment began, the pilots concentrated on trying to shield their loved ones from the dangers and uncertainties that lay ahead. Baz found himself flicking between channels on the television, searching for news of the Afghan war while at the same time trying to reassure his family that everything was going to be all right out there.

'We're all human, and you find yourself trying to protect your family from what's going on. I told them that we were flying a bullet-proof machine, an invincible aircraft. We knew in theory how rugged the Apache was, but we also knew of its weaknesses, and the tactics of the enemy. Plus we knew how badly the Soviets had been hit in Afghanistan. But we did our best to keep all that from the family.'

A week prior to departure, the aircrew were issued with their desert combats and encouraged to wear them around camp. One evening, there was a pre-mission dinner and piss-up at the base. It ended up with thirty-odd blokes playing a game of mess rugby, a near-riot with a rugby ball, buckets of beer and no rules. Baz ended up with a shoulder injury and almost missed out on the deployment, and he all but broke the arm of his co-pilot, Tim: 'It was a crazed, alcohol- and testosterone-fuelled session, but it was all part of the bravado, bonding and madness that was needed to sustains spirits and deal with the pre-deployment tension.'

662 Squadron were finally ready for action.

3
SOLDIER FIRST

An oft-repeated saying in the Army Air Corps is 'soldier first'. This refers to the men of the Corps putting their soldier's attitude above all else, and relying upon a soldier's most basic instinct when going into battle. They knew that all the technology in the world could never beat the human senses, coupled with that soldier's intuition and instinct. Every member of 662 Squadron would be operating on the principle of soldier first when heading into Afghanistan.

At one-thirty on the morning of departure Baz said a lingering goodbye to his wife Tracy and daughter Jenny at the door of his darkened house, and took a taxi up to the base. En route, the taxi driver told Baz how proud he was of him and his fellow Apache pilots, but still charged him the full fare. No chance of a squaddie discount, Baz reflected ruefully as he handed over the money.

The members of 662 Squadron had made a collective decision to do the family farewells at home, in part because they were leaving in the dead of night. Tim, Baz's co-pilot, was saying his goodbyes to his wife Andrea and their young son before gently closing the door behind him. Steve was wishing his fiancée a fond farewell, and had earlier called his daughter Robyn at school in Germany to say his goodbyes to her. His co-pilot, Alex, was having an emotional leave-taking with his future wife, Mel.

The four airmen joined their twelve fellow Apache pilots –

eleven men and one woman – as they milled around at the gates of the airbase. Baz glanced at the sixty-odd aircrew, ground crew and support staff, feeling a mixture of relief that they were finally off and a sense of the invincibility of an Apache squadron going to war.

As they waited for the coaches to arrive, Nicola, the four-foot-something Regimental Padre, turned up and started handing out the sweets.

'It was just like we were off on a school rugby trip,' Baz remarks. 'And every one of us appreciated that small gesture.'

By three o'clock the two coaches carrying the squadron were speeding down a near-deserted motorway, when the lead vehicle did a massive, tyre-burning swerve. The driver had almost achieved what the enemy could only ever dream of – wiping out half a British Apache attack squadron in one go.

They reached the Joint Air Mounting Centre, a cavernous hangar at South Cerney Airfield, and boarded a battered double-decker bus for the short drive to RAF Brize Norton. The driver asked them not to ring the bell unless it was an emergency. That was a red rag to a bull. It was *ding-ding!* all the way, with the bus driver getting more and more angry. At least it would prevent him dropping off at the wheel.

On arrival at Brize Norton they were asked if they had any 'sharps' on them prior to boarding the aircraft. 'Nothing, apart from Baz's sharp wit and charm,' Steve replied with a grin. Neither RAF policeman smiled. To Baz and Steve's amazement, they proceeded to try to confiscate any aircrew knives, scissors and even nail clippers that they had in their flight luggage.

'Look, this is mad,' Steve remonstrated. 'We're Army and you're RAF: we're on the *same side*. What d'you think we're we going to do, attack the flight crew and force the pilots to fly us to Florida?'

Having finally convinced the RAF policemen to let them keep their sharps, the men boarded the waiting aircraft. The RAF Tristar was basic and stripped of all luxuries, but at least it was clean and there was lots of legroom. After take-off a stocky bloke in desert fatigues got to his feet and started handing out refreshments.

Baz nudged Steve in the ribs. 'Looks like the RAF's equivalent of an airhostess.'

The attendant made his way down the aisle. He paused at Steve and Baz: all he could offer was orange squash and a sausage roll, he said, as there was no hot food or drinks.

As he handed over a plastic cup of squash, Baz noticed that his hand was shaking.

'What's wrong, mate? You worried or something?'

The attendant gave Baz a wide-eyed stare. 'We're going to Kandahar,' was all he said by way of explanation.

He continued down the aisle and Baz and Steve noticed a row of stretchers strapped to the right hand side of the aircraft. They were empty, but on the return those stretchers might well be filled by wounded British soldiers. It was a sobering thought.

Several hours later, the Tristar approached Kandahar Airfield. It was four o'clock in the morning, and the aircraft was using the cover of darkness to sneak into the coalition base. The men of 662 Squadron donned their helmets and body armour in case of small-arms fire. The ageing aircraft began its lurching, corkscrew descent, heaving and plunging as it continuously changed height and speed to avoid lock-on by an enemy missile.

It was pitch black inside, with all lights extinguished in order to minimise the aircraft's visibility to the enemy. As they hurtled earthwards, the atmosphere grew eerily silent, apart from the screaming of the engines. There was no joking any more, and it struck Baz that the attendant might have had good reason to be afraid: he'd done the flight before and he knew what was coming.

The Tristar fell out of the sky and hit the tarmac with a juddering thud, braking hard to come to an abrupt stop on the battle-scarred runway. Baz sat in the darkness listening to a warbling howl that had started up. It sounded like the Tristar's auxiliary power unit (APU) was cutting in. That was odd, he reflected. Why start the APU when the main engines were still working? He could hear the diminishing wail of the turbofans as the power dropped to a gentle throb.

He turned to Steve. 'Weird. Sounds like they've started the APU. Maybe the aircraft's got a fault and that's why we've stopped so suddenly.'

Steve stared at Baz incredulously. 'APU my arse. That's the mortar warning alarm. Kandahar's just been mortared, you muppet.'

The men of 662 Squadron were forced to sit on the runway in the pitch dark as the enemy targeted the Tristar with mortars. Little could be seen or heard from inside the darkened fuselage, so no one could tell how accurate the barrage might be, but the odd crump of an explosion sounded uncomfortably close, sending shockwaves through the aircraft.

Welcome to Afghanistan, Baz told himself.

'It was a total reality check for us. From the first minute we set foot on Afghan soil the enemy were trying to kill us. The IRA used to say that the British Army had to be lucky all of the time, while they had to get lucky just the once. As we sat out there in that big white aircraft, we all of a sudden realised it was the same in Afghanistan.'

For three hours they waited, first for the barrage to end, and then while the runway was checked for unexploded ordnance. The enemy was targeting Kandahar Airfield with 107mm shells, which they had adapted to fire as mortar rockets from three or more kilometres away. The shells had the range but they were notoriously inaccurate, and the Tristar had escaped unscathed.

Kandahar Airfield (KAF) is the coalition's second most important base in Afghanistan, after Bagram Airbase near the Afghan capital, Kabul. Kandahar is primarily an American–run operation, but most of the coalition's troops pass through as it is the hub from which the war is prosecuted in southern Afghanistan.

Coalition forces operate in Afghanistan under the NATO-led International Security Assistance Force (ISAF). The key troop-contributing nations are the UK, USA, Canada, Australia, Italy, Norway, France, Holland, Germany, Denmark and Poland. At 7800 troops, the British ISAF component is second only to that of the USA.

British forces are concentrated forwards of Kandahar, at Camp
Bastion, their purpose-built desert base. But Kandahar Airfield
remains the British Harrier operating base and also the location of
Joint Helicopter Force, the tri-service (Army, Navy and Air Force)
command element for British Chinooks, Lynxes and Apaches in
theatre.

The Commanding Officer of 3 Regiment, Army Air Corps,
Lieutenant-Colonel Jon Bryant, would be stationed in Kandahar as
overall Commander of the Joint Helicopter Force. He was known
for being a no-nonsense individual. Having trained on the Apache
himself he knew from experience its capabilities, and the best way
to deploy the aircraft.

The men of 662 Squadron had a few days in Kandahar before
moving forwards to Camp Bastion. Those first few hours were a
surreal experience. They knew that they had arrived in an Afghan
airbase – the heat, the dust and the jetlag, coupled with the heady
smell of burning avtur (aviation turbine fuel), told them as much.
But at the same time they could have been forgiven for thinking
they had landed somewhere in smalltown America.

The terminal was a grand complex of buildings, constructed in
a series of glass-fronted curves like giant McDonald's arches, but
coalition troops were restricted to a purpose-built military base on
one side. Here, concrete and prefabricated aluminium buildings
clustered around a central boardwalk, the PX Mini Mall, complete
with the best the West has to offer.

There was a Pizza Hut, a Burger King, a Subway and a Tim
Hortons doughnut emporium, plus an AT&T phone centre. Nearby
sat the cavernous mess tents and a pair of warehouses. These housed
a space-age gym and the entertainment hall, with its visiting country and western bands and even Hooters calendar girls.

The men of the Squadron spent their days in briefing after briefing,
the key focus of which was the rules of engagement for Apache pilots.
MOD lawyers identified the main legitimate target types of the enemy.
In the back of every pilot's mind was the knowledge that all Apache
engagements are recorded, using an on-board camera, and that footage
can be used as evidence against them if ever a wrong move was made.

'The rules of engagement were of special interest to us,' remarks Steve, 'especially when you consider the damage our munitions can inflict, and the fact that we video every engagement on the gun tape. We knew full well that our actions would be reviewed at the end of every engagement, and that those tapes would be available to any inquiries.'

'Unlike fast jets, we can actually see an enemy soldier pick up a weapon or comms device,' Baz remarks. 'So we have to call it for ourselves in the moment: do we engage or don't we? At the end of the briefings we had a chat among ourselves. We decided that we'd talk about it in the air prior to engaging, and with time and experience this would become almost like a sixth sense to us.'

A Royal Navy pilot on an Apache placement with the Corps had spliced together several sections of gun tape from recent ops. He played this to the aircrew, talking them through various real-life scenarios. This helped in getting the pilots to envisage the complex and emotive situations that they might face, and how the rules of engagement might be applied to each.

One clip showed an enemy mortar barrage targeting a convoy of British troops. Clearly visible on the ridgeline above was an Afghan man using a mobile phone. Was he, as seemed likely, a dicker – a scout calling in enemy mortar fire? And if he was, was it legitimate to take him out and would the rules of engagement justify doing so?

'We had a final briefing by Pete Lowe, 664 Squadron's Weapons Instructor,' Steve remarks. 'He'd put together some gun-tape of recent engagements, and he ran through the footage pointing out both good and bad points. If we had to engage the enemy who were danger-close to out own troops, or Taliban fighters holding out near civilians, then our gunnery had to be exact. This was real footage with real Taliban and real weapons being fired, and we got the message loud and clear.'

When not stuck in briefings, the aircrews took full advantage of the PX Mini Mall's unreality, for there would be few such luxuries at Bastion. The aircrew felt the pressure mounting, and were eager to move forwards and up into the air over Helmand.

'We maxed out on great food, music shows, milkshakes and Burger King,' Baz remarks. 'It was great for a day or two, but no more. Because KAF is a long-established, multinational base, all the bullshit side of the Army is there, with rules for this and rules for that, saluting and wearing your headgear. We could do without all that, and we couldn't wait to start the job we'd trained so hard to do.'

'The food was gobsmacking,' remarks Steve. 'KAF was like a holiday camp . . . We overheard troops complaining about having to attend a ramp parade at four in the morning, when the coffins of those killed in action were to be loaded aboard a flight back to Brize Norton. One evening we were in the food queue and some guy was complaining that there was a lack of lobster on the menu. Contrast that with the realities of the front line, where blokes mightn't have fresh rations for days on end.'

On their last day in Kandahar, the reality of moving forwards into Helmand was suddenly brought home to the Apache aircrews. Strolling along the boardwalk, iced coffees in hand, Steve, Baz, Tim and Alex ran into an RAF loadmaster who they knew from previous operations. In contrast to most at Kandahar, the loadie had the classic thousand-yard stare – the shell-shocked look – of those fresh out of combat. His first words were to say how glad he was to be getting out of theatre and back to the UK.

A couple of hours earlier he'd been airborne in a Chinook, inbound to extract a unit of British troops. As they'd gone in to a hot landing zone they'd come under fire. Heavy-calibre rounds had punctured the Chinook's hold, narrowly missing him and his fellow loadie.

An instant later he'd found himself behind the Chinook's mini gun, a motor-driven six-barrelled Gatling gun, while the other loadie racked up the M60 machine gun. They poured fire onto the enemy positions. By the time they'd got the Chinook airborne again, the hold was thick with cordite fumes. As they flew out of there the aircraft looked like a sieve, sunlight streaming in through holes torn in the fuselage.

'The loadie's words hit home,' Steve remarks. 'As we supped those café lattes our minds suddenly switched from the mall to the reality of what was to come.'

The call came for the men of 662 Squadron to board the Hercules C130 for the flight to Camp Bastion.

'Thank God we got out when we did,' said Baz. 'We'd all of us put on weight, and you can only take so much brain freeze from milkshakes and iced coffees. We got out of Kandahar not a moment too soon.'

As he gazed out of the window of the C130, Baz noticed an expanse of vegetation stretching south from Kandahar. But once the aircraft gained altitude, a three-hundred-metre-high wall of red reared up in the distance – the start of the Red Desert. As they crossed that first massive dune, a sea of undulating sand rolled out before them, stretching to the horizon. The desert was raspberry-red in colour, and like nothing he had ever seen before.

The Red Desert gave way in turn to the jagged grey-brown of the dust and rocks of the Kajaki Mountains. Beyond that lay the Helmand River valley, a ribbon of lush green among a sea of drab rock and sand. This fertile belt stretches a dozen kilometres or so to either side of the Helmand River, and to coalition troops this area has become known as the Green Zone. It is covered in lush gardens, and poppy fields that show canary yellow and candyfloss pink from the air. Helmand accounts for much of Afghanistan's opium production, and the country's booming heroin trade.

The Green Zone runs from north to south the length of Helmand Province. To either side of this linear oasis lie barren desert and mountains, where there is little water or vegetation to sustain life. The Green Zone is home to the majority of Helmand's inhabitants – and to the Taliban and al-Qaeda forces fighting to take control of both this area and the rest of Afghanistan.

Therein lies one of the greatest challenges of the Afghan conflict. The war is being fought across the villages and fields of Afghan civilians so as to secure their freedom from the Taliban's oppressive rule. But the risks of collateral damage in the Green Zone – accidental civilian deaths or destruction of property – are unavoidably high.

That C130 flight gave the men of 662 Squadron a bird's-eye view of Helmand and the Green Zone, and in an instant the briefings that they had listened to back in the UK made sense to them. This, then, was the war zone, and the challenge of engaging the enemy from the air without killing innocent civilians suddenly seemed all the more daunting.

The approach to Camp Bastion was across a flat, featureless plain. Though desolate in the extreme, Camp Bastion's location is well chosen. It is like no other place on earth – a vast encampment of sand-coloured tents set amid the desert north of Lashkar Ghar, the capital of Helmand Province. It is a place inhabited only by nomads, and the soil is so waterless that not a blade of grass will grow. All of this means that there is zero cover for enemy forces.

Camp Bastion is the British Army's biggest construction since the Second World War. It has been purpose-built in the desert wastes, with deep boreholes that tap subterranean water supplies. The entire six-by-three-mile base is protected by razor wire, blast walls and ground radar that can detect an intruder as soon as they set foot on the surrounding plain. Camp Bastion is approached on the ground by a single rutted track, and over everything lies a layer of fine, talcum-powder-like dust, which in places is so deep it comes over a soldier's boot-tops.

Gazing out over the barren lunarscape, Baz noticed a convoy of trucks strung out across the distant horizon. Their dust plumes rose hot and silver-grey before the low sun, giving a clear indicator of their direction of travel. The convoy was bound for Bastion. These would be the 'jingly' trucks, Afghan lorries heavily decorated by jingling bells and chains, each like a mobile Christmas tree.

The jingly trucks moved in their hundreds through the deserts so as to avoid the threat of ambush on the roads, bringing supplies to Bastion. Drivers were paid six hundred dollars per supply mission, a fortune by Afghan standards. The Taliban had condemned any driver to death, and the burned-out carcasses of trucks littered the desert.

The Hercules put down at Camp Bastion, the men running off the aircraft's rear ramp and the backwash from the engines blasting sand into eyes and ears. Ranks of Hesco-Bastion walling – giant steel-mesh boxes lined with a special membrane and filled with dirt – shielded Rolla-Trac plastic matting walkways, which threaded between serried ranks of khaki tenting. It was as if an entire military base had been parachuted on to the surface of the moon.

Once away from the roar of the Hercules's turbines, the crackle of small-arms fire could be heard to the east, as some of the two thousand British soldiers at Bastion zeroed in their weapons on the ranges. To the west, there was the unmistakeable thwoop-thwoop-thwooping of a twin-rotor Chinook, as the aircraft thundered across the camp's perimeter.

As the aircrew of 662 Squadron headed for their quarters, the unmistakeable forms of a pair of Apaches rose into the air, noses dipping earthwards as they set course for a mission somewhere to the south. At the sight of that pair of aircraft, the men of 662 Squadron knew for sure that they had arrived. For the next three months, this baking slice of moonscape would be home.

Baz, Steve, Tim and Alex greeted the aircrew of 664 Squadron, those from whom they were about to take over. Mostly they were familiar faces, and the men were expecting to share a sense of camaraderie and rapport with their fellow Apache aircrew. But they found them to be strangely quiet and subdued. This lack of comradeship was unsettling. It was only later that they would come to realise that the aircrews were totally exhausted, and intent only on getting the hell out of there.

The four men slung their kit into the tent that they would share for the next three months. In each corner was a 'pod', similar in appearance to a fisherman's shelter and made from mosquito netting. This was split into two areas: there was a space for admin and storage, plus a fold-up bed. The pod was small and cramped, but at least it provided a little privacy and offered an escape from the other flight members.

Electric lights were strung from wires on the ceiling of the tent, and the floor was carpeted in more Rolla-Trac plastic matting. As Baz and Steve glanced about them it clearly wasn't luxurious Kandahar, but it was good enough. High up on one of the walls was an air-conditioning unit that was struggling to keep the interior cool. It was clearly fighting a losing battle.

662 Squadron had arrived in Bastion in the second week of May. In a little over twenty-four hours after their arrival they would be taking over as the Apache squadron on combat duty. There was much to organise before then. Briefings began almost immediately, in the Joint Helicopter Force Afghanistan – Forward ops tent. This was situated alongside the Royal Anglian Regiment's quarters, and was the nerve centre of the Apache attack squadron.

The ops tent consisted of a rank of laptop computers, a rack of comms equipment and a giant plasma screen for electronic briefings and video viewing – either live battlefield feeds or after-action viewing of Apache gun tapes. At computer stations scattered around the ops tent soldiers were typing up reports to be uploaded on to the battlegroup's live database system.

Computer screens were displaying the recognised air picture, which showed all aircraft as icons on a map of the airspace over Helmand, like an air traffic control picture. A second digital air map showed the helicopter asset tracking system: a beacon in each helicopter allowed its exact position to be tracked and displayed at all times.

To the rear of the ops tent was a crew rest area, consisting of chairs and a TV, plus facilities for making a brew. Behind that was a purpose-built crew shelter and debrief facility in which aircrews would go through their post-op debriefs and play their gun tapes. The Royal Anglians' Ops Room was a similar set-up, but with an additional plasma screen for displaying live video feeds from unmanned aerial vehicles, the pilotless, remotely operated surveillance drones.

Major Jules Franks, the Squadron's Officer Commanding (OC), led the briefings, which covered air traffic control and command of airspace, the procedure for pre- and post-op briefings, rotation of duties and so on. Major Franks was both the Squadron Commander at Bastion and an active Apache pilot who made up one of the flights. In coming operations he would find himself having to juggle his command role with that of fighting his aircraft in the thick of combat. He was known as an excellent commander, one who gave his fellow pilots' considerations paramount importance.

'The OC is a people person,' remarks Baz. 'He considers his soldiers first and foremost, and is a fantastic leader. He is pragmatic and totally capable, and leads from the front. He has to be as good as anyone else to be able to fly and fight his aircraft *and* command the squadron.'

The eight Apaches of 662 Squadron were broken down into four two-aircraft flights – Five, Six, Seven and Eight Flight. For the next three months, each flight would rotate through one of four specific duties, each of which would last for three days.

The first duty was Very High Readiness (VHR), the aircrew of which had to be ready to move at a moment's notice, day or night. The second duty was Airtest Kandahar, a rotation back through Kandahar Airfield in order to service battle-worn Apaches and pick up replacement aircraft.

The third was Duty Ops, spent either in the Ops Room at the beck and call of the OC, or air-testing Apaches around Bastion. And the fourth was Deliberate Ops, in which the aircrew would be tasked with combat, escort or other operations that could be scheduled well in advance.

In order of desirability, VHR was the top duty, followed by Deliberate Ops. With VHR, every waking and sleeping hour was totally unpredictable, and the aircrew never knew what was going to happen next.

'Excitement and adrenalin wise, it was VHR,' remarks Steve. 'You could get a call at the dead of night, and from being fast asleep you'd be out with troops in a matter of minutes. That was when the whole team effort really came into play. Ops would scramble the ground crew and drag them out of their pits to get the aircraft ready. The Ops Room would be buzzing, but all your briefing might consist of was, "You have to get there – like, yesterday!"

'You'd head out to the flight line and be sitting in the cockpit with the engines screaming, when suddenly you might get a call: "Cancel – close down". The anticlimax was unbearable. You'd head back to the Ops Room, only to discover that some fast jets had made it over target and eliminated the threat. If you were unlucky, the other flights would get all the juicy ops during VHR and you'd be left on your arse bones.'

As luck would have it, flight *Ugly* were the first to be put on VHR duty. Baz and Tim's Apache had been assigned the call sign *Ugly Five Zero*; Steve and Alex's aircraft was *Ugly Five One*.

The morning prior to the start of that VHR duty was spent collecting load-carrying jerkins (flight vests), body armour, a morphine injector and a one-handed tourniquet kit, magazines of ammunition and the SA80 carbine, plus zeroing in the weapon on the ranges. Back in the Ops Room, the aircrew did a hurried job of trying to memorise maps of the area, code names for the key British and allied bases, and the various aircraft and ground troop call-signs.

'It was a steep learning curve,' remarks Baz. 'There were times we felt totally unsure of what we were doing, if we're honest. As we tried to cram in all of that information it was a fairly solitary feeling, each person focusing on their own role. We hadn't worked as a team on a real combat mission, so there was a sense of worry about the task in hand. There was no big talk up: we just tried to treat it as being "what we do". All of the bravado of the mess rugby and Gila Bend, that was out the window now. Now, it was for real.'

That afternoon the men of flight *Ugly* climbed aboard their aircraft for a familiarisation flight, overflying key landmarks in the region. Nicknames were chosen for some of the more difficult Afghan place names so that the aircrew might better remember them during the heat of battle. After that, the two Apaches were taken down the aerial ranges, some five kilometres to the west of Camp Bastion. A couple of old Portakabins had been towed out into the desert; flight *Ugly* got to hit them with Hellfires and 30mm cannon fire to zero in their gun.

That evening the four airmen took a walk around the Apache flight line. At one end of the short runway was a circular turning area and refuelling point, and to one side sat the waiting Apaches, each contained by massive concrete blast walls. On the opposite side of the runway were the cavernous, open-sided canvas hangars, where the ground crews slept and sweated in the heat and dust blasted up by the aircraft's rotor blades. It was a brutal twenty-four hours on, twenty-four hours off way to work and live.

Each Apache was tended by a ground team consisting of an Arming Loading Point Commander, with six Air Troopers under him. Theirs was an exhausting task bereft of the highs' of flying missions. It was no wonder that the ground crews – 'groundies' in Army slang – had got piss-taking T-shirts printed up: 'WE WORK WITH CHOPPERS' read the slogan on the back, no doubt a reference to the aircrews.

But by the end of 662 Squadron's deployment, ground crew and aircrew would have forged an unbreakable bond, one that would win battles and save lives.

To the rear of the hangars was a makeshift regimental flagpole, with a black skull and crossbones flying from it. The words 'Chinthe Lines' had been carved into a wooden signboard beneath. To everyone's amusement, below that had been added the phrase: 'Now under new management'. Too right it was: 662 Squadron were taking over at Chinthe Lines.

The chinthe is a mythical creature, half-lion, half-griffin, from which the Chindits special forces of the Burma campaign took their name. Led by the maverick commander Major General Orde Wingate, and backed by General Bill Slim, one of the most talented Allied commanders of the Second World War, the Chindits took the fight to the supposedly invincible Japanese Imperial Army, employing unconventional warfare tactics *par excellence*.

Formed as the First Air Commandos, the Chindits used gliders to fly into remote jungle locations, from where they launched hit-and-run attacks behind the Japanese lines. The First Air Commandos were also one of the illustrious forebears of the Army Air Corps.

As the men strolled along the flight line, Baz pointed to one of the massive blast walls. 'Jesus, will you look at that.'

On one side of the concrete wall was painted a dramatic cartoon, depicting a half-Chinthe, half-Apache attack helicopter in action. Below it was the motto: 'Woe to he who is seen'. Next to that was a list of the names of those who had served in the previous deployment, plus a record of the rounds fired in anger by that squadron.

The men of flight *Ugly* were astonished to see that some 10,500 rounds of 30mm cannon had been put down during the previous three-month deployment, not to mention the rockets and missiles. It was an awe-inspiring amount of ammo to have expended, indicative of the sheer intensity of the combat missions flown.

Little did the four airmen know, but their own squadron's record would far exceed that figure by the end of their tour.

Baz had a hip flask that he carried with him on operations. Traditionally, he would share it with his fellow aircrew prior to their first mission. The four men took a swig of the fine, single-malt whisky, raising a toast to whatever was to come. Then the flask was stowed away for the return journey to the UK – which was a hundred days away.

4

DAY ONE, COMBAT

Day 1

The four airmen had decided to try to get fit during their Afghan deployment, or at least to keep the gut bulge to a minimum. That morning they queued early for breakfast and opted for cereal, as opposed to a full fry-up. As they sat in the mess tent in the pre-dawn silence, munching away, nothing felt very different from yesterday: but this was day one of 662 Squadron's combat deployment, and flight *Ugly* could be scrambled at a moment's notice.

After breakfast they headed over to the ops tent for the first, 7.30 a.m. briefing. They were met by the Chief of Staff, Ian McIvor, flight *Ugly's* permanent point of contact at Bastion base. Over the coming weeks, Ian McIvor was to prove the foundation upon which 662 Squadron would build a superlative combat record.

'He was our back-stop at Bastion,' Steve remarks. 'He's an ex-ranker, having been ground crew and a door-gunner. He was thrown into the job, controlling the whole of the Ops Room, sorting out shifts, monitoring us in combat and running the squadron when the OC wasn't around. He was calm, professional and thorough: sometimes he'd give us ten minutes grace and keep us in the air when HQ said we should get back. He told us if we were in a contact to let him know, and he'd get it cleared.'

The Met Officer gave a flying conditions briefing, which were, as usual, hot and dusty. Chewy Liner, the Regimental Intelligence Sergeant, came next with a briefing on movements of the enemy, plus any friendly patrols that were out on the ground, and how these might affect air operations. The Watch Keeper then briefed the aircrews on any missions planned for the day, including convoy escorts and re-supplies.

Next, the aircraft technicians outlined which Apaches were present on the flight line and how many were serviceable. The technicians were seconded to 662 Squadron from the Royal Electrical Mechanical Engineers (REME), and their task was to deal with aircraft servicing and repairs.

New aircraft were flown out from the UK in C-17 Globemaster transport aircraft to Kandahar Airfield, and flight-stressed or battle-damaged aircraft would travel back in the same way. Replacement aircraft were brought forward to Bastion as and when required. Seldom did an aircraft need to be returned to the UK in order to get it battle-ready again, as a full team of REME technicians were able to carry out most repairs at Kandahar.

The Camp Bastion doctors spoke next, giving a heads-up on the wounded soldiers brought in during the previous day's operations. 'There was one soldier shot in the face, who was touch and go on the Chinook ride into Bastion,' the doctor told them. 'After two hours' surgery we managed to save him. And the guy who was burned in the vehicle denial – he's already on his way back to the UK.'

As the Apache airmen glanced around the Ops Room they spotted a female combat medic standing beside the plasma screen. She was a real beauty, and they recognised her as one of the medics who went out on the Chinooks doing casevacs. The Apache aircrew had immense respect for the combat medics. Most were either TA or civilian volunteers, and they flew out unarmed and often under heavy enemy fire to rescue wounded British soldiers.

During the Chinook flight from battlefield to Camp Bastion, it was the combat medic's job to keep a wounded soldier alive. They would scribble the soldier's vital signs – blood pressure, pulse, blood group – on to his forehead using a marker pen. Few if any injuries could not be treated at the Camp Bastion Field Hospital, the base's state-of-the-art medical facility. If a wounded soldier reached it alive, the doctors reckoned they had a more than 95 per cent chance of saving him.

'As much as we like to crease the RAF, I can't imagine what it must be like to be in the back of a Chinook trying to resuscitate dying soldiers in the darkness of a blood-soaked hold and under enemy fire,' Baz remarks. 'We'd do anything we could to protect those casevac missions, and they'd do as much for us. We formed an unbreakable bond with the Chinook pilots, having total respect for each other.'

The briefing was finished off by the Squadron OC, Jules Franks, with a roundup of any other business. His final words were: 'End of brief: RS30.' RS30 stands for Ready Status 30 – meaning that the Very High Readiness flight was on thirty minutes' notice to move. That meant half an hour from being scrambled to having their aircraft in the air.

Flight *Ugly* had been allocated dedicated code words in case they had to be scrambled by radio from anywhere across Camp Bastion. These were known only to the four men of the flight, and command and control in the Ops Room. They had to be unique and highly memorable. The airmen chose the names of two characters from the TV sitcom *Only Fools and Horses*: *Ugly Five Zero*'s code-word would be 'Del Boy', and *Ugly Five One*'s would be 'Rodney'.

Once the briefing was over, the men of flight *Ugly* spent some time getting to know the Chinook crews. Being RAF, the Chinook pilots were all commissioned officers. That was one of the key differences between the RAF and the Corps: in the Corps, the majority of the aircrew came up from the ranks and were Sergeants, Staff Sergeants or Warrant Officers. Steve James himself was a Warrant Officer. Every Apache was commanded by the best man for the job, regardless of rank.

In theatre, the Apaches invariably went in ahead of the Chinooks to secure the airspace and ground prior to the casevacs going in. It was the responsibility of the Apache aircrews to clear the Chinooks in to land or not. As a result, Corps pilots who were more often than not Non-Commissioned Officers (NCOs) would be leading a flight of RAF officers. Sometimes the Apache aircrews could see the RAF pilots thinking, Hang on a minute – I outrank that guy and *he's* telling *me* what to do!

Having broken the ice with the RAF, the four airmen went out to check on the flight line. At the start of the day, each pair of pilots would be allocated an aircraft by its tail number. Flight *Ugly* had already been told which their aircraft were: tail number 172 was for *Ugly Five Zero*, 176 for *Ugly Five One*. Apaches 172 and 176 had already been dragged into the Very High Readiness-1 and -2 slots on the apron.

The pilots did a walk-around of the two aircraft, checking them over visually. When not on active operations, the Apaches were kept 'blanked up', with the aircraft's weapons pods and engines covered to stop sand and dirt getting into them. The interior of the cockpit was protected by a sun-reflecting shield, to prevent the aircraft heating up in the 45-degree temperatures.

Then they loaded their personal weapons and kit aboard. Alongside the SA80 carbine, a small bergen backpack containing magazines of ammo, a Camelbak water carrier, some biscuit rations and a compass was crammed into the cockpit. If the aircrew did have to ditch and go on the run, that grab bag was the key to their survival.

'As part of our survival equipment, I jokingly suggested we each take a French onion seller's outfit with us, complete with beret and black-and-white striped top,' remarks Steve. 'This would be our disguise if an Apache went down and we had to go on the run. However, we were unsure if the Taliban liked onions.'

From the flight line the men headed back to the VHR tent. As the crow flies it was barely three hundred metres between the VHR tent and the flight line. But it was a kilometre or more using the dirt roads that ran around the base perimeter. The VHR tent was adjacent to the Ops Room, and reserved strictly for the on-call crew. It would be flight *Ugly's* home for the next three days.

The VHR tent was a plush number compared to the standard accommodation, with real beds, a fridge full of cold drinks, easy chairs and a DVD player. To one side, a sheet of Rolla-Trac plastic matting and some old wooden pallets made a makeshift patio, in case anyone fancied trying to get a tan.

Steve, Baz, Tim and Alex flopped into the easy chairs, wondering what to do with themselves. They glanced around each other a little self-consciously. It was quite possible that 662 Squadron's first VHR duty might prove to be uneventful, which would be the mother of all anticlimaxes. Barely had the thought crossed their minds when the field telephone on the desk in front of them started ringing.

This was a dedicated line from the Ops Room, and it only ever rang to signal that the VHR crew were to scramble. Two rings was a call-out for the Chinook incident reaction team, most often signifying a casevac that required an Apache escort. Three rings indicated a callout for the Apache aircrews only. As the second ring died to silence the four men were sprinting out of the tent door.

Tim and Alex made directly for the ops tent, using a scaling ladder to vault over the Hesco wall that separated the two areas. Baz and Steve dived into the VHR Land Rover, gunning the engine for the flight line. Tim and Alex found the ops tent buzzing. Ian McIvor hurriedly outlined the mission: troops were in contact south of Sangin, near the allied base at Forward Operating Base (FOB) Robinson. A convoy of Royal Marines had come under attack and there were two T2 casualties. Flight *Ugly* were to shepherd in a Chinook on a casevac and escort it out again.

The injured men had suffered severe burns as their Viking armoured vehicle had been hit by an improvised explosive device. Their wounds weren't life-threatening, just as long as the burns could be treated quickly, which meant getting the wounded back to Bastion pronto. Tim and Alex turned to the Chinook's aircrew and ran through a basic flight plan, as Ian McIvor listened in. They would keep it as simple as possible and be sure to minimise any threat before clearing the Chinook in to land.

Over at the flight line, Baz brought the Land Rover to a halt in a cloud of dust and he and Steve dashed for the hangar. Inside, each of the Apache aircrew had a locker. The men grabbed their combat survival vests, checking that the armour plates were fitted, and that the GPS and radio were in the vest's internal pockets. Pulling on the heavy vests and their flight helmets as they ran, Baz and Steve made for the waiting aircraft.

They could see that the groundies had removed the blanks and sun shields, and were checking that the Apaches were bombed-up and fully fuelled. Reaching up for the grab-handles, they climbed the eight feet or so on to the Apache's bulbous flanks, and each lowered himself into the rear seat of his aircraft, threading his legs into the foot wells as he did so.

Each pilot was now surrounded by a wrap-around array of flight, navigational, communications and targeting technology. Reaching behind him, Baz grabbed the flight harness and shrugged it over his shoulders, clipping the central clasp and straps tight across his sternum. Then he groped around for the folded slabs of Kevlar armour, swinging them forwards until they slotted in to place to provide extra protection on either side of the seat.

Baz looked down: his stomach bulged out well past the extent of the protection provided by the armour plating. He told himself to breathe in.

'Every Apache pilot wishes they were a few inches thinner and a little shorter when the enemy rounds started flying close,' remarks Baz. 'We'd all of us lower our seats before take-off, so as to provide as small a target as possible.'

At this stage, neither Baz nor Steve had any idea what the coming mission might be, and they didn't particularly care. Their every effort was concentrated on getting airborne as quickly as possible.

First they flicked on the auxiliary power unit (APU), a tiny turbine in the rear that provides power to the aircraft's key systems prior to starting the main engines. The cockpit's interior was already hot from being under the full sun. The APU would enable the air-conditioning to run and cool the aircraft's main systems, many of which would malfunction in the heat.

Reaching into his pocket, Baz removed his data transfer cartridge, inserted it into a slot and punched a series of keys on the flight computer's palm-sized keyboard. The small data drive contained digital mapping covering the whole area of operations, including restricted flight zones, major towns and bases, and known enemy locations. This information was updated on a daily basis. Pressing another sequence of keys, Baz zoned his flight computer to speak to his wing aircraft, *Ugly Five One*, so that both cockpits had become part of a live digital chatroom.

A squelch of static in his headphones signalled his radio coming to life; Baz reached forwards to tune it in to the combat radio net of the ground troops. As soon as he did so he could hear reports coming in of the contact. The crippled British convoy was now coming under further enemy fire. He could feel the adrenalin pumping, and from the radio reports alone he knew that this was it: they were going out to a contact.

Splitting his mind into parallel zones, Baz began to run though the Apache's complex series of pre-flight checks at the same time as he monitored the radio traffic, while keeping a watch on the groundies as they removed the covers from the surveillance pod on the aircraft's nose.

To his right he noticed the Arming Loading Point Commander (ALPC) plugging in his intercom to the jack on the end of the Apache's stub wing. As Baz flicked his hands over the pre-flight controls – infrared systems: cooling to operational; radar systems: turning; daytime TV: running – the ALPC started to give him a rundown of the aircraft's weapons load.

'Okay Sir, you have two SAL Hellfire on each stub wing. You have nineteen rockets in each pod, so a total of thirty-eight – all flechette. And you are armed with three hundred 30mm rounds. Are you happy with the munitions load?'

'Roger that, Wing, and thanks.'

Each Apache had been fitted with an auxiliary fuel tank capable of carrying an extra six hundred pounds of fuel. This had both an up side and a down side. The extra fuel meant the aircraft had greater range and could spend more loiter time over target, but the weight had to be compensated for somehow.

The CRV7 rockets can carry different types of warhead: high-explosive incendiary semi-armour piercing (HEISAP) or flechette. Each flechette rocket contained eighty five-inch darts (flechettes) made from tungsten, one of hardest metals known to man. The flechettes fired out from the warhead in a lethal cone of death capable of piercing thick walls, trees and even armour. Eight rockets releasing 640 flechettes into an area the size of a football field was potentially a battle-winner *par excellence*.

Flicking his eyes between the pair of portable television-sized screens to his left and right front, Baz pushed a button to pull up the aircraft's 3D armament display. He checked that the flight computer could 'see' the munitions that he now knew he had loaded. After confirming weapons load, he turned to what was arguably the most important piece of kit on the aircraft, the helicopter integrated defensive aids suite (HIDAS) – the Apache's automatic defence system.

HIDAS provides defence against heat-seeking and radar-guided missiles, and it even detects the heat signatures of rocket-propelled grenades firing from the ground. As soon as it detects a threat it deploys the correct countermeasures to defeat it, while issuing a voice warning to the aircrew. HIDAS is the single most important go/no go piece of equipment on the whole aircraft. Without it functioning properly, he would not be clear to get airborne.

By now the APU had raised enough condensed air pressure to start the main engines. The aircraft's night vision and infrared surveillance systems had cooled to a level at which they could distinguish between hot and cold, which is basically how they function. And the air temperature in both cockpits was dropping to something like bearable.

Flicking the flight computer on to flight-controls mode, Baz asked it to carry out the all-important check made on every helicopter prior to take-off: that the hydraulic systems that moved the tail rotor and adjusted the pitch of the main blades were working. As the computer ran through those checks, Baz turned his attention to the fly-by-wire system. This is a lifesaver on the Apache, for it detects when normal flight controls have been lost – due to mechanical failure or enemy fire – and enables a simple, back-up system to kick in.

Glancing over at the Ground Crew Commander, Baz was given a thumbs-up: he was cleared to start engines. He reached down and

pushed the left engine power lever forwards. There was a whine
from above, which grew in pitch and intensity as the rotors started
to turn. The groundies swarmed around the left engine, checking
for leaks or fires, then moved over to the right-hand side of the aircraft. With both engines sending power to the rotors they rapidly
spooled up to speed. The ground crew did one final sanity check,
before clearing *Ugly Five Zero* to get airborne.

'This was the first mission and hearts were pumping,' Baz
remarks. 'But, amazingly, everything seemed so calm and professional: the training was kicking in and we had done similar missions
during Kush Dragon so we almost felt as if we'd been here before.'

Out of the corner of his eye, Baz noticed two figures sprinting
for the flight line. It was Tim and Alex, their heads bent low to
avoid the downwash of the rotors. Tim joined Baz in the cockpit
of *Ugly Five One*, squeezing between the barrel of his SA80 that
was jammed between the front seat and the door frame, and limbo-
dancing his way under the optical relay tube, the awkward gunnery
sight that sticks up into the front-seater's chest. To either side of that
are the pistol-grip columns that allow the front-seater to control
the weapons systems and laser.

Bulked out in body armour, survival vest and ungainly Kevlar
helmet, it was a miracle how the front-seaters ever made it in
there, Baz reflected. The rear seat was set considerably higher so
Baz had a sweeping view over Tim's head, whereas the front-seater
was tucked down in the bowels of the aircraft, his forward vision
dominated by the gunnery controls.

Baz noticed a message coming in via the computer net from
their wing, *Ugly Five One*. 'You ready yet, old men?'

Somehow, Steve and Alex always seemed to get flight-ready
before Baz and Tim. It irked Baz no end.

'Wankers,' was the one-word reply that he typed back at them.

'North of Sangin – TIC,' Tim's voice cut in over the radio chatter, sounding breathless from the run.

TIC stands for Troops in Contact. It was a phrase that was to
become wearily familiar over the coming months.

'We'll go low, you go high. I'll give you more en route.'

British Apaches deploy in pairs, keeping a minimum of altitude between their flight paths as a default mode to avoid air collisions during complex air manoeuvres. This was the 'low-high' reference that Tim, as flight leader, had made.

As Baz punched in a route to Sangin, Tim was fully occupied with the Apache's weapons systems. He snapped his helmet-mounted display (HMD) on to his helmet, bringing the monocle screen down over his right eye. Pushing himself up in his seat and glancing over the top of the bulky gunnery controls, he proceeded to 'bore sight' his HMD, lining up the crosshair with a red bullseye and pressing a synchronisation button.

Once this had been done, sensors in the rear corners of the cockpit created an invisible cone of infrared light around Tim's helmet. The slightest movement of his head would be detected by the sensors, enabling the weapons systems to be slaved to his eye line.

Baz did the same in the rear cockpit.

Tim turned his attention to the surveillance pod as he began running through his target acquisition systems. This being a day-time mission, they were likely to rely on the 127-times magnification video lens to find targets. On full zoom, narrow field mode the video was an extremely accurate way to find, target and kill the enemy. Once the pod was checked, he moved on to the weapons tests, the final checks before take-off.

'Ground override on,' Tim announced. This permitted the weapons to be tested prior to getting airborne. 'Ground crew: stand clear of the gun.'

The groundies moved away from the muzzle of the 30mm cannon. 'Roger, clear of the gun.'

Tim pushed forward a small Chinese-hat shaped button on his left-hand pistol grip control column. 'Actioning gun.'

There are 240 separate control buttons in the Apache's front cockpit and over a hundred in the rear. Each has up to four functions, and each has a highly distinctive shape and feel – a ribbed pyramid, a smooth Chinese hat, a rubbery rocker switch. This allows the pilots to identify the controls by touch and feel alone –

crucial for night operations when the aircraft would be showing no lights, the cockpit swathed in darkness.

Immediately Tim had thumbed the Chinese hat button on his pistol grip control column, the 30mm cannon sprang into life, its motor vibrating through the aircraft's floor. Reaching forward with his right hand, Tim stroked the force control pad and the 30mm gun traversed left, right, up and down in response to the movements of his thumb.

The Ground Crew Commander confirmed that the gun had full mobility: 'Fully left, fully right, fully up and fully down.'

'Safe. Acquisition source – fixed direct; laser codes – Alpha and Bravo; burst rate – twenty,' Tim announced, confirming the full range of the cannon's functions. 'Your gun,' he concluded, handing over to Baz.

While Baz did a repeat set of checks from the rear, Tim selected the rocket pods. 'Actioning rockets.' He ran though a similar set of tests for that system before moving onto the Hellfires.

'Actioning missiles – missile page. Trajectory – low, direct; acquisition source – fixed; range – three kilometres. Countermeasures – off. I can see two missiles present, all code Alpha, with one missile ready on the left hand rail. Check complete. Your weapon.'

'Roger, actioning missiles,' Baz confirmed as he again repeated the procedure from the rear. 'Checks complete. Armament panel – safe. No weapons actioned.'

It was time to get airborne.

'Pins, chocks and cords,' Tim announced as the groundies raced to remove the wooden blocks from beneath the aircraft's wheels.

The Ground Crew Commander gave a thumbs-up: 'All removed. Disconnecting. Have a safe flight'.

'Thanks buddy, see you in about two hours.'

'APU?' Tim queried.

'APU is off. Fuel is full and sufficient for the task.'

'Performance?'

Baz pressed a button next to his left-hand computer screen. 'VSSE is fifty-six knots and we have 95 per cent inside ground effect and 105 per cent outside.'

'Roger that,' Tim confirmed. 'Harness check – locked and tight.'

'Locked and tight.'

'Lights.'

'Calcutta.' This meant that that the Apache was showing no lights, as in the black hole of Calcutta.

'Tail wheel and parking brake?'

'Tail wheel is locked; brakes are off.'

'Weapons systems?'

'Arm safe switch is on, ground override off and no weapons actioned.'

'Checks complete. Let's go!'

As Baz taxiied the lead Apache out on to the runway, he made a call to the tower and got final clearance to get airborne. Normally the aircraft would do a hover take-off, lifting into a vertical hover. But here at Bastion things were different. They were at an altitude of three-thousand feet, in furnace-like temperatures and with a heavily bombed-up and fuelled-up aircraft. In thin air the rotors produce less lift. The only safe way to get airborne was to do a running take-off, which was why the heli-runway had been built.

Baz lined up the Apache on the 230-metre runway. Reaching down with his left hand, he grabbed the collective, a lever the size and shape of a knobbly handbrake, and eased it upwards. In doing so, a system of levers and rods changed the pitch of the four rotor blades, making them cut into the air more deeply. This increased the airflow over the aerodynamic wing-shape of the blades, in turn boosting lift. When the force of the lift became greater than the weight of the Apache it should rise into the air.

But as the pitch of the blades increased so did the drag, and engine power had to be increased to stop the spinning rotors slow-ing. On the Apache, as with most modern helicopters, this is managed automatically by a system called FADEC (fully automatic digital engine control). A system of sensors detects changes in the collective and the rotor pitch, boosting power as soon as it is required.

Baz eased up the collective still further, the machine bucking and straining as the rotors slapped at the air above. The increase in rotor speed and drag created a powerful torque reaction which would tend to make the fuselage spin in the opposite direction to the rotors once the aircraft took to the air. This is countered by the aircraft's tail rotor. As Baz raised the collective he applied pressure to the left floor pedal, increasing power to the tail rotor and countering the torque from the main blades.

Baz was now some sixty seconds into the delicate dance of foot, hand and eye that would get the aircraft airborne. He did a final visual check that the runway ahead was clear and boosted power to 55 per cent, increasing pressure with his left foot as he did so. With his left hand playing on the collective, his right rested on a lever between his legs, the cyclic, which is in effect the Apache's steering wheel. As he eased it forwards the orientation of the main rotor shifted slightly forwards, and the rear wheel of the aircraft lifted free of the runway.

With the Apache balanced on its two front wheels, Baz did a rapid scan of the imagery on his HMD, the monocle-screen sitting over his right eye. He had to get the aircraft's nose below the artificial horizon line by one degree, at which point it would be angled exactly right to gain enough speed for safe take-off on the short runway. If the nose-down attitude was insufficient, the aircraft would run out of runway; if it was overdone, the 30mm cannon beneath the aircraft would plough into the tarmac. And if he pushed the cyclic too far without enough power on the collective, the spinning rotor would tilt too far forwards and smash in to the nose of the aircraft.

Releasing the brakes, the Apache lurched forwards. As it accelerated towards its take-off speed, Baz danced on the foot pedals, minute adjustments keeping the line straight on the runway. As the forty-five-knot speed was reached, Baz eased the collective power towards maximum and the eight tonne machine lifted gently in to the air. Boosting lift with the collective still further, and pushing the cyclic forwards to raise airspeed, Baz hit the speed at which the Apache could keep flying after a single engine failure. He immediately pushed the cyclic lever to the far left, shifting the rotor orientation slightly and banking the aircraft into a sharp left hand turn.

At the end of the heli-runway was an ammo dump, and over-flying this had to be avoided at all costs. The sharp left turn increased the torque on the rotor blades so power had to be boosted to almost 100 per cent. With the twin turbines screaming into the tight turn, Baz reached out and flicked the counter-measures suite on to semi-auto-matic. In this mode the HIDAS detectors would be fully operational but the defensive flares could only be triggered manually. Without taking this precaution the decoy flares might accidentally trigger, with catastrophic consequences if they landed in the ammo dump.

Steve followed Baz's lead, and for the first ten kilometres they kept their aircraft low and level in an effort to fox any dickers – enemy spotters who might be trying to guess the Apache's desti-nation. As they did so, both pilots were continuously playing with the cyclic, minutely adjusting the aircraft's trim as it reacted to changes in wind and air pressure. Once Camp Bastion had faded into the haze behind them they took the aircraft up to six thousand feet on Tim's orders to go 'high-high', and pushed the airspeed up to the Apache's 258 kph cruising speed.

The tactic to get from low to high altitude in the quickest time without being vulnerable to enemy fire is called the Wells Manoeuvre. It takes the aircraft up in an unpredictable series of movements that make tracking it from the ground next to impos-sible. 'High-high' meant above the threat band, at which level the aircraft was safe from most, if not all, ground fire.

Having reached that altitude, Baz put a call through to *Crowbar*, the air traffic control unit at Bastion, giving a brief outline of their area of operations and nature of mission.

'*Crowbar, Ugly Five Zero*. Mission number 3450, routing *Shop, Susan*. Request picture north.'

'ROZ *Susan* UAV four thousand feet. Picture north clear.'

Crowbar was giving a warning for their intended flight path. An unmanned aerial vehicle (UAV) was operating within restricted operating zone (ROZ) codename *Susan* – part of the airspace the Apaches were routing through. Generally, they would be alerted to any areas where there might be artillery fire, air activity or enemy actions that might restrict the Apache's ability to fly.

After checking with *Crowbar*, flight *Ugly* were finally cleared into the contact. From the call out to being airborne would normally take some forty-five minutes, but here at Bastion they had managed it in a fraction of that time. Corners had been cut and the groundies had sweated blood to get them moving, but they all understood why. Lives depended on the Apaches getting into the air and over the battlefield in double-quick time.

It was a twenty-minute flight north to Sangin, and for the first time since the telephone had rung Baz found himself with a moment to catch his breath. First priority was to get some details from his front-seater as to the nature of the mission.

'So Tim, what're we going into here?' Baz asked, speaking into the radio attached to his helmet.

As Tim briefed him on the coming mission, Baz tried to collect his thoughts. Getting airborne had been frantic and he was soaked in sweat from exertion and the aircraft's hot interior. Ever since they had been told to scramble he'd barely had a moment to consider what the mission might be. Now, as he pushed the Apache onwards, he found his mind totally focused on the wounded British soldiers on the ground, and their brothers in arms who were taking fire. Baz was in the tunnel vision of the flight into combat; all other thoughts were blanked from his mind.

'When you're going into battle everything else goes out the window. All the bravado from before, thoughts of home, your family, the mortgage, the kids – all of that is gone. You're a far different person from the one your mates perceive you to be on a daily basis. In that cockpit on the run in to battle you know that everything you've done before is building to this moment. That tunnel vision is vital to the process, but it can prove dangerous as well.'

Behind and above the lead Apache, Steve was having similar thoughts: 'I'd been waiting on the runway thinking, this is it: the only thing that can stop this now is if the aircraft doesn't function. Let's go! There were those few moments' silence as we asked for final clearance, and then we got the "go". I lined up, and before I knew it I was running off the runway and almost crashing into Baz, so keen was I to get going on my first flight duty.'

It was tempting to follow the extraordinary ribbon of green and blue that stretched below the aircraft into the distant heat haze – the Green Zone of the Helmand River valley. That would lead directly to the target. Sangin, like most human settlements in Helmand, huddled on the banks of the river, the grey-brown desert crowding in from either side.

But Baz kept the flight well to the left of that for the Green Zone spelled danger. It was from there that they were most likely to be engaged by ground fire or missiles as the enemy kept to the thick cover of the bush and the shadows. And if an Apache had to make a crash landing it was better to do so in the empty desert wastes than in the heart of enemy territory.

As Baz gazed out of the cockpit of the lead aircraft he spotted a column of coal-black smoke barrelling into the ice-blue sky up ahead. It was oily and angry, and it could only come from burning diesel fuel, engine oil and rubber – a vehicle on fire. No doubt about it, that had to be the crippled Viking armoured vehicle.

They were still several kilometres out yet the complex navigational kit on board the Apache had been rendered all but superfluous. That pillar of smoke was the location of the contact and all Baz needed was his Mk I human eyeball to draw him onwards to the field of battle.

As the smoke loomed ever larger in the aircrew's vision, *Ugly Five Zero* tried to make contact with the ground troops using the secure radio system. Sangin sits in a wide valley carved out by the Helmand River, and only to the south is it clear of the barren, raggedy grey mountains. With the two Apaches approaching via the south, making direct radio contact should prove no problem.

Baz's front-seater, Tim, made the call. '*Widow Six Nine*, this is *Ugly Five Zero*, do you read me?'

Each unit of British ground troops has a Joint Terminal Attack Controller (JTAC) embedded within it. The role of the JTAC is to liaise with coalition air power, and each has a dedicated *Widow* callsign.

There was a burst of static in the crew's headphones: '*Ugly*, this is *Widow Six Nine*. You are loud and clear.'

'Inbound two Apaches, one Chinook casevac. ETA three minutes, standard weapon loads. Request area of operations update.'

'We're in a defile five clicks south of Sangin. We're on a narrow
track, high ground to the east and a wadi to the west. We've got a
Viking hit and four casualties, three with burns and breathing difficulties. We're taking incoming rounds from the high ground.'

'Visual the smoke from the burning vehicle: I'll use that as my
marker for the talk-on. Do you have an LZ for the casevac?'

'LZ is three hundred metres to the east of the burning Viking.
LZ is hot, repeat hot. We're taking incoming rounds and there's a
mobile enemy presence in the area. Watch out for a dark-coloured
saloon car: suspected enemy mortar team. Coordinates for the LZ
are 23649685. Repeat, 23649685.'

'Roger 23-64-96-85. Overhead in two minutes.'

The instant those coordinates were given Alex punched them
into the flight computer of *Ugly Five One*, and sent them across to
Ugly Five Zero via the data net. Alex was always the fastest at imput-
ing grids, storing and sending them.

There were four casualties now, and they sounded more serious
than first reports had suggested. Baz relayed that information to the
Chinook as Tim slaved the video lens on the nose pod to the coordinates of the ambush. Even at this distance, some six kilometres
out, the 127-times magnification lens provided a stable and clear
picture.

As he studied the area, Baz realised that this was a classic ambush
situation. He could envisage how the enemy had put the attack
together and what assets they would have used to do so. The
convoy of Viking tracked vehicles had been on a relief mission,
driving up to FOB Robinson, a British base to the south-east
of Sangin. The commander had taken the standard precaution of
avoiding the roads and driving through the open desert, but the
tracked vehicles would have kicked up a cloud of dust visible for
many miles.

A small and mobile enemy unit – most likely a civilian-looking
car or even a motorbike – would have tracked the convoy, working
out its likely destination from the direction of the dust trails. They

would then have raced ahead to a known bottleneck, where the convoy would be forced to follow a given route.

Working quickly, they would have buried a mine or perhaps an improvised explosive device (IED) on the trackside and retreated to a vantage point. If it was a mine, the weight of the Viking would have set off the explosion. If it was an IED, it was most likely that a mobile phone signal would have been used by the watching enemy to detonate the charge. It was a raw and basic – yet effective – form of warfare, and standard operating procedure for the enemy in Helmand.

It was also notoriously difficult for coalition ground forces to guard against, especially as the mine-laying team would look no different from the civilian population until the very moment of setting the ambush. In fact, they would do everything in their power not to draw attention to themselves.

Once the ambush had been triggered the enemy would have hit the convoy with small-arms fire and mortars, hoping to capitalise on the confusion and alarm caused by the initial explosion. And if, as was now the case, a Chinook came in on a casevac mission, that was the target that every enemy fighter prayed for. From their bird's-eye view of the battlefield, Baz knew that they had to find and nail that enemy force to allow the Chinook to go in safely and extract the wounded.

'We knew that they were good at setting an ambush on the fly. And this ambush site was very well chosen: it was totally open, yet left our troops little room to manoeuvre, so it was an ideal killing ground. One thousand metres to the east was a main road, and it was there that the saloon car had been spotted dicking the convoy.

If the *Ugly* airmen could find that car they'd be halfway there.

5

DEL BOY AND RODNEY

As the two Apaches powered in over the ambush site, Steve radioed the Chinook to the rear and asked the pilots to establish a holding pattern over the desert. That would leave flight *Ugly* free to go in and clear the LZ. Like the Apaches, the Chinook had only a limited amount of fuel, so now the race was on to find and kill the enemy. This was the name of the game in Helmand, and for the first time flight *Ugly* were about to be tested.

The pair of Apaches set up in wheel formation above the battlefield, one opposite the other in a circular orbit. The pillar of black smoke pluming into the sky formed the axis around which the aircraft circled. Down below the Viking lay in a blasted heap, smoking debris clearly visible all around, its buckled sheet metal and shattered interior a red-hot inferno as the flames billowed and roared.

It looked like a mine strike: nothing else could have so comprehensively torn the Viking apart. Behind the stricken Viking was a snake of armoured vehicles, the occupants of which had dismounted and taken up all-around defensive positions. To the east of the column of smoke a group of soldiers could be seen in box formation, securing a landing zone where the Chinook could put down and collect the wounded.

To the north was a high ridge. No doubt the enemy were up there somewhere, watching and waiting. To the south was a steep drop to a riverbed far below. There was no way out of the ambush but forward along the track that was blocked by the crippled

Viking. Numerous hulks of burnt-out vehicles, both military and civilian, littered the ground, testament to how popular this was as an ambush site. There were any number of potential vantage points from which the enemy could snipe at the column below.

In the terse radio chatter that followed, the four pilots went over what had happened the previous day. A Danish patrol had been hit by a mine and the enemy had quickly brought down accurate mortar fire on the ambush site. If there was a mortar team down there somewhere there was no way that flight *Ugly* could allow the Chinook to go in. One mortar round dropped on the Chinook and the aircraft would be finished. Flight *Ugly* would have to find and kill the enemy first.

For five minutes the pair of Apaches continued to fly their search orbits, straining their eyes to spot any enemy movement, but there was nothing. The frustration in each aircraft was palpable: ground troops were being hit by sporadic sniper fire and there were injured men who would die if the Chinook was unable to put down.

Suddenly, out of the corner of his eye, Tim spotted something – the blinding flash of sunlight on glass. There was movement on the road, some seven hundred metres up ahead of the ambush site. He slaved the video lens to that movement and it immediately picked up the image of a maroon-coloured saloon car crawling at slow speed along the highway.

As *Ugly Five Zero* relayed the coordinates to *Ugly Five One*, all four aircrew felt a kick of adrenalin. The two aircraft moved in to take a closer look, each sensing that this could well be the enemy mortar team that the *Widow* had warned them to look out for. In this part of the world vehicles are uncommon. Generally they are owned or used by people with money or influence such as warlords, businessmen and drug-traffickers, or the Taliban.

Eyes glued to the 127-times video picture, Baz, Tim, Steve and Alex watched the vehicle slow to a halt. The two Apaches held an orbit some three kilometres distant so as not to alert the car's occupants to the fact that they had been spotted. Three figures got out, two dressed in white robes, the third in the black dishdasha and headgear that so often indicated a Taliban commander. The men in white moved off the road, descending into a dark pit that looked like a borehole or a well.

The man in black crouched in full view at the side of the vehicle. He turned and stared in the direction of the crippled British convoy, his face unmoving in the bright sunlight, one hand shading his eyes. The other hand fished around inside his black robes, emerging with what appeared to be a camouflage-coloured pair of binoculars. The man in black lifted them to his eyes, seeming to train them on the convoy below. As he did so, Tim prepped the 30mm cannon, ensuring it was armed, locked-on and ready to fire.

Baz's soldier's sixth sense was screaming: this had to be the mobile unit that the *Widow* had alerted them to, and there had to be a mortar tube hidden in that well. But as of yet none of the three men had shown any weapons, and there was still just a chance that they were up to something innocuous.

Each of the four airmen ran the rules of engagement through his mind: was what they could see enough to justify opening fire? Tim voiced his thoughts over the radio net: 'I know what it looks like, but is there any way that it could be innocent? Like a family getting water? Like the guy squatting down praying or something?'

'I reckon I can see something inside that well,' came Steve's calm reply. 'It's black as hell in there, but can anyone make out a dark tube shape? Any of you lot see it?'

Baz strained his eyes. The two men in white did seem to be leaning over something, but it was mostly hidden in deep shadow. Was it a mortar tube? It was hard to say for sure. Either way, there was no way in which they could allow the enemy figures – if that's what they were – to launch a first strike onto the convoy below. With the clock ticking and the Chinook still orbiting out over the desert, a decision had to be made, and fast.

'I can see a dark shape, which could be a mortar tube,' Baz confirmed to Steve. 'We see two guys down there, and one with the binos. What d'you reckon – are we clear to fire?'

'Alex and me, we're happy,' Steve replied. 'He has the binos and he has two men down in the well, and the guy has definitely been observing the area of the convoy.'

It was time to check with the *Widow* on the ground.

'*Widow Six Nine*, this is *Ugly*,' Tim intoned into his radio. 'We've got eyes on a maroon sedan, six hundred metres to your north on the main roadway. Three males of fighting age dismounted, no weapons visible. Two appear to be preparing what looks like a mortar tube hidden in a well. The third is observing your position via binoculars. Is that your suspect vehicle, and are we cleared to fire?'

'That's the vehicle. I'll clear it up the chain. Stand by.'

The *Widow* made a call to Bastion, seeking clearance to engage the target. As he did so, the four men in the circling Apaches kept their eyes glued to the scene below them. At any moment they were expecting to see a white-hot muzzle flash rent the shadows and an 81mm mortar round to go smashing into the exposed ranks of the convoy below them.

The tension in both cockpits was agonising as they waited for the *Widow* to come back with a green light. It was normal operating procedure for the air cover to seek clearance via the *Widow* to open fire, especially in tough situations like this one where a suspected enemy force appeared to be unarmed. But even so, the wait was frustrating as hell.

There was a squish of static and *Widow Six Nine* was back on the air.

'*Ugly, Widow Six Nine*. You're cleared to engage.'

The four airmen breathed a collective sigh of relief. 'Roger. Engaging now.'

The decision to open fire on unarmed figures was never taken lightly. As *Ugly Five One* was in a better position to fire first, Tim told them to engage with a warning burst. Alex moved the crosshair sight on his video screen a hundred metres to the left of target, flicked up the trigger guard on his pistol grip control column and pulled the trigger. An instant later there was a juddering growl from below the cockpit floor as the 30mm cannon churned out a ten-round burst.

For six seconds or so nothing happened as the high-explosive rounds sped the three kilometres to target, then the desert to one side of the saloon car exploded in a sheet of dust and flying sand.

As *Ugly Five Zero* came around on target a second ten-round burst slammed into the desert, this time closer than the first.

The 127-times video image was without sound but the picture was crystal clear. At a hundred metres or less distance the impact of the high-explosive rounds must have been deafening for the figures at the roadside. But not a man among them had so much as flinched.

The figure in black kept his binoculars glued to his eyes, his focus on the convoy below. It was almost as if the warning shots had never been fired, let alone torn into the earth a hair's breadth away from his position. The man in black made not the slightest effort to raise his hands in protest or wave the Apaches off. In fact, he was acting as if they weren't even there.

'Perhaps he's deaf,' Steve remarked sarcastically.

Further ten-round warning bursts were fired, each round creeping closer to the borehole. The last of *Ugly Five One*'s rounds tore into the desert barely twenty yards in front of the crouching man but he didn't so much as stir. As the dust from the rounds settled not a man among the three of them had made the slightest effort to move.

'Perhaps they're blind as well as deaf,' Baz added.

It was either that, or these were some of the bravest men under fire that the aircrew had ever encountered. The lone figure in black turned to those behind him and began issuing instructions. There was a series of rapid movements in the shadows of the well, as if readying a mortar to fire.

The men of flight *Ugly* knew that this was it. *Enough*. No way was this normal behaviour. This was an enemy mortar team and they had to take them out before they got rounds in the air and hit the British soldiers in the pass below.

Both aircraft turned towards target and opened up, the 30mm cannons on their chin turrets spitting fire and pumping twenty-round bursts at the target. As the rounds impacted the flash of exploding shells rent the circle of darkness, razor sharp shards of shrapnel tearing apart whatever was hidden in there.

Within the closed confines of the well the effect of the 30mm rounds would be murderous: no living thing would be able to survive.

Further rounds slammed into the rim of the structure and tore into the desert at the feet of the crouching man, the whole area erupting in sea of exploding sand.

Suddenly a lone figure emerged through the haze, running away from the kill zone. It was the commander, black robes flying as he raced like the wind. It was beyond belief that he had survived the onslaught: 120 30mm rounds had been unleashed on the target. But somehow he had done so and now he was running for his life.

He raced ahead, *Ugly Five One* tracking him with the cannon and opening fire, rounds slamming into the desert at his heels. Just as they seemed to catch him, the commander dropped his binoculars and doubled back to fetch them. The high-explosive rounds tore into the desert where he'd just been standing. Binoculars in hand, the man in black dived into the cover of some mud-walled buildings, just making it in there alive.

As the dust cleared above the well nothing stirred. There were presumably two men down there in the darkness, their white robes lacerated and streaked with red where the rounds had torn them apart, their lifeblood leaking on to the hot sand. Hopefully, there was also a twisted and buckled mortar tube lying there alongside the two dead men.

Baz felt nothing above a sense of a job well done. The enemy must have had balls of brass to stand firm under fire as they had done. And when the commander had finally broken and ran he'd covered some three hundred yards like an Olympic sprinter. It was no mean feat considering he was doing so at three-thousand feet, in forty-degree heat, wearing sandals. Baz couldn't help but respect their bravery, and he hoped to God that down in that blasted well was the evidence to prove that they had been right to engage.

Ugly Five Zero held her position orbiting above the well. *Ugly Five One* split from her wing aircraft, heading off to rendezvous with the Chinook and clear it in to the landing zone to pick up the four casualties. With the mortar team eliminated, it should be safe enough to do so now. The aircrew of *Ugly Five Zero* combed the ground below for further signs of the enemy. As they did so, Tim radioed in a report.

'*Widow Six Nine*, this is *Ugly* – mortar team eliminated. Suspect two dead in well. One got away and is holed up in a compound three hundred yards to the west of the well head.'

'Good work, *Ugly*! Take out whichever building he's hiding in and let's finish the job.'

'Negative, *Widow Six Nine*. There're too many unknowns in there. We're holding station. Let us know if you need us for anything else.'

For all the aircrew knew, the compound to which the enemy commander had fled could be a family home with women and children inside. All it had been was the nearest slice of cover that he could find from the attack helicopters. No way were they going to take that compound out. There was, however, no reason why they shouldn't deprive the enemy of their vehicle.

From two kilometres out *Ugly Five Zero* set up for an attacking run on the saloon car, unleashing a single Hellfire missile. With the aircraft's laser painting the target, the Hellfire homed in on the point where the laser beam bounced back from the skin of the vehicle.

Eight seconds after launch there was a streak of black at the top of the Apache's video screen as the missile plummeted earthwards, blowing the vehicle into the air. As it tumbled back to earth the fuel tank exploded and the whole of the road was engulfed in flames. Baz was relieved to see the flash-explosions of ammunition cooking off inside the car, for it meant that the passengers had been carrying weapons after all.

While Baz and Tim had been Hellfiring the vehicle, *Ugly Five One* had escorted the Chinook into the LZ. It had collected the four wounded and the big helicopter was already heading back towards Camp Bastion with the casualties on board. Flight *Ugly* had one last task to do prior to disengaging from the battlefield: the crippled Viking had to be denied to the enemy.

The Viking all-terrain protected vehicle is state-of-the-art troop transport that, as its name suggests, can go almost anywhere. It is amphibious and its caterpillar tracks can surmount most obstacles. The one-millon-dollar vehicle has recently been introduced to the

British Army. It contains top-notch weaponry and communications kit that would need to be destroyed to prevent it falling into enemy hands.

The Hellfire is designed as an anti-tank weapon, its shaped charge burning through all known armour. For a second time *Ugly Five Zero* lined up for a Hellfire hit, this time on a British military asset. The Viking is a two-part vehicle, the front and rear compartments being articulated in the middle. Having warned friendly forces of the impending missile strike, that first Hellfire tore into the front compartment of the Viking, the cab disintegrating into twisted plates of buckled steel.

As *Ugly Five Zero* prepared to Hellfire the Viking's rear compartment, Steve came up over the radio net.

'Let's not be greedy here, guys. How about leaving the second bite of the cake for us?'

'We thought you needed a diet, Fatso,' Baz replied. 'Go on then, it's all yours.'

'Can you believe those guys?' Steve said to Alex, his front-seater. 'They're that greedy, doing the whole of the Viking on their own when they know we're here.'

Alex gave a good-natured shrug. He aimed his laser at the rear compartment of the Viking, holding the sight on target, which in turn fed the weapons processors with all the necessary information to direct the missile. He pulled the trigger, the Hellfire leapt off its rail and seconds later the Viking and the missile met face-to-face in a burst of flame.

Having turned both front and rear compartments of the armoured vehicle into twisted metal hulks, the Apaches remained on station for a further ten minutes. They provided top cover as the British convoy extricated itself from the ambush position and got safely underway. Then, with a final farewell to *Widow Six Nine*, the pair of aircraft turned for home.

As they did so, the four airmen counted the cost of the battle so far: four British soldiers wounded and a British Viking destroyed versus two enemy fighters dead and an enemy vehicle obliterated. And, hopefully, there was an enemy mortar accounted for too.

Had the Apaches not arrived on station, the cost to British forces might have been far greater indeed.

Baz settled in for the short flight back to base, his mind still on the battlefield. They were the first of the Squadron to have engaged the enemy, and for sure it had been a good fight. Baz felt certain that they had saved British lives, which was a fine feeling. The men of flight *Ugly*, young guns and old dogs alike, had behaved with calm and true professionalism. As for the Apaches, they had performed like the mighty chariots of death that they were. No doubt about it, this was the aircraft to take into the Afghan battlefield and a column of British ground troops had borne witness to that fact.

All four airmen were also aware that they had killed: not up close and personal on the end of a bayonet, but in the high resolution of the video screen where the man's every facial expression was visible. Each hoped to hell that they *had* been enemy fighters, and not some innocent villagers out collecting water at their well.

Either way, they were soon going to find out: upon arrival at Bastion there would be a full debrief with the OC and Chief of Staff, at which time the gun tapes would be played. And, as always, far more would be visible during the controlled playback on a giant plasma screen than could ever be seen in the Apache cockpit during the heat of battle.

Ten minutes later the pair of Apaches settled on the baking hot runway, their rotors slowing to a thwooping stop as the turbines shut down. Baz, Tim, Steve and Alex emerged from their sweaty cockpits and gathered at the foot of the aircraft. Almost without thinking they shook hands. This wasn't about celebrating a first kill or the squadron being blooded. This was about the men of the flight acknowledging a job well done – that they had finally proved themselves, and their machines, in combat.

'Well done lads,' said Baz. 'We did well out there. We worked as a team and we did what we had to do. Bloody well done.'

Turning to the groundies who had gathered excitedly around the aircraft, the four pilots gave them a quick summation of the mission. Baz and Steve had done their time as ground crew and they knew what a thankless task it could be: days on end spent

rearming, refuelling and pushing and pulling aircraft in the suffocating heat and dust. Without the groundies, the Apaches would be
going nowhere fast. It was important to share with them a sense of
the importance of what they had done that day.

As the ground crew listened to the unfolding story of the operation – the first combat mission of 662 Squadron – there was a
growing sense of a shared purpose and of teamwork. This was the
first time that they had ever had to rearm an Apache after munitions had been fired in anger, and they suddenly began to
appreciate the value of what their sweat and toil made possible.
Four wounded British soldiers might have died on the field of
battle had the Apaches not flown so rapidly, and so potently, into
combat.

No matter how intense future operations were to become, the
post-mission handshake was to become a defining tradition of flight
Ugly. It was one that the other aircrew would mercilessly rip the
piss out of, but as far as the four airmen were concerned it went to
the heart of their fighting spirit. It cemented the four of them as a
team and as a flight. It signified that they were happy with the way
the mission had unfolded, and that they had made it back alive.

'No other flight shared such a close bond, and it did cause some
rivalry,' remarks Baz. 'We'd go running together around the base
perimeter, we'd hit the gym to pump iron and we'd chill out
together over a *Band of Brothers* DVD. Shaking hands on the flight
line was our way of saying we'd done okay out there. During the
drive to the ops tent we'd talk about how things had gone so we all
felt good about it prior to the debrief. We were equally good a ripping into each other if we felt things had not been done well as a
flight.'

In that first post-op debrief the men of flight *Ugly* relived the
whole mission, playing back the gun tapes on the plasma screen.
Tim led the discussion, talking through exactly what their gun
tape showed and explaining the decision-making process that had
led to them opening fire. Alex followed, outlining any further
points that could be gleaned from the perspective of the rear aircraft's gun camera.

When played back on the big screen the gun tape revealed much that had previously been hidden. In the depths of the darkened well the gaping muzzle of a mortar tube could clearly be seen. The four airmen had behaved exactly as they should have done in the circumstances, engaging an enemy well within the rules of combat that had been dictated to the squadron some forty-eight hours earlier back at Kandahar Airfield.

Questions were fired at the four airmen by the Squadron OC, Jules Franks, Ian McIvor the Chief of Staff and the Intelligence Officer Chewy Liner. But the conclusion of that first debrief was that Del Boy and Rodney's had indeed been a job well done.

'For many of us, this was the first time doing what we'd trained to do, and what the machine is designed for,' remarks Baz. 'Afghanistan was the coming-of-age for the Apache squadrons and for us as a flight.'

The post-op debrief was also an opportunity to learn the lessons of combat in order to do it better next time around. If anything, the gun tape suggested that the aircrew had been overly cautious in engaging the target. It had been a clear case of an enemy operation and no warning shots had been required. In firing them the aircrew had alerted the enemy to the fact that they had been spotted, which in turn had risked them lobbing off some mortar rounds while they were still able. That, in turn, had put the lives of British soldiers on the ground at risk.

While all of this was clear on the big screen, it was a different matter when in the aircraft in combat and with the possible threat of disciplinary action hanging over one if the wrong decision was made. It was a delicate balancing act between protecting British forces and avoiding civilian casualties, and woe betide any pilot who called it wrongly. It was made all the more difficult because the enemy deliberately dressed like civilians, hid their weapons whenever possible and tried to hide among the wider population.

After the debrief the four airmen felt both relieved and vindicated. They headed back to the flight line to give the ground crew a fuller presentation on the day's mission, and to say a big thank you for the job that they had done getting them airborne in

record time. They pulled up the gun tape on an Apache's screen
and the ground crew gathered around the cockpit to see playback
of the combat images.

Steve gave an impromptu briefing: 'As you can see, we're fighting against a well-disciplined, stupid or simply very brave
enemy . . . The enemy commander stood firm under seventy
rounds of 30mm before he was forced to get up and run. Either
way, you've got to respect an enemy who can do that. We learned
some respect for them out there today and we couldn't have done
jack shit without you guys here backing us up.'

The groundies declared themselves 'lit up' by what they had
seen. Seeing those images really made the job feel worthwhile, for
it showed where and how the rounds they hefted around had been
utilised. They decided to start a 'Taliboard' in one of the hangars –
a scoreboard of the number of enemy soldiers, vehicles and big
guns taken out by the Apaches. Two men, one mortar and a
maroon saloon car opened the scoring.

'Nothing beats getting a debrief and to see some of the video
from the Apaches,' remarks 662 Squadron's Ground Crew Leader,
Dave Janie. 'It demonstrates to us why our job is so important. A
refuel and rearm which would normally take forty-five minutes
using all the checking systems in the manuals and cards could be
done in under fifteen minutes if we adjust the rulebook to the
needs of combat, when soldiers' lives on the ground depend on the
Apaches getting back to target a.s.a.p.'

Seeing the way the impromptu briefing had affected the groundies,
Steve decided that more of this should be done. He would prepare a
weekly brief with clips of the gun tape to show to the groundies and
the REMEs. It was important to do so. It was a very, very long
chain from repairing, rearming and refuelling the aircraft to flying and
fighting it, and it was good for the support troops to see what their
hard work was for. It also showed that this was a team effort, and how
from the lowest rank up everyone played their part.

'Over dinner in the mess tent we expected everyone to be
buzzing about this first mission,' Baz remarks. 'We were waiting for
someone to come and ask but the other aircrew kept their distance.

Professional rivalry came in here, and as no one asked we kept our silence. It was really bizarre.'

That evening, a note was pinned up on the 662 Squadron noticeboard. It read:

Three members of the University of Kabul archaeological department were in Helmand today when they discovered the Holy Grail hidden in a disused well. They were ecstatic at the find, realising that it would bring them international recognition and fame. The team leader spotted a British military convoy in the distance . . . He tried in vain to get their attention, even using his binoculars as a crude signalling device, when suddenly out of nowhere there was a flash of lightning and 'whoosh' – their car was blown to pieces. Locals believe that this may have been the hand of Allah, punishing the men for disturbing the forgotten burial site and important relic. Others feel that it was the hand of the Apaches who had mistakenly identified the men as a Taliban mortar team.

The flight *Ugly* aircrew had a good laugh over the note. They weren't bothered by its piss-taking tone, and would have expected nothing less from their fellow aircrew: squaddie humour always did tend to be in-your-face and provocative.

The four men retired to their pods knowing they were on permanent standby. Before sleeping, Baz wrote the following in his combat diary:

We were the first of our squadron to engage with the enemy and we were ecstatic. On the ground we went through long sessions reviewing our tapes and debriefing. We learnt many lessons that day, and we decided that in future if the opportunity arose we would go after the target more aggressively and until we were certain it had been destroyed.

In a few hours' time, flight *Ugly* would be doing exactly that and more.

6

BEHIND ENEMY LINES

Morning, Day 2

From the very first hour of being allocated Very High Readiness (VHR) duty, an operation had been mooted that each of the flight *Ugly* pilots dearly wanted. A combined force of British troops was to be flown into the deserts of Helmand in a lightning raid. The target was an enemy vehicle convoy believed to be carrying sophisticated weapons supplies including anti-aircraft weapons.

The Apache pilots felt this to be a particularly personal mission, for anti-aircraft weapons constituted the chief threat against helicopters.

The force was to be flown onto target in a Chinook. Two Apaches were to lead the assault, putting down a barrage of fire on to enemy positions prior to the Chinook setting down the force to launch a ground attack. Those running the arms shipment were believed to be the 'foreign' Taliban – Pakistani, Chechen, Saudi and North African diehards who would fight to the death to stop their weapons systems being destroyed or captured.

The target was several hundred kilometres distant from Bastion, in the midst of the enemy badlands. The mission was at the very limit of the Apache's range, and as such it represented an awe-inspiring challenge. Flying at low level using nap-of-the-earth tactics, the lead Apaches could allow for zero navigational error across hundreds of kilometres of desert terrain. If they were off target even slightly the mission would have to be aborted for the aircraft had very little loiter time over target.

This would be the first time that 662 Squadron had been into action on a mission of this sort, and the potential for failure was high. Even so, the men of flight *Ugly* wanted this mission bad.

'Get the navigation wrong or the route, and it'd be fuel-critical,' remarks Steve. 'A couple of hours is the normal time we can stay airborne, and on this mission you'd be going in flat-out in any case. The convoy was carrying anti-aircraft weapons, which was what made it a priority target. And that meant the Apaches could be met by anti-aircraft fire, which was pretty worrying.'

Strictly speaking, this mission wasn't flight *Ugly*'s for the taking as they were on VHR duty. It should have been flown by Captain Charlie Hudson's *Greenpeace Flight*. The rest of the squadron reckoned that *Greenpeace Flight* were a bunch of tree huggers, hence the flight's nickname.

For twenty-four hours *Greenpeace Flight* had been on standby. Like any operation, it might suddenly get the 'go', or it could equally be cancelled at a moment's notice.

Just to keep the aircrews guessing, in the dead hours of the morning flight *Ugly* were stood to for the mission. As they waited in the darkness for the 'go', they reckoned that their chances of getting it were slim. With the approach of first light they lessened by the minute, for the assault would doubtless be going in under cover of darkness. The four men waited with bated breath, the brightening sky presaging dawn, the skyline shot through with bolts of burnished steel.

'Everything was being kept close to the chest until the last moment,' Baz remarks. 'But enough detail had come through to know that this was a mission to destroy the enemy. The tension was mounting: would it be "go" or "stand down"?'

At dawn flight *Ugly* were stood down and *Greenpeace Flight* resumed their standby duty. Baz, Tim, Steve and Alex headed for an early breakfast, feeling not entirely disheartened. It was too late for the air assault to proceed, or so they reckoned, and who knew what dramas might be facing them that morning on VHR duty? After a good feed they headed to the ops tent for the first briefing of the day.

But as they settled in the Ops Room went haywire: all of a sudden
Greenpeace Flight had got the 'go'! The attack had to proceed immediately. Within minutes the two Apaches of *Greenpeace Flight*
were airborne, their squat forms turning away from the direction
of the spectacular sunrise. As they flew in to attack the aircraft
would be doing so from out of the rising sun, so perhaps the time
of day gifted them a tactical advantage.

Whatever the reasons behind the sudden call to go, all that the
flight *Ugly* aircrew knew was that they had failed to get the mission.
The four men were left to listen and watch as the distant operation
unfolded via the radios and giant plasma screen in the Ops Room.
There was still just a chance that they might be called out to join
the assault if things didn't go to plan, but they reckoned that was
unlikely.

The pair of Apaches and the lone Chinook thundered over
sleeping villages and across desert wastes, their only observers at this
hour being the goats dotted among the sparse vegetation. The
attack helicopters had gone heavy on Hellfires as it was believed
that the vehicle convoy would be heavily armed and would attack
any approaching military vehicles or aircraft without warning. It
therefore needed hitting hard, as allowed by the rules of engagement. This was *Greenpeace Flight*'s first-ever combat mission, and
if they got the navigation wrong it would all be over before they
got a chance to fire in anger.

Some 160 kilometres out from target the two Apaches dropped
height, hugging the desert terrain and pounding forwards, the
Chinook behind them following suit. They would remain at this
altitude until they reached their attack positions.

The soldiers in the Chinook's hold held an assortment of weapons:
most carried assault rifles with under-slung 40mm grenade launchers;
several sported the drum-fed light machine gun (LMG); all had
grenades and plastic explosives; plus there were several portable light
anti-tank weapon recoil-less rifles (LAWs).

Together the soldiers packed enough firepower to take out a
small army, and with the Apaches in the vanguard to soften up the
enemy they had every confidence that they would do so.

During the last ten minutes of the flight into target there was the scream of the alarm from the Apaches' HIDAS defence system as it detected an enemy ground threat. But, flying at low level, the aircraft were past the danger before their defence measures could even engage or deploy. That was the beauty of flying nap-of-the-earth into target: by the time an enemy might have spotted the pair of Apaches they were already skimming low across distant sand dunes.

The rising sun was clawing skywards from the rim of the Afghan desert as the Apaches bore down on to target. With the attack occurring in daylight, the aircrew had decided to employ their daytime target acquisition optics to the max. The aircrew punched in the GPS coordinates of the enemy convoy they'd been given on their data pads.

Even before the convoy was visible in the crisp dawn light, the 127-times video cameras were slaving to those coordinates and searching ahead for the enemy, the 30mm cannon tracking the nose pod as it scanned the horizon.

Three kilometres short of the target grid, Lex Brome and Andy Wawn, the Apache pilots, threw the two aircraft into maximum rate of climb, the G-forces crushing them into their seats as the aircraft powered upwards. Seventy-five seconds later they had reached several thousand feet of altitude. A sea of golden desert rolled out before them, dune tops kissed by the rising sun, their troughs lying in impenetrable shadow.

Beyond lay a scattering of mud-walled buildings, to the north of which stretched a dense finger of green where a tree line traced the path of a little-used desert road. Within the densest thickets of that tree line the enemy had hidden their vehicles.

With the video lens slaved to target a flash of movement was detected as the enemy woke up to the arrival of the Apaches in the sky overhead. A figure ran out of the tree line, a rocket-propelled grenade poised on his shoulder as he prepared to fire. With the rising sun in his eyes the RPG operator was momentarily blinded, and that gave Charlie Hudson, gunner of the lead Apache, the moment he needed to nail him.

With the weapons systems armed, the Apache opened up with

its 30mm cannon, the gunner aiming with his crosshair sight fixed on the enemy rocket man below him. The chin turret flared a white sheet of flame as a twenty-round burst cut the dawn sky, spent shell casings glinting in the sun as they tumbled through the desert air.

Seconds after firing the first rounds hit: the large calibre shells punching into the desert before exploding, the soft sand muting the power of the blast. The 30mm cannon is an area weapon: each twenty-round burst saturates a patch of territory with high-explosives and shrapnel. The desert around the enemy figure erupted, the concussion of the explosions sending shockwaves through the enemy positions in the tree line.

As the dust cleared the body of the RPG gunner could be seen slumped on the ground, the launch tube lying beside him. For the enemy convoy it was one hell of a wake-up call.

Angry bursts of tracer snaked up towards the Apaches as the enemy responded with their RPK machine guns from positions hidden in the tree line. The RPK is a reliable and accurate Soviet-era 7.62mm weapon with a range of a thousand metres. The Apaches were operating at the maximum extent of the weapon's range, but still it made it all the more urgent to find and kill the enemy.

The aircrew switched to their forward-looking infrared sensors, seeking to probe the tree line for the body-warmth signatures of the hidden enemy fighters. Suddenly an RPG streaked out of the tree line. Its motor trailed a blue-grey swirl of smoke as it rocketed skywards, the projectile clearly visible to the Apache pilots as it raced towards them.

The Apaches' HIDAS alarms were screaming, the system detecting the flare of a rocket firing at ground level. The RPG is a simple, basic weapon possessing no guidance system apart from a manual sight.

The maximum range of the RPG is a thousand metres. The 2.5-kilogram warhead has a kill radius of 150 metres. With the grenade set on airburst mode, the warhead could send blast and shrapnel over a wide swathe of airspace.

The pilots threw their aircraft into emergency evasive measures, pulling a series of ear-popping manoeuvres across the sky. The grenade exploded, throwing a dirty black pall of smoke laced with shrapnel across the clear air, the blast wave beating a warning tattoo in the Apache's interior.

Momentarily a figure appeared, sprinting out of the cover of the trees. He had an RPG launcher clutched in one hand, and a back-pack with half-a-dozen spare grenade rounds strapped to his back. He raced for the open ground, seeking a vantage point from which to sight the aircraft and open fire. Targeting the Apaches through the dense foliage of the tree line was all but impossible, which was forcing the enemy to break cover.

As he levelled the RPG at his shoulder, the Apache's gunners were too quick. The 30mm cannons roared and this time the rounds were bang on target, tearing into the body of the lone fighter. As one round exploded in his backpack, it set off the motors of the spare grenades that he was carrying. All of a sudden the enemy figure was blasted off his feet, spinning over and over like a Catherine wheel, his body trailing a wake of blue-grey RPG smoke as it spun through the air.

The limp figure came to earth with a sickening thump, the backpack rockets still coughing fire as he lay unmoving in a cloud of dust and smoke. Apache front-seater Stew Peach spotted more figures appearing out of the tree line. One made a beeline for the downed RPG operator, doubtless intending to retrieve his weapon. Exploding rounds of 30mm chased his heels, beating him back to the cover of the woods.

The Apache's 127-times magnification video cameras picked out figures diving for the ditches and cocking their weapons. But they had shown themselves, and that made them vulnerable. Twenty-round bursts of 30mm pounded their positions, raking the trees with high-explosives and shrapnel.

As the cannons found their target there was an almighty explosion at one end of the enemy positions and a sheet of flame boiled through the tree line. A truckload of RPG rounds had been hit, the 30mm rounds setting off the grenades in a series of explosions that ripped through the foliage.

Gouts of oily smoke belched skywards from the burning vehicle. One end of the tree line was a sea of fire now, branches transformed into burning skeletons, the twisted wreckage of a Toyota pickup truck clearly visible in the inferno. The enemy had been hit hard and by complete surprise, and they had taken serious casualties.

But a well-trained and motivated adversary can quickly regain order and initiative. As if to prove this, a third RPG operator darted out of the tree line, his launcher hefted skywards. There was a flash of flame as he fired on instinct, barely pausing to aim, and ran back towards cover.

The lead Apache pilot glanced at the target, switched to manual, slaving the gun to his eye line, and fired off a burst of 30mm rounds. The shot was off-axis, with the cannon swivelled ninety degrees away from the direction of flight of the aircraft, but it was bang on. The rounds cut the RPG operator down before he could make the tree line.

Three RPG operators had been taken out, but how many more might there be in there? All it would take was one lucky shot, or a hidden operator with an anti-aircraft weapon, and an Apache could go down. If that happened and the aircrew survived, they would be far from friendly forces and totally reliant on their SERE training.

With limited loiter time fast running out, the Apaches needed to hit the convoy hard to put the enemy's heads down for long enough to get the soldiers in to land. The Chinook was still circling out in the open desert, waiting for the Apache's signal to drop the troops onto target.

From five kilometres out the two sleek attack helicopters began their bombing run, each with four CRV7 rockets primed to fire from weapons pods on the stub wings. The 2.7-inch rockets cannot be independently aimed. The aircraft itself needs to be lined up on target before the salvo can be released, which basically means flying down the enemy's gun barrels to ensure a direct hit.

As the first Apache powered in towards the tree line, muzzle flashes from within the shadowed ditches showed where the enemy were firing. The aircraft held its line and there was a smudge of dirty-brown smoke from the pods. Four rockets leapt ahead, each armed with eighty flechettes. As the rockets bore down towards target, 320 darts fired out at Mach 1 in a cloud of tungsten death. The darts tore into the tree line, slicing through metal, wood and flesh alike.

Once the second Apache had fired its rocket salvo, aircraft commander Stew Peach gave the Chinook the all-clear to land. The Apaches turned to escort in the Chinook, providing top cover in case enemy forces were lurking in the region of the LZ. The giant helicopter was putting down deep in enemy territory, and they had to be prepared for anything.

Even before the rear wheels had touched down the ramp was dropping, the soldiers charging down the metal chute and into all-around defensive positions. Once all were dismounted they moved quickly through the open desert. The soldiers advanced towards the tree line, taking out the few surviving enemy fighters that continued to fight.

Within minutes the position was declared clear, leaving only the intact vehicles and weapons supplies to be destroyed. The soldiers checked over the Toyota Hilux pickups, searching for the anti-aircraft weapons that they'd been told to look out for. Then they rigged the vehicles with plastic explosives, detonators and fuse wire. As the attack force melted back into the desert for the rendezvous with the Chinook, they set off a series of explosions behind them, blowing the enemy vehicles sky-high.

Just to make doubly sure that all weapons and vehicles had been rendered useless, the Apaches lined up on the two least-damaged pickups and fired their laser-guided Hellfires. Further explosions ripped the convoy apart as first the Hellfire warheads hit and then the ammunition in the pickups ignited in a giant orange fireball.

As the Apaches turned for home, not an enemy fighter was left alive nor a vehicle intact. And none of the assault force had suffered casualties. By anyone's reckoning it was a job well done.

The success of this mission gave the aircrews of 662 Squadron a massive boost. It proved that their lack of experience was not an impediment to prosecuting such risk-laden operations. So started an excellent partnership between 662 Squadron and the ground forces they supported, one that would see them working together closely over the coming weeks.

As the two Apaches of *Greenpeace Flight* set a course for Camp Bastion, the men of flight *Ugly* sat enveloped in silence in the Ops Room. During the last fifteen minutes of the air assault there was nowhere else that they would rather have been than in those aircraft, braving enemy fire and taking the fight down their very gun barrels.

The air assault was over and the ground forces had discovered anti-aircraft weapons stowed in the enemy vehicles. In due course efforts would be made to trace who might be supplying the enemy with such deadly weaponry.

Between 1978 and 1988 the then Soviet Union had waged a decade-long war in Afghanistan, which was part of the wider Cold War power struggle in the region. During that time the Soviets had lost over three hundred helicopters, many of which were shot down by the Afghan mujahidin using anti-aircraft weapons, a weapon that had revolutionised the modern battlefield, challenging air superiority as never before.

Now the Apache aircrews of 662 Squadron knew for sure that the enemy had, or at least were in the process of acquiring, new anti-aircraft weapons. During that morning's operation a convoy carrying them had been well and truly taken out, but how many others might have made it through okay?

662 Squadron's Intelligence Sergeant, Chewy Liner, was also able to reveal how flight *Ugly*'s Sangin operation of the previous day had concluded. The British convoy had extracted itself from the ambush without further incident.

It was mid-morning by now, and *Greenpeace Flight* were undergoing their post-mission debrief. An American Apache helicopter put in an unscheduled appearance at Camp Bastion. The US aircrew had been flying out of Kandahar and decided to drop in to report a target that needed destroying. The Americans crew their Apaches in a very different way from the British Apache squadrons. Whereas in the British set-up both pilots are more or less on an equal footing, in the US helicopters the rear-seater is fully in charge.

As there was nothing much happening on VHR duty, the four airmen of flight *Ugly* invited the American pilots for a brew. They took their seats under the cavernous arch of the mess tent, the American rear-seater doing all of the talking. He had apparently spotted an enemy anti-aircraft missile system and was keen to pass the coordinates across to the British Apaches, so they could take it out.

The US Apache's front-seater kept trying to object that they weren't 100 per cent certain that it was an enemy missile system. But the flight commander kept telling him to keep quiet. What did he know? He was just a front-seater! Eventually the British airmen asked the American pilot to play their gun tape so they could see for themselves what the weapons system might be.

What they saw when they played the gun tape on the Ops Room plasma screen was a white, oblong building with a long black tube mounted on the flat roof. Far from being a missile system, the weapon looked like a recoilless rifle, plus the white building bore a remarkable resemblance to a typical Afghan National Army (ANA) outpost.

Baz called over the aircrew from *Geek Flight* – named for their geeky obsession with military hardware and technology – for a second opinion. Sure enough, the four pilots – Dean, Dave, Nick and Garie – confirmed that the weapon was a 105mm recoilless rifle, a bazooka-like anti-tank weapon. Furthermore, the white building was an ANA outpost: the giveaway was the Afghan flag flying above the building.

Despite the dangerously misguided targeting skills of the aircraft's commander, the American pilots were friendly enough and they stayed for a bite of lunch. Over a tray of coronation chicken rolls, the US pilot tried to steer the topic of conversation away from the so-called enemy missile system. But the flight *Ugly* aircrew wouldn't let it rest. They kept asking him why he hadn't taken it out if he had believed it to be an enemy position.

The delight of the American Apache's front-seater was clear as his commander got a right royal grilling. Seemingly unperturbed, the rear-seater proceeded to boast about how he was the famous American Apache pilot who had taken out half the Taliban Navy. Surely the British aircrew must have heard about that?

The men of flight *Ugly* looked at each other in bewilderment. The Taliban Navy? What was this guy on? Afghanistan was a land-locked country, so it was a little unlikely, to put it mildly. They weren't overly sad when the two American airmen headed for their aircraft and took off to return to Kandahar.

There had been a serious undertone to the whole exchange. American Apache crews flew all of their missions at nap-of-the-earth level, which meant that they only ever had a split second in which to locate, identify and decide to kill a target. It was hardly surpris-ing when there were incidents of so-called friendly fire – wounding and killing of their own, or Allied, troops – or of collateral damage, where civilian people and buildings were hit. In contrast, British Apaches attacked using high orbits, from where they had ample time to study the battlefield and identify targets.

The story of the ANA outpost was a case in point: the American aircrew had been convinced that it needed taking out. For a reason that remained unclear they'd asked their British allies to do the attack, but either way the outpost had come that close to getting blasted by Hellfires and 30mm cannon fire. It was unforgivable, and no way to win hearts and minds in Afghanistan.

It was true that the ANA often dressed like Taliban, and they drove the same Toyota pickups as the enemy. But a simple radio call to the nearest *Widow* call-sign would have identified any ANA presence in the region. Or if that had failed, a call to base would have linked up the Apache aircrew directly with ANA head-quarters. But the dead giveaway had been the Afghan flag, fluttering in the breeze on the flagpole.

'*Geek Flight* were the experts at guns and gadgets of all kind,' remarks Steve. 'Within seconds of seeing that tape they'd identified the weapon, and then they pointed out the obvious: the Afghan flag, plus the men in the compound were wearing ANA uniforms.

Good job the pilot hadn't just tipped in and shot it up! I saw a smile on the junior pilot's face as we pointed all this out. But the fact that they had taken on the Taliban Navy – that had us gasping.'

Little did the men of flight *Ugly* know, but their next sortie would have them doing the very same thing.

7
SINK THE TALIBAN NAVY

Afternoon, Day 2

Shortly after the US Apache had departed, the flight *Ugly* aircrew were enjoying another brew in the canteen when a call came over the radio that they would learn to know and love: 'JHF calling Del Boy and Rodney . . .'

The last words were lost in the scramble as chairs were shoved backwards and the four men raced for the door. As they thundered out on to the Rolla-Trac walkway, their minds were racing. What would their mission be this time, they wondered? As before, Tim and Alex made for the ops tent as Baz and Steve headed for the flight line.

On the face of it, Tim and Alex's mission briefing was remarkably similar to that of the previous day: a Viking had been hit in an ambush to the south of Sangin and there was a T1 casualty requiring an urgent casevac. The Apaches were to escort in a Chinook to pick up the wounded.

The Viking had been moving from Forwards Operating Base Robinson towards the District Centre at Sangin. It had been hit while in the centre of Sangin town, a place where only recently had life started to return to normal as British troops brought law and order to the war-torn region.

For eleven months the British-garrisoned District Centre had been under siege from Taliban forces, a siege that had earned the town the nickname of Sangingrad, after the epic siege of Stanlingrad during the Second World War. On 5 April 2007

Operation Silver had been launched to relieve Sangin, involving a thousand NATO troops.

As the US 82nd Airborne Division launched a heliborne assault from the south, 250 Royal Marines attacked from the north with further support provided by Dutch and Estonian troops and Canadian artillery in support. The siege had been truly broken, the enemy putting up only light resistance. But now the Taliban were trying to re-infiltrate and destabilise the town, upsetting the calm that British troops were building there.

Today's ambush was their first big hit since the siege of Sangin had ended. The Viking had been struck by an RPG and the follow-up attack had been ferocious, as a group of heavily armed enemy fighters had targeted the British convoy with assault rifles and machine gun fire. A contingent of Force Reaction Troops had come out of the District Centre to link up with the convoy and secure the area. But even so, this would be a cluttered, urban battlefield and the Apaches would have to be triply careful if they were to fire on the enemy without causing civilian casualties.

As Baz ran through the flight checks at warp speed, his hands flicking over the myriad controls, his radio was tuned in to the frequency of the ground troops in contact – the Royal Anglians. Details of the attack seeped into his fevered mind, the scope of the threat becoming ever more clear as they did so.

Within minutes the pair of Apaches were airborne, the lone Chinook swinging in to their rear as they set a course north-east for Sangin. The Chinook pilots had been briefed on the basic plan of action by Tim, back in the ops tent. As the Chinooks were based within easy reach of the Apaches at Camp Bastion, linking up for missions was relatively simple. Once in the air, any updates from the *Widow* on the threat, or the casevac plan, would be relayed via the Apaches to the Chinook pilots.

As the three aircraft neared Sangin it was decided that the Chinook would be held back over the open desert. The only safe place to carry out the casevac was at the Sangin District Centre, and the casualty would first have to be moved there by the ground troops. That would take time, and until then the safest place for the Chinook was flying an open-desert orbit.

The first sign of the contact was a solid pillar of smoke that dominated the horizon. The Royal Anglians had called in a US fast jet – an F16 – to take out the crippled Viking and deny it to the enemy. The F16 had dropped a five-hundred-pound JDAM (joint direct attack munition), a GPS-guided smart bomb. Only in this case, while the JDAM had obliterated the armoured vehicle it had also ripped apart the buildings to either side. The destruction was clear to the Apache aircrew as they arrived over the battle scene. Hopefully there hadn't been any Afghan civilians taking cover in those buildings.

For the second day running, *Ugly Five Zero* and *Ugly Five One* set up in wheel formation over the battlefield, the centre of their orbit being a burning Viking that had been hit in an ambush. Once again, *Ugly Five Zero* radioed the Joint Terminal Attack Controller (JTAC) on the ground, *Widow Six Three*, asking for a heads-up on the battlefield situation and how the Apaches might best be utilised. And once again, they asked that the casualty be removed to a usable LZ, in this case the District Centre towards the centre of the town.

But it was there that the similarities with the previous day's battle would end, for today's was to develop a darkly menacing character and a momentum all of its own. The *Widow* outlined the battlefield scenario as quickly as he could. Some fifty soldiers from the Royal Anglians were on the ground at the ambush site, which was now secure. A force of twenty enemy fighters was moving south out of the contact area between the road and the river.

As they were dressed like regular Afghans, there was every danger they would mix with the civilian population and the opportunity to kill them would be lost. Once again, the enemy would have succeeded in wounding, perhaps fatally, British soldiers, and getting away with it scot-free. British soldiers were in hot pursuit, but without the Apaches' eyes in the sky there was every danger they would lose the enemy in the bewildering array of alleyways, lanes and woodland running down to the river.

'One more thing,' *Widow Six Three* added. 'We reckon they've hidden their weapons in a cache somewhere, so they're making like unarmed civilians. If there's any more I'll let you have it soon as I hear.'

From their orbit above the town the airmen of flight *Ugly* scanned the terrain below for any sign of enemy movement. None of their sophisticated imaging systems would help them here: the streets were clogged with townspeople, the lush vegetation running down to the riverside dotted with rich fruit and vegetable gardens. Four pairs of eyes scanned the terrain but the trouble was distinguishing friend from foe. There were scores of people on the move down there and any one of them could just as easily be an innocent farmer as an enemy fighter intent on escape. It was hugely frustrating.

A phrase from his Northern Ireland days came into Baz's mind: if all else fails try thinking like the enemy. He put his mindset into that of an enemy fighter: where would he be heading if he was trying to escape the vengeful British troops?

On the far side of the Helmand River lay a tiny village that was a known sanctuary for the Taliban; that much they had been alerted to by the *Widow*. The village was opposite and a little to the south of the ambush site. Reaching it would involve crossing the river but that was no major drama: it was a kilometre or so across and small boats plied its waters running a ferry service to and from either bank.

The rear-seater of an Apache sits higher than his co-pilot and has a better all-around-view from the cockpit. Baz traced a straight line with his eyes from the ambush site to the point on the nearside bank that would present the easiest river crossing. A series of deep irrigation ditches followed that line to the river's edge. Had Baz been one of the fleeing fighters, that was the cover he would have used to escape.

As soon as he'd seen those ditches, Baz voiced his thoughts to Tim and to their fellow aircrew in *Ugly Five One*. As they talked it over, there was a growing certainty – a sixth sense, if you like – that this was the enemy's escape route.

Flight *Ugly* adjusted their wheel formation so that the centre of their orbit became the near side of the Helmand River. As they did so, Baz caught a glimmer of movement far out on the river – the flash of water on a boat's prow. A powerful craft was moving across from the far bank, its bow wave shimmering in the midday light. It was aiming for a bare, rocky island in the middle of the river. That would be the pick-up boat if the enemy were planning a river-borne escape with the far village as their hideaway.

Tim decided to split the flight, with *Ugly Five Zero* covering the nearside of the river and their wing aircraft covering the far side. As Baz and Tim slaved the aircraft's 127-times video lenses to the riverboat's location, they began feeding details of what they could see to the *Widow* on the ground at Sangin.

'*Widow Six Three*, this is *Ugly*. We're orbiting over the river, five hundred metres to the south-east of the ambush site. We see a motor boat heading across river from the far side: it's empty of pas-sengers, so it could be a pick-up.'

'*Ugly, Widow Six Three*. Roger that.'

Baz scanned the heavy vegetation of the riverbank directly below him. As he did so, he spotted further movement and a second boat appeared, nosing out from under the trees into the open water. He alerted Tim via the radio net.

'Tim, I have another boat, low, nine o'clock, against the eastern bank.'

Tim relayed the new sighting to the *Widow*.

'*Widow Six Three*, this is *Ugly*, now there's boat two and this one's got four fighting-age males in it. It's heading out from the nearside bank, making for what looks like a rocky island in the river centre. Could be the rendezvous point with boat one.'

'Fighting-age' males are deemed to be those from their teens to their early forties.

'Roger. It's the right location to find them. You have eyes on. What's their description?'

'Four men, white robes and dark turbans. Two carrying dark-coloured backpacks. Look to be in their late twenties. All with beards, but none visual with weapons. It's a small rowing boat with a tiny outboard so it could have been moored in cover awaiting their getaway. Then a link-up on the island with the fast boat and they're away.'

The motorised rowing boat chugged out into the river, its prow turning upstream as it fought against the current. Sure enough, it set a course for the rocky island. As it did so the motor boat on the far side set out to meet it, the rendezvous point clearly being the island. From their bird's-eye view the four airmen spotted further movement on the far bank: a white vehicle had pulled to a halt at the riverside. That would be the pre-arranged pick-up point, to take the enemy fighters to the nearby village.

The Apaches circled the river crossing, the aircrew discussing what they could see and running through various possible scenarios over the intercom. As there were only four figures in the boat below them, the remaining sixteen had to be escaping by a different route. Odds on they were also going to try for a river crossing, and they would be doing so a little to the south – further out of town and downstream.

Tim decided to divide forces. While *Ugly Five Zero* would remain on station, its wing would fly a search pattern over the river to the south in an effort to locate more of the enemy.

As *Ugly Five One* broke from the orbit and headed downstream, *Ugly Five Zero* received a call from the *Widow*. His men had reached the riverbank, from where they had eyes on the motorised rowing boat, which was moving remarkably quickly. It was already half a kilometre or more downstream and across river from their position, and approaching landfall on the rocky island. It was out of effective range of their weapons; had it not been for the Apaches it would have made a clean getaway.

The British soldiers had been able to observe the boat and its passengers with their binoculars. They had seen them dumping their weapons in the woods then moving on to the river as if they were unarmed civilians. They were certain that these were the men who had ambushed the convoy.

'*Widow Six Three, Ugly* – are you asking us to engage?'

'We can confirm – *repeat, confirm* – that those are the enemy soldiers we were in contact with.'

'Okay, but are you asking us to engage?'

'Affirmative.'

'Okay, this is the situation: we understand it's odds-on they're the ones who ambushed the convoy. But they're unarmed and they're sitting ducks. We are unsure if we're cleared to fire. If we are, we want cover right from the top. As high as it needs to go. Get us that clearance and we'll do what's necessary.'

'Affirmative. Stand by.'

As the aircrew of *Ugly Five Zero* waited for the call back, they could feel the nervous energy eating away at their guts. It was one thing to engage the enemy in the full flow of combat, quite another to shoot up four unarmed men in an open boat as it puttered across the blue-green waters of the Helmand River on a sunny afternoon. This wasn't the sort of combat mission the aircrew had ever imagined flying. War could be hellish, and this was it in all of its dirty, muddled ambiguity.

'It was our second day in combat and we were faced with this,' remarks Baz. 'We didn't know what to do . . . None of us wanted this on our second day in theatre. You can see their faces, their expressions; maybe even their fear. They had no weapons and were defenceless in an open boat. Yes, we believed they were the enemy. We believed that they had ambushed and wounded British soldiers. But we didn't know it for sure. It was one hell of a thing to have to do.'

Out in the open desert the lone Chinook was still flying its holding pattern, awaiting clearance to go in and collect the wounded. Whatever the *Ugly* aircrew decided to do, they had better do it quickly. After a wait that seemed to last an age, but in reality was no more than a couple of minutes, there was a squelch of static on the radio as a call came through from the JTAC.

'*Ugly*, this is *Widow Six Three*: you are cleared to fire. This went up to Regional Command RC-South and the MOD lawyers at KAF. We confirm those are the same EF as who attacked us. We have eyes on and can confirm. You are cleared to engage.'

'Roger that. Engaging now.'

EF stands for enemy forces. Under the rules of engagement it was permissible to engage a positively identified enemy after a contact. That was the rule that was about to be put into practice now.

Baz and Tim turned to the target. The rowing boat had made landfall and three men had crossed the island. They were sitting on the rocky bank on the far shore, no doubt awaiting collection by the motor boat. It was holding off in mid-stream, as if sensing that something bad was about to happen. The fourth figure had remained with the first boat and was tying it up on the shore. The Apache pilots could sense that the men were aware of being hunted, and in the close-up images playing on the video screens they could all but sense their knowing.

Tim decided to fire warning shots, if for no other reason that to give the men a chance to surrender. He slaved the 30mm cannon to the video image and then moved the crosshair sight a hundred metres to the side of the target. That first ten-round burst thundered across the open river, the shells exploding on impact in mid-stream and sending gouts of white water arcing into the air. As the spray cleared, it cast a momentary rainbow across the river's surface, but not a man among the three had so much as moved. As for the pick-up boat, it did a rapid about-turn and made for the cover of the far bank.

Ugly Five Zero fired a second warning burst, each heavy-calibre shell erupting in a spout of water that trailed ever closer to the crouching men. Again, not so much as a movement; no gesture of resistance or fear disturbed the three figures' poise as they sat by the riverside. There was no attempt to put up their hands and surrender. Had the men done so, the Apache would have remained on station and overseen their capture.

With a flick of a fingertip on the targeting mouse, the crosshair sight moved until it was directly over target. There was the chunter of the cannon from below the cockpit as a twenty-round burst was fired, the alloy shell casings tumbling towards the waters far below. It seemed to take forever for the rounds to travel the three thousand metres or so separating the Apache from target. Time seemed to freeze to an agonising stillness for the aircrew . . . and then they hit.

Impacting on the hard stones, the high-explosive rounds transformed the shoreline into a whirlwind of red-hot shrapnel, shattered rock and fire. For five full seconds the 30mm shells slammed into the beach, rendering it a boiling cauldron of flame. As the dust cleared, where the three figures had once been there was now just a sluice of gore, a growing slick of red spreading downstream from the island.

Swivelling its 30mm cannon barely a fraction of a degree, *Ugly Five Zero* brought the gun to bear on the rowing boat. A second twenty-round burst was fired, this time the rounds ripping open the craft as if it were made of matchwood. Shattered planks spiralled into the air, turning end over end as they plummeted back towards the water below. As for the fourth figure, who had been hiding beneath the boat, his form had been all but obliterated.

With barely a pause, *Ugly Five Zero* peeled away from its orbit over the island to hunt for the motor boat out on the river. As the first ten-round burst of 30mm cannon-fire erupted in the craft's wake it darted under an overhanging cliff and an instant later was lost in the shadows. For now, at least, it was out of harm's way.

With the Apaches engaging the enemy on the river, the decision was made to get the Chinook in to do the casevac. The battle had moved some two kilometres south of Sangin town, so going in to the landing zone at the District Centre should prove safe enough. After a quick in and out the Chinook began the flight back to Bastion with the critically injured soldier on board.

Some two kilometres downstream of *Ugly Five Zero*, *Ugly Five One* was on the hunt. Steve and Alex were concentrating on their own search-and-destroy mission. They had found a third craft, this one pushing along in the slow current of the far riverbank with four figures on board. It appeared to be a carbon copy of what had taken place upstream, only this time the boat operator was being more careful, sticking to the cover of the overhanging trees. It made it hard to get a good sight of, or shot at, him.

Ugly Five One requested, and received, clearance to fire. Zooming in the 127-times video lens to narrow-field view, the aircrew prepared the cannon. Just as they were about to open fire

Steve realised that one of the figures in the boat was wearing a headscarf. It was a woman. As the two airmen studied the scene below them they noticed that one of the men was readying a motorbike for unloading. His face was clearly visible. He was an old man and far too advanced in years to be one of the enemy fighters described to them by the *Widow*.

As they watched, the boat pulled in to the riverbank and the motorbike was manhandled on to the shore. The old man kick-started it, the woman climbed on to the pillion and together they set off up a narrow track through the trees. It looked like a father and daughter, or maybe an Afghan elder with his young bride. Either way, this was a boatload of civilians. Thank God they hadn't opened fire.

Turning back to the river they began to search again, each circuit taking them closer to the village that was the known enemy refuge. A fourth riverboat was picked up, and this time there was little doubt that it was the right target. There were four robed men in the boat, which was making a beeline for a landfall directly below the village. *Ugly Five One* shadowed the craft as it docked. Three men got out, leaving the fourth with the boat.

As casually as they could, as if they were out for a day's stroll, the three figures made their way along a dirt track towards the outskirts of the village. As the Apache circled some two thousand feet above them the three figures made no move to look up or otherwise register its presence. Once again they were trying to behave as if the aircraft just wasn't there.

At the top of the dirt track was a small grove of trees. The three figures headed into the shade. Despite the cover of the foliage, the high-resolution video lens revealed to the crew of *Ugly Five One* exactly what the three men were doing in there: they were changing their clothes.

One figure swapped his white robes for a black shirt. Once he'd done so he emerged from cover and set off up the track towards the centre of the village. *Ugly Five One* stuck with the two figures in the shade to see who else might appear, and to track them to their base of operations.

Barely a minute had passed when a white estate car came bouncing down the track from the direction of the village. It passed by the grove of trees, as if it was unconnected to the waiting men, but proceeded to execute a U-turn some hundred yards further on. It drove by once more and stopped fifty yards ahead of the hidden men.

Two figures emerged from the car and moved through the tree line to link up with them. This was a planned meeting and the longer the Apache delayed its attack the greater the chance of the team being moved elsewhere, or of losing them. Of course, there was still just a chance that it could all be innocent, but the instinct of the watching airmen told them otherwise. It was the change of clothing that had been the giveaway.

Ugly Five One radioed their flight leader, plus the *Widow*, seeking clearance to engage. Once again a ten-round burst of 30mm warning shots was fired. The rounds impacted wide of the trees, the explosions clearly visible in the open farmland. There was no response from the four hidden figures and so the Apache proceeded to fire a twenty-round burst directly into the trees. The instant it did so, two figures came racing out, one taking the track down towards the river, the other diving over a wall in an effort to find cover.

The aircrew recognised the second figure as the driver of the vehicle. A decision was made to take that out before it might be used to effect an escape. Placing the laser guidance beam on the roof of the estate car, Alex selected the Hellfire and pressed the trigger on his left-hand pistol grip control column. It was like using a sledgehammer to crack a nut.

Seconds later the car disintegrated in a ball of flame, the front bumper being blown so high into the air that it fell to earth over a hundred yards away in an adjacent field. For a moment the aircrew mistook the lump of smoking metal for a dead body, so far was it from the vehicle. They presumed it had to be the corpse of the driver, until they recognised it as a scorched and twisted fender.

The mangled wreckage of the vehicle belched out flames and a thick cloud of oily smoke. Steve and Alex scanned the ground below but there was no more movement. Beneath the trees all was still. One dead body was clearly visible and a second figure was twitching about on the bloodied earth in the final stages of his death throes.

These men had clearly been part of a larger enemy operation – some of whom had got away and some of whom would be laying low. What was needed now was a ruse, a sleight of hand to flush them out from wherever they were hiding. Steve had just the thing in mind.

He placed a radio call to his wing and the two Apaches joined up in formation over the Helmand River, turning south as if heading for Camp Bastion. But as soon as they had disappeared below the horizon they did a swift about-turn and came back in again, fast and low, their rotors whipping the river to a frenzy as they thundered past.

The aircraft arrived back at exactly the same location, the whole manoeuvre having taken just five minutes to execute. As soon as they reappeared over the battlefield the aircrew slaved their cameras to the coordinates of the woodland. But five minutes was all the time it had taken for the scene below them to change almost beyond recognition.

'We could see that the wood line was crawling with people,' remarks Steve. 'There were dozens of figures and they had ponchos in which they were carrying the dead. They were running with the bodies and trying to get them back into the village. We could've hit those people picking up the bodies but we decided to give them at least a bit of dignity and let them gather up their dead.'

There were also more practical reasons for the Apaches to break off the contact. They had been in the air for over an hour and were getting close to the point at which they would have to return to base to refuel.

It was a twenty-minute flight back to Bastion, and during that time the aircrew took stock of what had just happened. Both aircraft had fired 160 rounds of 30mm and accounted for several enemy fighters – fighters who had ambushed a British convoy, destroyed a Viking and badly wounded a British soldier.

Not only that, they had then proceeded to hide among the town's civilian population, dropping their weapons in order to do so. Sangin had just found peace after eleven long months of chaos and blood-shed, and the enemy attack had been an effort to destroy all that. They had deserved to meet the consequences of their actions that day.

Or so Baz told himself as the flight neared Camp Bastion. But somehow he couldn't shake off an uneasy feeling. Something was nagging at him. For some reason he couldn't seem to get those images out of his mind; images of disintegrating body parts and the slick of gore left behind on that island beach. Those faces – young faces, the faces of men not carrying arms, faces rendered in inti-mate detail in his video screen – swam before his eyes.

He already knew that their wing, *Ugly Five One*, had been that close to shooting up a boatload of civilians. He hoped to God that his aircraft hadn't inadvertently done what their wing had avoided doing thanks to the aircrew's caution and vigilance.

'Anyone who says it's just a video game when attacking the enemy in an Apache is so wrong,' remarks Baz. 'This was close up and personal, the video capturing the true horror and our left eye seeing it all in full and vivid colour. But at the time there was no time to worry about that as we had to find and destroy the remain-ing enemy. We had taken out that boat to deny the enemy a future exit plan, but we didn't celebrate this attack. It was nasty work. We just concentrated on looking for more targets.'

One way or another, the gun tapes would prove it, Baz told himself. They would pore over the images on the giant plasma screen and reassure themselves that what they had done out there was the right thing.

Baz pushed his concerns to the back of his mind and forced himself to concentrate on getting the aircraft on to the ground safely. Landing at Bastion was never easy: it was always punchy, varied and fast. The luxury of a slow and straight approach was denied the Apache aircrews: there might be enemy forces lurking around the base and a slow and straight approach would make them vulnerable to ground fire.

As he lowered the power on the collective, reducing pitch and lift, he played with the right foot pedal to keep the tail rotor in bal-ance with the main. Using the cyclic, he was continually changing the aircraft's bearing to make a zigzag approach to the runway. As it drew nearer, Baz threw a switch to make the aircraft's stub wing – its stabilator – tilt forwards, which in turn forced the nose of the Apache downwards, allowing him an unrestricted view out the front of the cockpit.

He switched on the flight path vector (FPV) imaging system, a graphic appearing on the monocle screen in front of his right eye. Placing the FPV's three-dimensional image over the runway, Baz began to make continuous adjustments with all three controls – collective, cyclic and foot pedals – in order to keep the aircraft on line for the landing. Gently pulling back on the cyclic, Baz eased the aircraft into the last hundred feet of the approach.

Reducing air speed to forty-five knots, and with the FPV lined up on the end of the runway, he used the foot pedals to minutely adjust the aircraft's heading, guided by another icon on the monocle screen – the head tracker. With the head tracker indicating where the aircraft's nose was pointing, he played with the cyclic, so ensuring that the Apache had the correct attitude for landing. Gently lowering the collective he felt the aircraft settle its three wheels on the runway. They were down.

He taxiied over to the VHR-1 bay and powered down the engines, the rotors slowing to a thwooping stop. Having shut down the aircraft, Baz reached forwards to eject the Hi8 videotape from its carriage. But as it popped out a warning bell was ringing inside his head, the sense of alarm getting ever more insistent. The Hi8 cassette was refusing to eject fully. The tape had been chewed up in the mechanism and it looked to be completely ruined.

In conditions of intense heat, and with the air saturated by abrasive dust, the video decks did break down and tapes did get chewed up. But why did it have to happen now, on this of all missions? His wing aircraft's gun tape would be of little help: *Ugly Five One* had been two kilometres downriver when Tim and Baz's aircraft had obliterated the four unarmed men crouching on that island beach.

This was the nightmare scenario. Neither aircraft had any gun tape of the river island shoot-out.

8

WHO KILLED THE FERRY MAN?

Days 2–7

The four men dismounted from the aircraft and did their round of handshakes. But the atmosphere was quiet, tense and subdued. There was little of the high or the camaraderie of their first mission. From the flight line they headed directly for the debrief. During the short drive in the Land Rover, no one said very much about what they had just done. Of the two crews, *Ugly Five Zero* was by far the more subdued.

'We had a nagging doubt as to whether we'd engaged the right target,' Baz remarks. 'Plus the fact they were unarmed: we'd never done this to an unarmed target before.'

As per usual, the debrief was held in the remote debriefing facility, a secure metal Portakabin with a droning air-conditioning unit keeping it icy cool. Jules Franks, the Squadron OC, Ian McIvor, the Chief of Staff, and Ralf, an earnest RAF Intelligence staffer, gathered to view the gun tapes and hear the pilots talk through the mission. The trouble was, *Ugly Five Zero* had no recording. The Hi8 videotape had snapped very early on in the mission, and after that there was nothing.

To make matters worse, the first images shown on *Ugly Five One*'s tape were of the women and old man in the first boat – those that they had come close to shooting up. As those images flickered on the plasma screen: the old man being helped to lift his motorbike off the boat, the young woman jumping on sidesaddle, the pair of them trundling off up the track – you could hear a pin drop in the debrief room.

With the images playing, Steve and Alex began to describe how they had narrowly avoided killing that first boatload of people. Then they moved on to describe what they believed was the genuine target and the sequence of that attack.

'We were looking at Steve's tape of the woman, the old man and the motorbike, and thinking – oh shit,' remarks Baz. 'At that moment we thought maybe we'd sunk the wrong boat, engaged the wrong target. We had no pictures to prove otherwise. But the OC was adamant. He told us that we had sought and been given clearance to fire from the top, so it was legitimate. Sometimes in the heat the videotape does break, that's just how it is. So there was nothing that we had done that was in any way wrong.'

Having the backing and support of their OC meant everything to the four airmen. But when they came out of the briefing room they were still feeling shaken. As they walked back through the ops tent there was the usual barrage of good-natured abuse from the other flight crew.

'Hear you sunk the Taliban Navy then!'

'Nice one, Del Boy, come to the desert and shoot up a boat . . .'

'Only you lot could manage that!'

It was typical squaddie humour, and it was meant in the best possible way. But the jokes fell more than a little flat with men who were feeling bruised and uncomfortable with what they had just done.

Rather a full-on mission, like that experienced by *Greenpeace Flight* that morning, facing rocket-propelled grenades and anti-aircraft weapons from a diehard enemy, than what they had just been through. Anything rather than the ambiguity and uncertainty – and sense of guilt – again.

Because the 30mm rounds from *Ugly Five Zero* had impacted on a hard, rocky shoreline, the images of death had been intensely graphic. Normally the rounds half-bury themselves in the desert sand so all that can be seen is the brown puff of an explosion. But on that island beach, exploding on impact among the rounded pebbles, the effect had left little to the aircrew's imagination. That was what a human body looked liked when it was blown to pieces and – enemy or no enemy – it wasn't particularly pleasant.

Over dinner that evening the talk in the mess tent was all about the operation to take out the enemy convoy flown by *Greenpeace Flight* that morning. Barely a mention was made of flight *Ugly*'s mission. There was an odd, echoing silence on their table, especially when a fellow airman cracked a joke about the missing gun tape.

'Lucky the camera broke then, eh lads? Nice one!'

That evening, Baz wrote the following in his combat diary:

Even though we are killing the enemy in large numbers we probably all share the same sentiment – that we would rather have arrived in Helmand and left without firing a round of ammunition and that nobody had to die. We naively thought that our presence alone would have put the enemy off. However, that will never be the case with the fanatical Taliban fighters, and so long as they continue to attack and kill our troops, the honest people of Afghanistan and the Afghan armed forces, then we will continue to prosecute the mission to destroy them. It's a terrible thing to do but it must be done.

The following day was their last on Very High Readiness duty, and it proved to be a slow one. The flight was tasked to escort a Lynx helicopter flying a casevac mission, but the Apaches had little to do other than shepherding it into and out of the LZ.

Later there were reports of troops in contact in the Gereshk area, just north of Bastion. A British infantry patrol had been coming under sporadic mortar fire throughout the morning, and the flight was tasked with finding, and destroying, the mortar base plate. But an hour and a half spent searching the hillsides above the British positions turned up nothing of interest and the frustrated aircrew were forced to return to base.

In the evening the flight was stood-to for a deliberate ambush of an enemy convoy in the mountains to the far north of Helmand Province. But with the adrenalin pumping and the rotors spinning the mission was cancelled and they were stood down. Midnight marked the end of their stint as the VHR flight and the start of three days' duty at Kandahar Airfield. In a sense, it was the last thing that the four airmen needed.

They flew up to Kandahar in the rear of a Lynx. The Lynx is a multi-purpose utility and troop transport helicopter, but it is badly underpowered for daytime tasking in Afghanistan. Baz sat in the rear of the Lynx staring out at the dark desert and the star-lit sky. Now and again he picked up the eyes of the door gunner illuminated by the glow of his night vision goggles.

'In the back of my mind my thoughts kept drifting back to the riverboat shoot-up,' Baz remarks. 'I still couldn't seem to get those images out of my head.'

It was a surreal experience being back in Slipper City, as Kandahar Airfield has been nicknamed by British troops. There were a few Apaches that needed flight-testing or flying forwards to Bastion, but mostly Kandahar meant downtime. Here were the ranks of coffee shops, the clothing boutiques, the swanky showers and toilets, and the accommodation pods with their Ikea-style furniture.

But an ice-cold cappuccino glaze from Tim Hortons, with a country and western band providing entertainment just didn't appeal to the four airmen right now. In fact, the contrast between the atmosphere at KAF and what was going on in their minds could hardly have been more marked.

'We came off VHR duty and we had three days in which to do little more than think,' remarks Steve. 'Baz and Tim were more reserved than us, as they had no video. What they'd seen was horrific and not very pretty. Those were three days in which we didn't speak to each other very much at all.'

'I wasn't very happy,' Baz remarks. 'What we'd done was really horrific to look at. Even though we'd reviewed the videotape we still had no idea who we had killed. There was a lot of tension between us, and no one was talking and bringing it out in the open. It was all bottled up, which was just making things worse.'

In an effort to lighten the mood, Baz started to sing the Chris de Burgh song 'Don't Pay the Ferryman', but with slightly doctored lyrics: 'Who killed the ferry man . . .' It didn't go down very well, and not only because Baz was no songster. On one level the lyrics really hit home: just who was it that they had killed out there on that river? Was it the enemy, or was it an innocent group of boatmen? The mood was brooding and introspective; the flight's team spirit was being sorely tested.

Up until this moment the four men had been operating as a close-knit unit: they had been to the gym together, they had been running around the Camp Bastion perimeter in the cool of the evening and they had watched their DVDs together in the VHR tent when not on active missions. But now each man was sticking to his own space and his own company, spending time in his pod cocooned in his own thoughts.

'At the end of the day this was very personal,' remarks Baz. 'We could see them so clearly on that riverbank. Unless you're a sniper, or in close-quarters combat, you're never so up close and personal and intimate to the action and horror. I'd hate to fire and not feel anything: I'm glad we have feelings like we do. I'm glad that when I fire I think: have I done right? What was so strange was that we didn't talk to each other. Had we really messed up already, in the very first week? Would we always have this nagging doubt?'

It was Steve who took the initiative to lift the flight out of its morass. There had to be some way of finding out just who it was that flight *Ugly* had targeted during the riverboat shoot-out. He made it his mission to do so.

Validation of their actions during the Sangin operation came via their intelligence man, Chewy Liner, and also 3 Regiment's CO, Lieutenant Colonel Jon Bryant. The Royal Anglians had been able to give them real insight into the achievements of the Apaches operating that day. Sources had confirmed that the flight *Ugly* Apaches had killed seven Taliban on the river, two of whom were their top commanders.

Just as the Apache aircrew had suspected, the enemy had been extracting from the Viking ambush by riverboat. In addition to killing the seven enemy fighters, the Apaches had destroyed their escape boat and their getaway car. Between the two Apaches and the soldiers on the ground, eighteen enemy fighters had been killed, including high-rankers.

'When Chewy rooted out that info, to know we weren't wrong was just a huge relief,' remarks Baz. 'After three days of not knowing, the shadow finally lifted. It didn't mean a lot to anyone other than us, but we looked at each other with enormous relief on our faces. We finally admitted to each other that we'd all felt a bit odd about the whole period. We made the decision that from then on we would discuss our thoughts and problems openly with each other, as a flight, both during and after the tour.'

After three days in KAF the men of flight *Ugly* were desperate to get back to the real world – the Apache base at Camp Bastion. But their scheduled flight was cancelled. While awaiting a replacement the men ran in to Colin Norton, a fellow Apache pilot and one of the Six Flight crew – nicknamed *Super Six*. They were starting their own rotation through Kandahar, and they had been in the thick of the action during their own VHR duty.

While the *Ugly* aircrew had been buried in their pods, Colin Norton, flying with the Squadron OC, Jules Franks, had been tasked to escort a Chinook into the area of the Kajaki Dam, north of Sangin, a place that was to become an increasingly busy hub of operations. It had been an interesting operation, to put it mildly.

The Kajaki Dam was built on the upper reaches of the Helmand River to trap the snowmelt coming off the mountains and channel the water through a series of massive turbines to generate electricity. The dam was part of a massive US-sponsored project to irrigate the Helmand Valley, with a crosshatch network of canals branching off along much of the river's route. During the Cold War US money had been pumped into such projects in Afghanistan in an effort to help defeat the Soviet threat.

The irrigation grid was very clear from the air, and in many places it still provided the water that made the Helmand Valley bloom. Without water, agriculture and life would be largely impossible. But as for the power supply from the dam, that was another matter. In theory the dam's capacity should have been enough to provide electricity to most of the inhabitants of Helmand Province, especially those in the more northerly reaches of the valley. In practice, the long years of war and neglect had left the turbines in a state of disrepair, and electricity supplies were pitifully irregular.

One of the keys to achieving the coalition's aim of winning the hearts and minds of the people of Helmand was to get the dam up to 100 per cent power. Arguably, that one success would do more to bring people on side than anything else, and holding Kajaki was a vital objective. To get the dam working again would involve trucking in replacement turbines and spare parts, for which the roadways needed to be made secure.

It was for these reasons that a permanent British garrison had been established at the dam site, and patrols were being pushed out to clear and secure the surrounding terrain. For their part, the Taliban had vowed to drive the British out of the Kajaki region and had even threatened to dynamite the dam. Kajaki had become a key battleground.

During their missions over Sangin, flight *Ugly* had got sight of the Kajaki Lake, the intense milky blue of its snowmelt lying in dramatic contrast to the bleached brown-greys of the surrounding mountains. From the air it was an awe-inspiring sight. It had crossed Baz's mind that in a different time, and if peace ever came to Helmand, it would make a wonderful place to visit, a dip in the icy snowmelt offering the perfect antidote to the baking heat of the Afghan plains.

As it was, Kajaki was set to become one of the most familiar patches of terrain over which the Apaches of 662 Squadron would find themselves operating. Colin's *Super Six* flight had been on a bog-standard resupply mission escorting a Chinook in to Kajaki. On arriving in the area the local *Widow* call-sign had cleared them into the landing zone with words to the effect of: 'You are cleared in, the LZ is cold, we have neutralised the AAA and have not heard any more from him.'

The AAA was a heavy calibre anti-aircraft artillery piece that the enemy had brought in to the region to menace Allied resupply by air. 'Roger, running in,' had been Jules Franks's reply. But no sooner had those words been said than the AAA had opened up. BOP-BOP-BOP-BOP – rounds had barrelled past the Apache cockpit as the pilots threw the aircraft into evasive action and tried to spot the location of the enemy gun. As with RPGs, the HIDAS defences could do nothing against such ground fire.

'AAA in area! Area hot! I say again HOT,' the local *Widow* had reported, as if the aircrew hadn't already realised. It was just another indicator of how much the enemy were learning to hate the Apaches, and how determined they were to shoot one down. With guns like those they certainly had the means to do so. The resupply was aborted, at least until the gun could be taken care of, and *Super Six* flight were lucky to have escaped unharmed.

662 Squadron had flown two other significant missions while flight *Ugly* had been away. A flight of two Apaches had been sent on a seek-and-destroy mission into a remote area of Helmand. A high-ranking Taliban leader was known to be passing through the area and a Predator UAV was tracking his vehicle. The pair of Apaches had thundered towards target, with the pilot of the Predator sitting in his air-conditioned office in America keeping the UAV above the vehicle.

But sadly the Taliban commander had driven into a busy village by the time the Apaches had arrived over target. As he was parked up in a compound full of women and children the mission had to be aborted. But it had served to demonstrate the potential of the Apaches to work as a hit squad in conjunction with a Predator, without risking men on the ground.

The second mission had again involved high-value enemy targets. A meeting of Taliban commanders was taking place at night in a location south of Sangin. The aim of the meeting was to plan further attacks against Sangin town in an attempt to destabilise it. As the Apaches of *Geek Flight*, commanded by Nick Easton, had flown in towards target a thousand-pound JDAM bomb had been dropped on the compound by a fast jet.

But the JDAM had fallen short of the target and not all of those present at the meeting had been hit. The Apaches were tasked with taking out those who had escaped the bombing, the so-called leakers. They had gone in to attack, hunting down several leakers using their thermal imaging systems to direct their 30mm cannon fire.

Hearing about such missions only made the men of flight *Ugly* all the more keen to get back to Bastion. They were finally able to get out of Kandahar by hitching a ride on a Chinook that was routing to Bastion via Gereshk and Laskhar Gah. The Chinook was crammed full of weapons and personal supplies for the soldiers on the ground, including what was arguably the single most important item of all: their mail.

The Apache aircrew took full note of the advice offered them by the Chinook's dour door-gunner: enjoy the flight, but don't sit by the windows. Instead, they crawled into the centre of the hold and perched on top of a massive pile of kit, trying hard not to crush any of the mailbags. There was little room to move, especially as the floor and sides of the aircraft had been decked out in armour as protection against Taliban ground fire.

When the men arrived back at their Camp Bastion base they found it a whirlwind of activity. For the second time that day *Geek Flight* had been scrambled to support a Chinook on a casevac, having not long been back from a major firefight. It looked like flight *Ugly* might soon be back in action. They dumped their kit in their tent, the muggy heat and the gasping air-con unit signifying that they were home. It was a far cry from Kandahar Airfield, but entirely welcome.

In the 662 Squadron Ops Room Ian McIvor brought the aircrew up to speed. That day there had been intense fighting in and around the area of the Kajaki Dam. The 105mm guns of the Royal Artillery had fired a staggering nine hundred high-explosive rounds at enemy positions, and the local *Widow* had called in five airstrikes using five-hundred-pound bombs. Operations against the enemy were ongoing to the north of Sangin and to the south of Garmsir, both in known Taliban hotspots.

Flight *Ugly* would be assigned to Duty Ops the following day. That meant they would be ground testing the Apaches at Bastion, plus helping plan any deliberate operations that might be in the offing. And if the VHR and Deliberate Ops aircrews became over-stretched – running over the limit of their permitted flight hours – then flight *Ugly* might be in the hot seat again.

Their initial Duty Ops tasking looked to be a peach if ever there was one. First thing the following morning some thirty-odd nurses from the Camp Bastion Field Hospital were due a tour of the Apache flight line. The men of the flight had been allocated the not altogether unpalatable task of giving those nurses a run-round of the attack helicopters, the hangars and other facilities.

Steve and Baz were up early, Steve admitting that he'd slept even less than usual due to the excitement of the coming mission. Having spruced themselves up and donned their smart one-piece flying suits they headed up to the flight line, feeling a buzz of anticipation as the bus carrying the nurses drove up and pulled to a stop. Yippee – the girls had finally arrived.

But to their immense disappointment only four nurses got out, and three of them were men. Not only that, but the lone female nurse turned out to be in charge of the Camp Bastion sexual diseases clinic!

Baz and Steve did their best to hide their disappointment. Putting their frustrations behind them they did the walk-and-talk around the flight line, engaging the nurses in conversation. The airmen had immense respect for the medics' work and their positive attitude. They were amazed to learn that if a wounded soldier made it back to Camp Bastion alive the medical staff more-or-less guaranteed to keep him that way.

In addition to British and Allied troops, the medics were also treating a bunch of Afghan children who had been wounded in a recent US airstrike. US warplanes had mistakenly targeted a wed-ding party in a tragic example of friendly fire. And then there were the injured Taliban and al-Qaeda fighters who were being treated in the hospital.

The enemy combatant's attitude to the female nurses was appalling: they repeatedly refused to be touched by the 'dirty, infi-del women'. Once those enemy fighters were well enough they would be handed over to the Royal Military Police Special Investigations Branch for a little questioning.

Steve couldn't resist asking the lone female nurse if she had any customers for her sexual diseases clinic. Surely there couldn't be that many in a place like Camp Bastion?

'You'd be surprised,' she told him with a mischievous smile. 'I'm really kept quite busy.'

The run-round of the flight line hadn't been quite the lingering treat the airmen were anticipating. Once it was done they headed for the ops tent for the first briefing of the day. After the letdown of the thirty nurses, they were relieved to discover that some real missions were in the offing. Flight *Ugly* were being stood-to for an operation in the area of Garmsir.

Garmsir is the Taliban's unrivalled stronghold in Helmand, and it lies in the remote badlands of the extreme south-west of the province. Here, the Garmsir Box consists of a twenty square-kilometre cratered and blasted landscape reminiscent of a First World War battlefield. Tunnels, caves, trench systems and thick woodland provide ideal cover and routes of secure movement for enemy fighters, making it a nightmare for an attacking force.

Parts of the Garmsir Box resemble the Somme in terms of the number of bomb craters pock-marking the landscape. The whole area is a ghost land devoid of civilians. Settlements are long-deserted, the bombed and bullet-ridden buildings bearing witness to years of fierce fighting.

A heavy-calibre air defence weapon had recently been used in a ground attack role against British forces, and flight *Ugly*'s mission was to take it out. The weapon had been tentatively identified as a ZU23. The ZU23 is a Soviet-era anti-aircraft weapons system comprising twin 23mm cannons mounted on a two-wheel car-riage. It is a highly mobile weapon, and easily towed behind a Toyota pickup, the standard Taliban vehicle.

In a ground attack role, the ZU23 is devastating against lightly armoured vehicles. It is also a potent anti-aircraft weapon, accurate to 2500 metres and with a rapid rate of fire. Even today, batteries of ZU23s are deployed as standard air defence weapons with Russian airmobile units.

British forces had been trying to kill this ZU23 for some time, but with little success. Intelligence sources had reported that the weapon's specialist operator – believed to be a Chechen fighter – would be in a meeting with Taliban leaders that evening. Flight *Ugly* were to head in to Garmsir to target that meeting, with a contingent of soldiers following in a Chinook. Once flight *Ugly* had hit the meeting house the troopers would be dropped by the Chinook to finish off the attack.

Taking offensive operations into Garmsir was all part of the British strategy of going mobile and causing the enemy a series of morale-sapping defeats in their heartland.

Just after last light that evening flight *Ugly* got the call to go. After a very quick briefing with the Chinook crew and the commander they headed for the flight line. As Alex was sick his place on *Ugly Five One* had been taken by Dean Attril, one of the *Geek Flight* aircrew.

The two Apaches lined up on the runway, fuelled up and Hellfire-heavy, and began the taxi for take-off. To either side of them the dim low-luminance bulbs that line the runway glowed faintly in the gathering darkness. Taking off in an Apache during the hours of night was always more challenging than a daytime lift-off, and Baz and Steve were concentrating 100 per cent on getting their aircraft airborne for the coming mission.

Baz eased up the power on the collective, preparing for a running take-off, all the time scanning the monocle-screen over his right eye – the helmet-mounted display. The image displayed there was the picture produced by the aircraft's night vision system – the forward-looking infrared (FLIR). It showed the runway ahead as a series of eerie fluorescent green dots and lines, the lighter heat sources standing out from the colder, blacker shade. At the same time his left eye could see the darkened world outside the cockpit as it actually was for real.

As Baz released the brakes and the aircraft accelerated away the image in front of his right eye showed objects passing the cockpit noticeably earlier than they were in reality. The infrared sensors are positioned in the Apache's nose pod, some twelve feet in front and four below the pilots. As the runway flashed past, Baz's right eye was seeing as if it was positioned on the Apache's nose, whereas his left eye was seeing things as it normally would. The experience was distinctly unnerving.

Twenty minutes after easing their aircraft into the air, the flight *Ugly* airmen crossed over the dark shadow of the Helmand River before pushing onwards into the open deserts and Garmsir. Hugging the contours of the rolling terrain, the pilots searched ahead using the aircraft's FLIR sensors, which transformed the darkness of night into the weird glow of infrared daylight.

All of a sudden the HIDAS alarm started blaring in the lead Apache as the aircraft's defensive sensors detected an enemy missile locking on. The weird, disembodied female voice of the HIDAS warning system began identifying the threat while simultaneously computing how best to counter it.

'Short range missile, six o'clock. Launch. Launch. Launch.'

There was a massive flash of blinding light as a fountain of white exploded in the dark sky all around the aircraft. Scores of flares fired off from the Apache's rear launchers, mounted just forward of the tail rotors, surrounding the aircraft in a sea of burning white and turning the darkness into a harsh metallic daylight. Each flare burned with a ferocity that far outmatched the heat from the Apache's exhausts, enveloped as they were in the aircraft's icy Black Hole system. They provided a confusion of different hot points for the missile's infrared guidance system to lock on to.

Leaving the blinding pyrotechnic show in its wake, the Apache powered onwards, Tim and Baz breathing a sigh of relief as it did so: the HIDAS really did seem to be as good as the instructors had claimed. To the front there was a second massive burst of light as the Chinook's defensive flares fired off, that aircraft also sensing and responding to an enemy missile threat at ground level.

As the burning flares fell to earth they set fire to dry crops lying in the fields and the thatch of farmers' huts. Either the flares from the Chinook or the noise of the low-flying aircraft caused a buffalo to rear up on its hind legs. As it did so, the farmer holding on to it was pulled into the air, hanging on grimly to the end of a rope. It was hardly ideal hearts and minds stuff, but the aircrew couldn't help but laugh at the spectacle.

There was a sudden burst of angry ground fire, as if in response. Threads of tracer laced the dark sky, seeking the cockpit of *Ugly Five One*. The ground fire redoubled until the Apaches were flying through a mesh of fluorescent green tracer. Steve dropped his height to some sixty feet or so, the other aircraft following suit while the Apache gunners slaved their sights to the muzzle flashes, searching for targets.

'Guess that's the Afghan way of filing a low-flying complaint,' Dean remarked over the radio net. 'Back home it's an angry phone call. Here they've got a different way of doing things.'

The contours of the Garmsir hills could be seen rearing out of the desert plain. It was there that the aircrew would hunt down and engage the enemy. Ten minutes out from target the four airmen learned that the meeting was breaking up. Unbeknown to the Taliban, their gathering was under observation by a Predator UAV and it was picking up images of people preparing to leave. A fast jet orbiting high overhead was ordered to drop three five-hundred-pound bombs before the opportunity was lost.

A call came through to the Apaches from the special operator piloting the Predator. The airstrike had gone in and the compound had been flattened. However, ten or more leakers had made it away and were hiding in a nearby wood line to the south-west of the target building. Among their number could well be the operator of the ZU23 gun. The Apaches were retasked to go in and hit those leakers, after which they would escort in the Chinook to drop the soldiers. The crack ground troops would mop up any surviving enemy and ensure the ZU23 had been destroyed.

With the Chinook holding off in the desert, the Apaches power-climbed to three thousand feet, like eagles searching for their prey. The target building was visible from several miles away as it was a blazing ruin. Baz picked out the tree line where the enemy had to be hiding and Tim slaved the nose pod to his sightline. As the FLIR detectors scanned the area they picked out the glowing hotspots of two figures, one of whom was clearly standing.

Seconds later Tim pulled the gun trigger and a twenty-round burst of 30mm cannon fire tore into their position in the dark woodland. The two figures instantly disappeared from view. Both Apaches turned their fire on the trees now, raking them with repeated 30mm bursts. Either the enemy were dead or they had well and truly gone to ground.

Breaking contact, the flight *Ugly* aircrew were informed that the mission was being aborted. The ground attack had been cancelled and the Chinook was to return direct to Bastion. The Apaches were to move immediately northwards to assist ground troops in a major contact.

As the aircraft turned in that direction they could see a 105mm barrage being fired out of Forwards Operating Base (FOB) Dwyer on to enemy positions around Delhi, a largely deserted village with a British base attached. It was there that British forces were engaging the Taliban fighters. The eastern checkpoint of FOB Delhi had been under a fierce enemy assault for seven hours, taking heavy machine-gun fire and dozens of RPG rounds. The Apaches were tasked with finding and destroying the enemy fighters.

On arrival over the battlefield the Apache pilots scanned the terrain below them for the enemy. But the FLIR image was unclear and muddled by blinding tracer so the aircrew switched to night vision goggles. Night vision goggles (NVGs) employ similar technology to forward-looking infrared, but the goggles clip on to the helmet, dropping over the user's eyes like a bulky set of spectacles. Sometimes they proved more effective, especially at a distance.

But even with the NVGs the aircrew were unable to detect the enemy, and by now the aircraft were running low on fuel. In an effort to help them find their targets the ground troops asked the Apache pilots to watch their tracer. Using their .50-calibre heavy machine guns, they poured bursts of fire into the enemy positions but the tracer rounds ricocheted all over the place, spinning off for miles into the fiery darkness. As far as the aircrew could tell, the focus of the fire appeared to be a ruined building directly below them.

Believing they had located the enemy position, the Apaches went in to attack. Using their 30mm cannons they pumped burst after burst of heavy-calibre rounds into the ruined building in the hope of angering the enemy and provoking them into revealing themselves. But there was no reaction from anywhere below and it seemed likely that the enemy fighters had gone to ground in the warren of hideaways that honeycomb the Garmsir Box.

Steve and Dean noticed a lone heat source moving across a crater directly below them. One long burst of 30mm rounds and the glowing blip was no more. With fuel levels at critical and their three hundred rounds of 30mm all but exhausted, the aircraft broke off the contact and set a course for Camp Bastion. Time after time this would prove to be the pattern of battle: that as soon as the Apaches appeared the enemy would make themselves scarce.

It showed how much the enemy were getting to know, and to fear, the sleek black attack helicopters.

9

UGLY, WIDOW CALLING

Days 8–14

The following morning, intelligence reports came in that eight enemy fighters had been killed in and around the Garmsir compound. The night vision sensors on *Ugly Five One* had actually malfunctioned over the battlefield, leaving Dean with an image that was like having 'a thick gherkin squashed over the eye'. It was amazing that he'd seen anything, yet his rounds of 30mm had been bang on target.

Most importantly, the attack had destroyed the ZU23 gun. The threat of the anti-aircraft weapon had been removed – at least for now.

It was flight *Ugly*'s first day on Deliberate Operations, not that they would have known it. The previous three-day stint on Duty Ops had seen them fly two combat missions against enemy targets, one against the ZU23 in Garmsir. Increasingly, each of the four flights of 662 Squadron were being called to man operations as the need arose, disregarding which of the four duty rotations they were on. Whether on downtime or not, they were being asked to step up to the mark. *So be it*. The aircrew had waited long enough to prove their machines and themselves in combat.

The only real limit on the intensity of operations was time. Each Apache aircrew had a daily limit of flight hours: once fourteen hours had been flown the crew was theoretically grounded. The limit was imposed to avoid the danger of aircrew exhaustion. There was also a 350 hour monthly limit imposed on the squadron as a whole. The Apache was an expensive aircraft to maintain and operate, and any significant overflight of planned hours would affect the Army's ability to keep the Apache flying.

The men of flight *Ugly* had been warned to carefully husband their flight hours. A major deliberate operation was in the offing and they were earmarked for it. Their flight had had a busy first week of the deployment and their hours were running: they would need to be careful. This was to become a major tension of the tour – the conflict between conserving hours and doing right by the soldiers on the ground, who were increasingly relying on the Apaches for close air support.

While awaiting the 'go' on that deliberate op, the four airmen decided to have an action-themed week of DVDs. A laptop was propped up on an upturned box in the centre of their tent and the full *Band of Brothers* DVD set was broken out. When they tired of watching Easy Company in action during the fight to liberate mainland Europe, the four men headed for 662 Squadron's makeshift gym. To one side of a hangar-tent was a DIY awning – a camouflage net that provided shade. Various ammo boxes and assorted pilfered junk had been welded to steel bars to make up a set of weights.

Following a good workout the four men would take a dip in the groundies' 'swimming pool'. Some of the more enterprising ground crew had got a couple of inflatable pools sent out from the UK. They were little more than paddling pools, but the groundies were forever throwing pool parties and trying to entice the female nursing staff to take a dip. Their efforts were largely unsuccessful; instead they got Baz, Tim, Steve and Alex piling in after a sweaty gym session.

Oddly enough, one of the few affordable items in the Camp Bastion stores – the NAAFI – were swimming hats. Among the forty-two-inch plasma screen TVs, the sunglasses and sun cream, there was also a wide range of swimwear on sale, including hats and goggles. Why on earth the NAAFI was stocking swimwear in a British Army camp in the midst of one of the most arid and barren places on earth defied explanation. Even in the groundies' pool there was little scope for putting in a few lengths.

Steve James couldn't resist asking the NAAFI store man why he was stocking swimwear, especially when the coolers kept running out of cold drinks and chocolate: 'I asked him why he was selling all these swim hats and goggles . . . He just shrugged and told me they get a bulk order shipped out from the UK, and whatever came with it came with it. Camp Bastion had got the full range of swimwear. That's just how it was.'

After their cool-off in the pool, the four airmen generally did a pre-dinner run around the camp perimeter. At around five o'clock the temperature started to drop and they would jog either a three-, five- or eight-kilometre route, depending on how energetic they were feeling. After the Garmsir op, and the relief of knowing that the Sangin riverboats were bona fide targets, the flight was rebuilding its team spirit once more.

The months of May and June are renowned for bringing sand-storms in Afghanistan. On day two of flight *Ugly*'s Deliberate Ops duty, 24 May, the temperature was red-hot, the weather close and brooding. As dark shadows boiled on the dirty horizon to the west of Bastion, those old hands who knew what this signified warned the aircrew of 662 Squadron to batten down for a major storm.

The Apaches were blanked up and wheeled into the hangars as the dark tempest bore down on the British base. In an instant the ferocious winds hit, transforming the ominous stillness of the morn-ing into the raging semi-darkness of a howling monster of a sandstorm. It was unlikely that there would be much flying that day.

When the sandstorm had blown itself out the Sky TV presenter and ex-*EastEnders* actor Ross Kemp paid a visit to the Apache flight line. Kemp explained to the aircrews that he was filming a documentary series on the British war effort in Afghanistan. His father had once served with the Royal Anglians, and he was now embedded with their troops. He was following the stories of four young soldiers from their UK departure to the end of their Helmand tour. Shortly, he would be heading into the badlands up around Sangin.

Ross Kemp got a warm reception from the Apache aircrews, who respected him for taking the risk of going to the front line with British troops. Flight *Ugly* agreed to give him an interview concerning their recent operations, but only on the condition that their faces were obscured.

'He was doing a fine job telling the story like it is,' Steve remarks. 'We admired him because the Sangin Valley is one of the most hostile and dangerous places on earth. His story would cover the ground war and our role within it. We showed him around the flight line and the aircraft, and one of our flights gave him a candid interview, but all without faces showing!'

The Apache attack helicopter squadrons were attaining a high level of respect, and fear, among a battle-hardened enemy. There was always a possibility that Apache pilots might be targeted in the UK – especially if their faces were shown in the media, or if their real names were used. After the 7/7 terror attacks on the London Underground, and abortive plots to kidnap and behead British soldiers on leave, such fears did not appear unjustified.

But right now at Bastion the aircrews had more immediate concerns to deal with: the burning heat constituted a growing impediment to 662 Squadron's ability to function properly. Aircraft could be blanked up and sheeted down in the hangars to protect against sandstorms, but the heat was another problem entirely. If the aircraft's interior overheated the complex computer systems could be tripped, rendering the Apache inoperable. More worrying still, the Hellfire missiles could actually 'cook off' (spontaneously combust), blowing the aircraft sky high.

In an effort to deal with such problems, the aircrews spoke to the US Apache operators, who had many more years' experience on the aircraft. A few simple precautions involving disconnecting batteries, and extra ventilation, seemed to work wonders with the flight computers. As for the Hellfires, a makeshift solution was hit upon. Groundies and aircrew joined forces to build some sandbagged storage bunkers right on the flight line. The Hellfires could be kept in the shade and only loaded on to an aircraft's stub wings when it was about to get airborne.

It was a simple yet effective solution. Unfortunately, MOD health and safety officers heard about the bunker construction and decided to pay a visit. The bunkers were apparently a 'non-standard modification to standard procedures' and so constituted a health and safety issue. There was a danger that a member of the aircrew or ground crew might trip and fall into one and injure themselves. Indeed, it was just conceivable that an Apache might crash into one.

The heath and safety officers ordered the groundies to demolish the newly constructed Hellfire storage bunkers. In response, 662 Squadron's aircrew and groundies proceeded to give this officious bullshit the short shrift it deserved: they invited the health and safety officers to sit astride a Hellfire as it heated up to forty-five degrees Celsius (113 degrees Fahrenheit), just to check whether it was safe at that temperature . . . The MOD health and safety lot seemed to value their manhood, for that settled the issue.

The one serious impediment to operations that the squadron could do little about was altitude. Camp Bastion sits at three thousand feet above sea level; up around the Kajaki Dam the mountains rear up to some nine thousand feet. Once fuelled-up and bombed-up, the Apaches were heavy in any case. The slower their speed, the more an aircraft was vulnerable to ground fire. The greatest fear when operating around Kajaki was that the enemy might be on the highest peaks, waiting to hit a British helicopter.

The main British observation post at Kajaki is well situated: it sits on a high ridge that overlooks the lake. It was garrisoned by a tough contingent from the Royal Marines. They knew they were very much on the front line due to the daily attacks they were suffering. Enemy forces had several advantages over the defenders, including their familiarity with the terrain and their knowledge of the location of any minefields. These had been lain by Soviet forces during their war in Afghanistan and little or no de-mining work had been done since that time.

Enemy forces had marked off safe passage across the minefields using pathways of white stones. An enemy fighter must have crossed the minefields and shinned up the British base's unused flagpole, unfurling a white flag – the universal symbol of surrender. At sunrise this was in full view of the British troops in their nearby observation post. Each time they tried to get to the flagpole to remove the white flag they were targeted by sniper fire and mortars.

Eventually flight *Ugly* was stood-to for a mission to hit the flagpole with a Hellfire, taking out the mast and the white flag with it. But, apart from being a waste of a missile, it would also be a waste of valuable Apache flight hours. Plus the enemy had proven that they had eyes, and accurate fire, on the flagpole and perhaps the real motive was to lure in a British helicopter to a well-prepared ambush.

The mission to Hellfire the flagpole was finally cancelled and the offending flag was taken out by a mortar team. After the aborted flagpole mission the men of flight *Ugly* were itching to get in the air. Day ten of their deployment marked the flight's return to VHR duty. Just to make sure that they would get airborne as quickly as possible, Steve booked himself an internet session for that morning. It had become a rule of the flight that whenever he did there was bound to be a call-out that stopped him getting online – and online time was precious.

With some five thousand troops at Bastion and only thirty computer terminals, online time had to be booked in advance. Troops at Bastion were allowed just twenty minutes' talk time a week to phone home – that was until someone realised that the inmates of Britain's prisons were allowed thirty minutes of free weekly calls, whereupon the soldiers' allowance was upped to the same. Other than phoning, time at the computer terminals was a rare opportunity to make contact with home. Yet whenever Steve tried to get online with his fiancée Tracey, the flight got stood-to for a mission.

'The morning of the twenty-fifth, I'd booked my internet access. So I said to Baz, "Here we go, I can guarantee us a contact – I've booked my slot on the internet." Baz laughed, but we all knew it was true: every time I booked it we got the call-out.'

'Reports had come in of the Taliban massing in the Sangin area, with more than 150 fighters and two twin-barrelled AAA guns,' remarks Baz. 'Steve had booked his internet session for 1030 hours, and we were always called out when Steve booked a terminal – it was the law. Today would be no exception. Not only that, but Tim had just told me to put on a DVD, as today was going to be boring as hell. At 1020 hours the phone rang and we got the call-out.'

It was a typical VHR mission. A British convoy had been ambushed to the south of Gereshk and a WMIK Land Rover had been hit by a mine blast. The weapons-mounted installation kit (WMIK) Land Rover is a lightly armoured open vehicle armed with a .50-calibre heavy machine gun on the rear and a general purpose machine gun (GPMG) to the front. The vehicle's main drawback is that it provides little protection against mine blasts or RPGs, and British soldiers were taking casualties as a result.

Three men had been injured and one was an urgent T1 case. Flight *Ugly* were to escort in a casevac Chinook and attempt to find and kill enemy forces that were hitting the crippled convoy. Gereshk was just a short flight east of Bastion, but with a T1 casualty every minute was precious.

The aircrew scrambled for the flight line and soon the Apaches were airborne and leading the Chinook in to the coordinates of the landing zone. Shortly after getting airborne the aircraft were crossing over the Green Zone, and suddenly there was the wail of the HIDAS alarm. Almost instantaneously the voice warning identified the threat as a surface-to-air missile (SAM) launch at medium range and the automatic defences cut in.

'As the HIDAS sensed a missile launch at medium range, the aircraft fired off decoy flares,' remarks Baz. 'It's an uncomfortable moment as you both look in the direction indicated for the launch site, trusting the system to defeat the threat, when what you really want to do is a rapid seat-of-the-pants manoeuvre to defeat it.'

Trusting in the HIDAS system, both Apaches thundered onwards. The decoy flares had presumably foxed the SAM or whatever it was that had been targeting the aircraft. But as the Apaches approached the ambush location the *Widow* call-sign came up over the radio, alerting the flight to a sudden change in the location of the landing zone. He had to shout to make himself heard over the deafening chunter of a .50-cal heavy machine gun, together with the howl of incoming rounds.

The *Widow* alerted the incoming Apaches to the presence of dickers on a ridgeline above the convoy. The enemy had by now learned how British forces reacted to an ambush and taking casualties. The dickers were on the lookout for where the ground troops were establishing the LZ. They would position their forces accordingly, so that when the Chinook and the Apaches arrived they could hit them with airburst RPGs and SAMs.

Before the casevac Chinook could go in, the dickers would have to be put out of action. That was the first priority for the Apache aircrews. With the Chinook held in an orbit over the open desert the Apaches set up in wheel formation above the ridge, scanning the heaped boulders and rocky crevices for any signs of life. They were looking for a figure using a mobile phone or a radio, and with eyes on the stricken convoy below. As nothing was visible to the naked eye the aircraft switched to their forward-looking infrared scanners, but could detect no man-sized heat blobs on the ridgeline.

The pilots felt their frustration levels rising as they flew search orbit after search orbit but still found nothing. Their failure to locate the dicker didn't mean that he wasn't there. The infrared scanners were far from infallible, and a skilled Taliban fighter trying to stay alive would be doing his best to remain hidden and undetected.

Did they clear in the Chinook, Baz wondered, knowing that enemy forces had eyes on the LZ? Or did they hold off in the hope of finding the dicker, knowing that all the while British soldiers on the ground were in dire need of medical attention?

All of a sudden there was a squelch of static on the radio and the distinctive twang of an American pilot came over the net. He was flying a B-1 Lancer bomber routed over their location. He'd been listening in on their radio chatter and was apprised of the situation. He was out of bombs, having just completed his attack run, but was there any way in which he could help? Might a fly-past over the ridgeline keep the enemy heads down for long enough to get the Chinook in?

The B-1 Lancer is a semi-stealth variable-sweep-wing aircraft with a flight speed of Mach 1.25. It is the US military's replacement for the B-52 Stratofortress heavy bomber and has a similar size, range and payload. In addition to its awe-inspiring size, the jet-black aircraft has a sleek, deltoid shape and a decidedly sinister look. Although the aircraft had no bombs on board, the enemy weren't to know that and the pilot's offer was readily accepted.

The giant black form came roaring in over the ridge at about the same altitude as the Apaches. As it drew level with the British attack helicopters, the American pilot could clearly be seen in the aircraft's tiny cockpit, perched above the arrow-sharp nose. He gave a thumbs-up and proceeded to give his best show of force.

As befitting its status, the B-1 carries an array of defensive systems, and the pilot fired off his MJU-23 decoy flares. A giant fan of burning white arced out from the B-1's tailplane, the fiery halo like a false sun hanging over the ridgeline. Selecting afterburners, the US pilot pushed the throttles fully forwards and accelerated away from the battlefield, the screaming vibrations echoing around the high ground.

As the flares drifted earthwards the casevac Chinook swept in to pick up the casualties, the pair of Apaches shepherding it in towards the LZ. It disappeared into the brown-out of a rotor-driven dust storm, the hold ramp lowering as it did so, and, with the rear wheels barely touching the earth, the wounded soldiers were loaded.

The Chinook's twin rotors rotate in opposite directions, a design that gives the aircraft superlative power and lift. It is especially capable in 'hot and high' conditions such as those found in Helmand. Within minutes the Chinook was airborne again and the convoy of vehicles was cleared to move out of the ambush zone.

En route for base Tim received a call from the Chief of Staff, Ian McIvor, asking if either aircraft had fired any munitions. If they had, McIvor would have to remain alert for the debrief and review of the gun tape. Tim reported that no rounds had been fired, to which the Chief of Staff's only response was relieved laughter. He'd been on the go for more than forty-eight hours and could do with a break.

Ian McIvor had a love-hate relationship with flight *Ugly*: they always seemed to fire off more munitions than any other flight and caused him the worst post-mission headaches.

'By now we had picked up the nickname "Spray and Pray" flight,' Baz remarks. 'The other flights took the piss that we'd fire at anything and, due to our poor gunnery skills, when we fired everyone in Helmand prayed! Steve argued that the evidence of the flight's high gunnery skills was there for all to see on the gun tape, but that didn't stop the piss-taking.'

On arrival at Bastion, the aircrews taxiied their aircraft in to the VHR bays and shut down the engines. As the VHR flight was permanently on standby the pilots often had to eat on standby too. Food boxes were passed up to the pilots. They looked inside, hoping for the tasty bacon and tomato rolls that went down a treat in the heat and dust. Instead they found a couple of rock-hard sausage rolls and a bag of crisps. The sausage rolls were about the last thing any soldier would ever willingly order from the canteen.

The aircrew were ravenous, so they bit into the sausage rolls in any case, only to get a mouthful of pastry as dry as dust together with rancid reconstituted meat. Choking on the pastry, one of the pilots found himself blowing it all out of his mouth, flakes of white floating around the cockpit like a surreal snowstorm. He grabbed a water bottle to rinse out his mouth, only to find its contents boiling hot from lying in the sun. And that was lunch.

What was the deal with the crap food, the airmen asked the groundies. The bemused ground crew explained that MOD health and safety had paid a visit that morning. The bacon sandwiches had been judged a health hazard as the hot conditions might cause the meat to go off, so risking food poisoning. Bacon sarnies were henceforth banned from the flight line: only sausage rolls would be allowed.

Let's get this straight, an incredulous Baz Hunter reasoned. We've just been out on a combat mission that got targeted by a

SAM, and that level of risk is acceptable. However, the risk involved in eating a bacon and tomato sandwich is not. This is unreal.

The sausage rolls were inedible. The solution proved to be to leave them sitting on the hot metal of the aircraft's stub wing for an hour or so. Pastry and filling alike melted in the intense heat, rendering the gooey mass vaguely edible. At least it could be swallowed without the need for chewing. This was also a good method for making tea to wash down the revolting mess. A bottle of water with a couple of tea bags in left on the stub wing produced a great brew.

Just after midnight the flight got its second call-out of the day. This time there were troops in contact down at Garmsir, and four British casualties. By the time the flight had got airborne one of those injured soldiers had died and the others were fast deteriorating. As the aircraft powered south towards Garmsir, the Chinook drew ahead as its top flight speed exceeds that of the attack helicopters. But when the Chinook arrived over the battlefield the pilots found that the LZ was unsecured: there was nowhere to go in and land.

It was hardly surprising. There was a fierce firefight raging on the ground, with tracer arcing back and forth between British forces and the enemy, and mortars firing off. With the Chinook holding off to the west, the Apaches headed in to support the British troops. As they approached they could see tracer snaking out from the British positions and supporting mortar fire coming out of the Garmsir District Centre. Both tracer and mortar rounds were hitting an area known to British forces as the West Wood, where fires were burning from a recent barrage of 105mm rounds.

As the pair of Apaches homed in on the West Wood the enemy turned their guns on the British attack helicopters. All of a sudden a curtain of tracer lit up the night sky ahead and around the Apaches, blinding the pilots who were flying on night vision goggles. NVGs are designed to be used in low light situations: any sudden and intense light source can cause a 'white out', blinding the user. Exactly that had happened to the Apache aircrew.

'As we flew in there was this massive firefight,' Steve remarks. 'Tracer was going off everywhere and there was so much coming up around the aircraft that we had to fly on instruments only as it was blinding us and we couldn't see where we were going.'

All battlefields are noisy and confusing. Visibility is uncertain and communication difficult, even from the bird's-eye view afforded by an Apache. But this one really took the biscuit. The area below was a jumbled mass of enemy fortifications – a series of interconnected trenches, bunkers and tunnels. Finding and targeting the enemy was going to be a nightmare.

As the Apaches hunted above and across the enemy fortifications, fighters popped out of cover and loosed off fire at the aircraft, the bullets tearing at the air all around them. The Apaches traded fire with fire, hitting back with their 30mm cannons and trying to find and kill the enemy before they darted back into cover. Repeatedly the attack helicopters pounded the enemy positions with bursts of 30mm cannon fire.

The brave Chinook pilots decided to go in on a hastily prepared LZ. The British soldiers were too badly injured to delay the casevac any longer. The pilots went in to land in complete darkness, navigating on NVG alone and with *Ugly Five One* shadowing them and trying to talk them on to the LZ.

As the downwash of the two giant rotors hit the ground the aircraft was engulfed in a storm of dust. The Chinook disappeared into that dust cloud, the aircrew relying on a small meter that indicates lateral and vertical movement to feel their way on to the ground.

'They went in totally blind, relying on their piloting skills, training and God to get them safely on to the ground,' remarks Baz. 'We have a very high respect for those RAF airmen, who risk their lives to go into dangerous locations, often at night and under heavy fire. At times like those we are glad of the fact that we are Apache pilots sitting high above it all!'

Barely a minute later the twin rotors emerged out of the dust and the Chinook clawed skywards, heading north at treetop level for Bastion. No sooner had the Chinook disappeared into the dark

night than the pilot came up over the radio net. He asked Tim to
relay the casualty list to Camp Bastion Field Hospital: one dead;
one needing amputation of the leg from the hip; one requiring
possible amputation of the arm and leg; and one with burns and
breathing difficulties.

British forces had suffered four casualties, one fatal, and still the
fighting was far from over. The Apaches are fitted with superior
radio equipment to the Chinooks and so they have better comms
with base. Having sent the casualty report through to Bastion, *Ugly
Five Zero* received a call from the *Widow* on the ground. He was
shouting to make himself heard over the ferocious battle-noise.

'*Ugly*, this is *Widow Seven Three*. One of the soldiers on the
casevac – he's left a LAW on the ground where he was hit. Can you
take it out?'

'Roger. We'll give it a go. But it's likely beyond our capabilities.'

The light anti-tank weapon (LAW) is a 66mm man-portable
one-use rocket. In the confusion of the firefight the injured soldier
had left his LAW behind. But somehow, and in spite of his injuries,
he had had the foresight to mark its position. He had done so using
a secret technology.

The *Widow* was asking the Apaches to hit and destroy the LAW
in order to deny it to the enemy. But trying to locate the marker
from several thousand feet in among the confusion of a darkened
battlefield, when half-blinded by tracer, was never going to be
easy.

Switching to forward-looking infrared, the aircrew pulled up the
fluorescent green glow of the battlefield on their computer screens,
hoping the marker might give a distinctive reading. The terrain
below was marked out in a series of indistinct contours, the picture
reflecting slight differences in the temperatures of each section of
ground. A building that had held the sun's heat within its thick
mud walls was visible as a set of bright green regular lines against
the dark of the desert. A vehicle was a solid block of bright green,
its engine glowing warm in the cold night air.

All of a sudden Tim noticed movement: the glow of what
appeared to be a figure emerging from an enemy position. As *Ugly*

Five Zero circled above, the figure seemed to crouch in the bush. Was it an enemy fighter heading into the no man's land of the battlefield, drawn by the marker to retrieve the LAW? As the 30mm cannon on *Ugly Five Zero*'s chin turret swivelled towards the target, slaving to the image on the screen, Steve's voice came up over the radio net: 'I've got bingo fuel! Repeat, bingo fuel! Must return to Bastion.'

After the long flight to Garmsir, and the chaotic fight above the battlefield, *Ugly Five One* was on 'bingo fuel': it had just enough to make it back to base. In the intensity of combat, coupled with the sensory overload of the Apache's night-time targeting systems, time raced for the Apache aircrews. Each of the *Ugly* airmen had been immersed 100 per cent in a parallel reality – that of fighting and flying the aircraft – in which an hour seemed to flash past in the blink of an eyelid.

Almost without realising, both aircraft's fuel supplies had reached critical levels. If either ran out of juice over Garmsir they would face going down in the heart of enemy territory. Resisting the temptation to engage the heat blob on the ground, Tim broke contact and set the quickest course for Camp Bastion. Better that enemy soldier live to fight another day and the LAW remain where it had fallen than to gift an Apache aircrew, and perhaps an entire aircraft, into the hands of the enemy.

Flight *Ugly* made it back to Bastion sipping on reserve. It was approaching five o'clock in the morning and the first slivers of dawn were piercing the dark sky to the east of the base. As they went to leave the cockpits each pilot checked his urine sack – a specially shaped bag. The pilots used them if they had to relieve themselves in flight, and periodically they did need emptying . . .

The exhausted airmen headed directly for the VHR tent. It was time to snatch a few hours' precious rest. Before sleep came Baz wrote the following in his combat diary:

Today made us think what it's like to be in the Chinook. The doctors in the back of the Chinook working in half-light to administer life-saving treatment to the casualties as the aircraft bucks and weaves its way back to Bastion. We have high regard for our doctors, medics and nurses and the amazing things they do to save soldiers. There was an annoying article in the press recently that there are not enough helicopters in Afghanistan, and that the time it takes to extract casualties from the battlefield is far too long – sometimes hours. Yes, more helicopters would be great, but the real truth is that the British military make every effort to pick up and extract casualties. The aircrew are on immediate standby, similar to Spitfire pilots awaiting the call to scramble in the Second World War, and when launched are far faster than that. The crews have a no-holds-barred, will-go-anywhere attitude, even under heavy fire, to extract wounded. There is nothing higher up the list of priorities. And the medics on the aircraft and the Chinook crews are among the bravest men and women I have ever had the privilege to meet.

There was little let-up during day two of the flight's VHR duty. They escorted a Chinook into Sangin on a casevac to pick up a T1 and a T2 casualty. But as the Chinook lifted off it suddenly plummeted downwards and actually slapped its belly on the surface of the Helmand River before the pilot wrestled it back into the air.

Ugly Five One made radio contact with the Chinook aircrew only to discover that in the hot and high conditions the aircraft had suffered a single engine failure shortly after take-off. Somehow the pilot had managed to bounce his aircraft off the river to get airborne again and he limped back to Bastion on just the one engine.

A second casevac followed, although this one was to extract casualties from a vehicle accident around Garmsir. A third call-out came, this time from an Afghan National Army unit operating in the open desert with British troops embedded as an on-the-spot training force. A vehicle had been hit by a mine and there were two T2 and one T1 casualties. There was no trace of the enemy by the time the Apaches had arrived and so they returned to base without having fired a shot.

Before coming off their VHR duty and revolving through Kandahar Airfield, Baz had to fly the Regiment's Commanding Officer, Jon Bryant, on a familiarisation and range training exercise.

Having fired off the 30mm cannon using the various automatic targeting systems Baz decided it was time for a small competition using the helmet-mounted display (HMD), the manual system that locks the gun to the pilot's eye line.

Baz also decided it was time to cheat a little, to ensure that he would win. With any HMD shot the range has to be set manually. Most pilots found it most effective to leave the range on a set distance. Baz informed his CO that he found the 1500-metre setting recommended in training produced the most accurate results. In fact, the 1000-metre setting generally proved most accurate and 1500 metres would very likely cause an overshot.

Trusting Baz's advice, the CO duly selected 1500 metres and overshot his target. He followed that with an excellent range correction and his second shot was bang on target, which meant that Baz had to beat two shots. Carefully setting his range to 1000 metres, Baz proceeded to hit the target first time around.

'Being a competitive dad I decided to cheat a little,' Baz remarks. 'On my go I hit the target first time and, just to show off, for the next nine rounds as well. It wasn't the best of tricks to play on your commanding officer, especially if you got found out!'

Prior to setting off on their rotation through Kandahar Airfield the four airmen would learn of a fascinating snippet of intelligence that had come in via 662 Squadron's Ops Room. Intelligence collected during the night of the recent Garmsir operation, during which the Apaches had gone down to bingo fuel, had picked up the following heated exchange between a Taliban commander and one of his minions:

Taliban Commander: 'Get out of cover and shoot down the mosquitoes.' ('Mosquito' was the disparaging term the enemy used for the Apaches.)
   Fighter: 'I'm going to.'
   Commander: 'If you don't get out there now and shoot one down, then I'm going come down there and shoot you myself.'
      Fighter: 'I will attack the mosquitoes. Just give me time to go and pray first.'

Garmsir was the enemy's de facto forwards mounting base for the whole of Helmand Province. It was there that newly recruited fighters crossed the border from the frontier provinces of Pakistan. Once in the Garmsir Box they were allocated to their units and had their first taste of battle. It was not unheard of for young recruits to be shot by their battle-hardened commanders for showing fear or refusing to obey orders.

But the enemy's fear of the 'mosquitoes' was becoming greater even than their fear of their own commanders.

10
OPERATION KULANG

Day 15

British and Allied forces were now operating on two main fronts in Helmand: in the north of the province, around the Sangin–Kajaki–Musa Qaleh triangle; and in the extreme south of the province, around Garmsir. Shortly, a third front was to be opened bang in the middle of those two areas of operations, in central Helmand.

Here, a series of planned operations were intended to strike hard against known enemy positions, wrestling control of key terrain from the Taliban. British and Allied forces would go on the offensive using combined airmobile and land operations across the entire length of Helmand Province.

This meant in turn that the aircrews of 662 Squadron, Army Air Corps, were likely to become even more in demand than they were already. In part it was the presence of a full Apache attack squadron in theatre that was enabling the opening up of British operations. Air Chief Marshal Sir Jock Stirrup, the head of Britain's armed forces, had hailed the achievements of the Apache Attack Squadrons by stating that their deployment had placed them at the 'cutting edge of British military power'.

'We might not have expected the degree of ferocity that the fighting would sometimes reach at its peak,' he remarked of Afghanistan. 'But we were ready for it, and we were ready because of the quality, training and courage of our forces on the ground. But we were also ready because we deployed the best attack helicopter in the world, and because it was crewed and maintained by people who are amongst the most able anywhere.'

But before going on the offensive in central Helmand there was a little local disturbance to deal with up around Sangin. The inhabitants of the village of Kang had decided to take the initiative by driving the hated Taliban out of their area. But retribution had been swift and brutal. Vengeful Taliban forces had captured the leaders of the uprising, including the village headmaster, hanging them from a nearby tree and then beheading the bodies. This was just one of many atrocities that had occurred over recent months.

And so the mother of all operations was planned to push the enemy out of the Upper Sangin Valley, their last stronghold in the area around the Kajaki Dam. The key terrain of operations would be the Green Zone band of vegetation tracing the course of the Helmand River south from the Kajaki Dam to Sangin. For several days now the Apache aircrews had been 'briefed to death' on the coming mission, which was codenamed Lastay Kulang: Pashtun for 'Sledgehammer Hit'.

No doubt about it, Op Kulang was going to be the real deal. Over several days a two thousand-strong force would push the enemy out of their bases across the region. That force would be spearheaded by a thousand troops from 12th Brigade, the bulk of whom were the Royal Anglians. In addition, soldiers from the 1st Battalion, Grenadier Guards, would be operating alongside Afghan National Army troops. This force would advance north from Sangin town, clearing the Green Zone and killing all enemy forces that they encountered.

The Royal Anglians' Recce Force — a highly mobile unit of specially trained troopers — was already active in the area, probing enemy positions by force and gathering intelligence. Prior to the main assault going in, a cut-off group — a unit positioned to ambush retreating enemy fighters — would be established by the Danish Mobile Operations Group in the desert to the west of Sangin. Danish troops were also tasked with keeping the enemy holed up in Musa Qaleh, their stronghold to the north of Kajaki, so preventing any reinforcements being set out from there.

At the northern end of the Upper Sangin Valley US troops from Task Force Fury – made up of the US 82nd Airborne Division's 4th Combat Team – would advance south in a ground attack convoy. At the same time a massive US air assault would go in. This would consist of three waves of helicopters: Chinooks and UH-60 Black Hawks inserting troops and weaponry, with Apache attack helicopters in support.

In Op Kulang the enemy were to be crushed between the hammer of British troops advancing from the south and the anvil of US forces in the north. Some one thousand enemy fighters were dispersed throughout the Upper Sangin Valley. Normally an attacking force would want to have three times the number of troops as the enemy when assaulting a well-defended area. In Op Kulang coalition forces outnumbered the enemy two to one and the deficiency was to be made up by air power – most notably, the British and US Apaches.

The ground attack plan seemed straightforward enough to the Apache aircrews. It was the US air assault plan that was causing them some problems. Eighteen Chinooks would be heading into the region of Kajaki Sofle in three waves of six aircraft. They would be landing on an eight hundred square-metre landing zone in the dark and in the brown out conditions of a rotor-blown dust storm, and with a bare few minutes separating each wave of aircraft.

As if that wasn't daunting enough, the area of operations was an enemy stronghold populated by battle-hardened fighters armed with rocket-propelled grenades, heavy machine guns and surface-to-air missiles. Intelligence reports cited Taliban leader Mullah Agha, together with a hundred diehard fighters, digging in around the Kajaki Sofle area, directly in the path of the planned US air assault.

The Apache aircrews knew that this was a high-risk operation, which was all the more reason to want to be part of Op Kulang. Flight *Ugly* hadn't exactly been promised Op Kulang, but this was the deliberate operation for which they had been warned to conserve their flight hours. Two weeks into their deployment and the aircrew felt as if they had got only the scrappy, itty-bitty missions.

In contrast, Op Kulang was scheduled to last for several intensive days, during which enemy resistance was expected to be at its fiercest.

Flight *Ugly* wanted Op Kulang bad.

However, as luck would have it, Op Kulang was pegged to start on the morning of flight *Ugly*'s last day on VHR duty, after which the four airmen were scheduled to rotate on to downtime at Kandahar Airfield. The timing could not have been worse: as British forces advanced into the badlands the four airmen would be heading off for some enforced R & R. Barring a miracle, tasking during Op Kulang would almost certainly fall to *Greenpeace Flight*, who took over VHR duty from flight *Ugly*.

No way were Baz, Tim, Steve and Alex willing to sit out Op Kulang in the PX Mini Mall in Kandahar while being serenaded by a country and western band. Having first convinced the Squadron OC and Ian McIvor, the Chief of Staff, they opted to remain in Camp Bastion, forming a reserve standby aircrew. That way, if the squadron became seriously overstretched they might just get a look in. They didn't have high hopes, but better that than to mope around Kandahar supping Frappuccinos.

Two days prior to the mission start time a British convoy of 120 vehicles including fuel lorries, heavy trucks, towed artillery and tracked Viking armoured vehicles set out from Camp Bastion. They moved up through the open desert to their start lines. The convoy had been throwing up a huge plume of dust, allowing enemy forces to track and target it. During that first day's tortuous drive over dry riverbeds, rocky plains and deep sand, a Viking struck a mine, killing a Royal Anglian signaller instantly. The following day a mortar vehicle hit another mine, resulting in two British wounded.

Undeterred, the Royal Anglians gathered on their start lines for Op Kulang. At first light on the first day of the operation, A Company, in conjunction with Estonian troops, advanced into the enemy hot spot around Putay village. Initial fighting was intense but the enemy were driven out of the area. B Company then moved on the enemy stronghold of Jussalay, where there was fearsome combat at close quarters, the British troops being targeted by machine gun fire and RPG rounds. Eventually, the Royal Anglians pushed the enemy out of the area and were able to declare it secure.

The Royal Anglians' C Company then moved forwards with the aim of linking up with the US 82nd Airborne troops from Task Force Fury who would be inserting by helicopter under cover of darkness at Kajaki Sofle. C Company advanced via the enemy stronghold of Mazdurak, the scene of some of the fiercest engagements of their deployment so far. Sure enough, enemy forces put up ferocious resistance from several different firing points and C Company had to call in mortar fire to clear a route through.

It wasn't long before Charlie Hudson's *Greenpeace Flight* got the first call-out of Op Kulang. A unit of enemy fighters were holed up in a compound with thick mud walls and were causing the Royal Anglians some serious problems. Their advance force was pinned down and they needed air power to break the enemy's resistance. Two Apaches from *Greenpeace Flight* tore in over the battlefield, raking the enemy position with bursts of 30mm cannon fire. The lead aircraft followed that with a Hellfire missile, which punched a neat hole through the roof of the main building. After that the enemy guns fell silent.

Surveillance aircraft were flying above the battlefield feeding back images to Camp Bastion via live video relay. The four airmen of flight *Ugly* were able to see the action unfolding on the plasma screens. They sat there in frustration as *Greenpeace Flight* got into the thick of things. Then *Geek Flight*, on Deliberate Ops, got their first call-out of the day, escorting a Chinook into FOB Robinson, the fortified allied base south of Sangin town. The flight *Ugly* airmen were left twiddling their thumbs.

En route to FOB Robinson, *Geek Flight* was diverted to a *Widow* calling for urgent close air support to take out an enemy position. From a jumble of mud-walled buildings Taliban fighters were putting down accurate fire on to British forces as they tried to advance. *Geek Flight* arrived over target, only to find that a B-1 Lancer stealth bomber had got there before them. The lead Apache proceeded to film through its gun camera as the B-1 dropped two two thousand-pound bombs on to the target in quick succession.

But as the dust cleared from the B-1 airstrike the enemy commenced firing once more. *Geek Flight's* lead Apache lined up on target and unleashed sixteen flechette rockets on to the complex of buildings. A total of 1280 five-inch tungsten darts saturated the compound, the clay walls offering little resistance to their penetrative force. The flechette strike covered every square foot and the enemy guns fell silent.

As *Geek Flight* turned for home, *Greenpeace Flight* was scrambled again – this time to support a unit of the Royal Anglians in a cut-off position on the banks of the Helmand River. The British soldiers were positioned to the north of Wombat Wood, a notorious Taliban ambush position. Advancing south-east, their intention was to sandwich the enemy between their force and the river. If the enemy tried to use the river as an escape route they would be highly visible, especially from the air. *Greenpeace Flight* took up orbit over the eastern bank of the river, searching for signs of the enemy.

Sure enough, a large group was spotted gathering on the river's rocky beach. As the Apaches kept watch the 105mm artillery guns firing in support of the Royal Anglians were preparing to pound that position with a devastating barrage of fire, as were the Royal Anglians' own Mortar Company. All of a sudden, the lead Apache noticed some toddlers playing in the shallows. As the aircrew zoomed in their cameras, they could see women washing clothes in waters shadowed by overhanging trees. While the enemy were known to drop their weapons and mingle with civilians, there were few here that would fit the bill as Taliban fighters.

From its bird's-eye view of the battlefield, and with its unrivalled optics, the Apache provided a matchless platform from which to get a full sense of the unfolding action. There was no way in which the figures on the beach were retreating enemy fighters. *Greenpeace Flight* put in a radio call to the *Widow*, reporting exactly what they could see. This led in turn to the mortar and artillery barrage being cancelled, averting a possible massacre of the innocents.

With the approach of 2100 hours – the start time for the Task Force Fury air assault – Op Kulang was already sixteen hours old.

There had been several further call-outs for the Apaches, mostly casevac escorts, but flight *Ugly*'s services were yet to be required. The tension in the 662 Squadron Ops Room was mounting as the hour of the US-led air assault neared. If there was a high-risk stage to Op Kulang, the airmobile assault onto the Kajaki Sofle landing zone was it.

A British surveillance aircraft had moved northwards at ten thousand feet in anticipation of the air assault by the US 82 Airborne troops. As that first wave of Chinooks swept forwards towards the LZ, each carrying some forty crack US troops, Baz had a bad feeling about the mission. There were British Chinooks involved in the air insertion that had flown out from Bastion, linking up with the US aircraft en route. Baz hoped and prayed that none of those brave British aircrew with whom they had already been in action would hit trouble, and ditto for the American crews.

The first aircraft swept in at high speed and at tree-top level, putting down on the LZ with hardly a shot being fired. As that first wave lifted off the second was already inbound to the LZ. Once again, the giant helicopters put down into a cloud of rotor-driven dust with barely a round being fired by the enemy. But as the Chinooks went to lift off again the Taliban sprang their ambush.

A series of flashes on the shadowy ridgeline eight hundred metres above the LZ showed where a barrage of rocket-propelled grenades had been fired. The lazy trails of the rockets laced fire across the night-dark valley as the grenade rounds bore down on their targets. The Chinooks and Black Hawks struggled to lift free of the dust-entombed LZ, each clawing at the darkened skies with its thrashing rotors.

Just as the aircraft got airborne an RPG round ploughed into the cockpit of the Chinook nearest the ridge, the 2.5 kg warhead blasting the armoured steel and Perspex capsule apart. An instant later there was a second explosion as another, more powerful projectile ploughed into the ninety-eight foot long aircraft amidships.

Effectively crewless and losing power, the stricken aircraft plunged earthwards. The sixty-foot diameter rotors hit first, slicing into the rocky soil and shearing off with the terrible scream of tearing steel. The aircraft impacted side-on and front-first, ploughing into the boulder-strewn hillside. The nose crumpled on the ground, the Chinook shuddering as it did so, and finally buckling in two where the second projectile had all but sliced it through the middle.

There was a stunned silence in the Camp Bastion Ops Room: the live video images showed the stricken aircraft coming to rest in a pall of smoke, dust and flames.

All of a sudden the airwaves went haywire.

'*Flipper*'s down! *Flipper*'s down! *Flipper*'s down!'

Flipper was the call-sign of the stricken US Chinook. American Apache attack helicopters went in at low level to hit the positions on the ridge. But anti-aircraft guns opened up, putting up a wall of tracer. The Apaches flew right into it and within moments they were being pounded by the heavy-calibre rounds.

The Apache is designed to take and survive a hit from a 23mm shell, providing flight time for it to limp back to base. As a crippled Apache turned for home it was targeted by SAMs, the aircraft's flares shooting off in a halo of fire.

'The plan had been put into place four days prior to the op going in,' Baz remarks. 'Three waves of Chinooks going into a known enemy stronghold . . . In some ways we weren't surprised when the Chinook went down. But as we heard the disaster unfolding on the airwaves we knew there were still more aircraft to go in on that LZ – how many more might we lose? It was fellow aircrew and we were all thinking about the numbers involved – it was a big number that we'd lost that day.'

Amid the alarm and confusion and chaos of the battlefield, intelligence revealed what experienced and tactically astute fighters they were. They had a second force positioned some four hundred metres to the south of the downed Chinook and they were preparing to head into the LZ for a follow-up attack. Taliban commanders had vowed to capture an Allied soldier alive if they dared venture into the Upper Sangin Valley. If that second enemy force reached the downed Chinook they might capture the surviving aircrew – that's if there were any left alive.

Up on the ridgeline an enemy mortar team was setting up position to fire on the downed Chinook should a rescue party arrive. The Taliban had clearly planned this ambush carefully and with possible foreknowledge of Op Kulang, and possibly even the location of the LZ. They had manoeuvred themselves into a prime position either to capture the surviving aircrew or to hit any rescue force that might arrive at the downed aircraft.

'The American helicopters were going in at low level, they were vulnerable,' remarks Baz. 'In the Ops Room we had a massive plasma screen that breaks down into four screens, and from that we got the real-time updates on what was going on. So we knew the Chinook had gone down, but we didn't know for sure if it was British or American. The airwaves were blocked with the over-chat but we all knew that it was the first helicopter to go down in the whole of the Helmand campaign.'

Fortunately the first two waves of aircraft had dropped enough troops from the 82nd Airborne to be able to secure the LZ. A force went out and surrounded the wreckage of the Chinook in all-round defence, engaging the enemy in a fierce firefight. With *Flipper* having well and truly gone down, the 82nd Airborne troops began to collect the dead and prepared to blow up the remains of the aircraft in order to deny it to the enemy.

In the aircraft's shattered interior they found seven dead soldiers: five of them were the American aircrew, one was a Canadian soldier and one of the dead men was British. Had the enemy hit the Chinook as it went in to land there would have been forty-odd soldiers on board and it would have been an even greater catastrophe.

As reports came up over the radio net of one dead British soldier it only added to the confusion felt by the 662 Squadron aircrew. What was a British soldier doing on board an American Chinook inserting troops from the 82nd Airborne Division? The British soldier turned out to be part of the British Army's Combat Camera

Team, a team of cameramen who film operations deemed too dangerous or sensitive for the mainstream media.

With *Flipper* having been shot down, it was now that flight *Ugly* finally got the call to stand-to for their first mission of Op Kulang. As they waited to get the 'go', Baz wrote the following in his combat diary, with it perched on his knees in the Apache's cramped cockpit:

> We have been stood up to provide crews for escort duties for the Chinooks who are required to make vital supply runs to the forward troops. The situation has deteriorated and the likelihood of further attacks on helicopters has increased due to Taliban successes. The death toll now runs at seven, including a British passenger.
>
> As this was going on there was a call for a Lynx to pick up a compassionate case from the Brigade Recce Force, in the middle of battle and from a desert HLS [helicopter landing site]. The Army are fantastic when it comes to casualty evacuations or compassionate cases. They turn everything on to get the soldier home as soon as humanly possible with no regard to cost.

A 'compassionate case' generally meant a soldier with compelling personal reasons to get home – more often than not a death or illness in the family.

Minutes after Baz finished writing that diary entry flight *Ugly* were cleared to get airborne.

11
FLIPPER'S DOWN

Days 16–21

Flight *Ugly* got the 'go' in the early hours of the morning of day two of Op Kulang. The mission was a complex resupply flight. They were to escort two Chinooks flying weapons and food, first to Sangin then followed by a drop-off with the Task Force Fury troops on the Kajaki Sofle landing zone – where call-sign *Flipper* had been shot down. Then there would be a final resupply drop at the British base at Lashkar Ghar.

The mission briefing had been incredibly detailed as the aircraft would be on the limits of their range and the flight plan would have to be tight in order to make it on available fuel supplies. If the mission went awry the aircrew would either have to locate a refuelling point or ditch in the open desert – neither of which was a simple proposition when operating over the Upper Sangin Valley.

The flight *Ugly* Apaches lifted off from their Bastion base, linked up with the pair of Chinooks and headed north-east – first stop Sangin. But problems arose almost immediately, with one of the Chinook pilots refusing to route over Sangin and insisting on changing the flight plan. The pilot was only recently back in theatre. He knew Sangin as a notorious hotbed of enemy activity, which, until recently, it had been.

Eventually the Apache aircrew were able to convince him that Sangin was well and truly held by British forces and that no hostile fire would be coming up at them from the town. By the time they had dropped their supplies with the Brigade Recce Force in Sangin the fuel plan was already looking stressed.

The aircrew waited on the ground for what seemed like an age as the 82nd Airborne troops prepared to clear them into their position. Two faulty grid references were passed up to the Apache aircrews, by which time the aircraft were running even tighter on fuel. Just as they got airborne for the flight to Kajaki Sofle, *Ugly Five One* was ordered to split from the flight and head north to the Kajaki Dam area. Two British Chinooks were on a resupply mission to troops on the ground up there and they needed an Apache escort.

Ugly Five Zero continued with the original mission, pushing up the left hand bank of the Helmand River towards the American ground troops. The Chinooks were carrying urgent supplies of water, ammo and food. In an effort to beat back the enemy and push out from the LZ, the US 82nd Airborne troops had run out of mortar rounds and in many cases were down to their last few magazines of ammo. Linking up with the American ground convoy or C Company of the Royal Anglians had so far proven impossible and the airborne troops were in dire need.

As *Ugly Five Zero* powered in towards the LZ Tim and Baz discussed the attack on call-sign *Flipper* and how best to avoid the threat from surface-to-air missiles. The first projectile into the Chinook's cockpit was believed to be an RPG, but the second impact was rumoured to be from a SAM.

All of a sudden the HIDAS warning alarm started blaring. A SAM had locked on to *Ugly Five Zero*. In an instant Baz's worries about dwindling fuel supplies went out the window as the HIDAS voiced the bearing and distance of the enemy threat. In the seconds that followed, defensive flares bloomed in a crest of fire to the rear of the helicopter and an arrow-shaped missile hurtled past below, chasing the fiery trails of the flares.

The moment of danger was over in a flash but the fear remained. Baz and Tim found themselves laughing with nervous relief. Only seconds before they had been discussing the missile threat, and from the very area from which that SAM had just been launched.

'As soon as the aircraft feels threatened the flares go off automatically,' Baz remarks. 'Yet it was still a frightening moment. In fact, to be honest, we were shitting ourselves.'

Ugly Five Zero shepherded in the two Chinooks to the Kajaki Sofle LZ. The US 82nd Airborne troops had thrown a ring of steel around it and the supplies were quickly unloaded. Eight wounded American soldiers were hurried aboard the empty Chinooks. This was testimony to the ferocity of the fighting since the three waves of aircraft had touched down on the LZ.

A group of handcuffed Taliban prisoners were also loaded onto the aircraft, itself a sign of the combat-readiness of the US troops. The Taliban rarely, if ever, willingly surrender: they only do so when out of ammunition or seriously wounded. The 82nd Airborne's 4th Brigade Combat Team had only been formed in January 2006, some sixteen months earlier. Here at Kajaki Sofle they were doing what they had been trained for and had accounted for themselves well.

Once the two Chinooks were airborne the three aircraft climbed in a corkscrew spiral to gain height above the LZ. But as they did so *Ugly Five Zero* suffered a second SAM lock-on. Again the alarm wailed and the flares fired, the HIDAS defences appearing to defeat the missile threat. Tim and Baz set a course to get the hell out of there as quickly as they possibly could.

Next stop was Lashkar Gar, some thirty minutes to the south and the last of the mission. En route it quickly became clear that fuel was too tight to make it. The aircraft would try to put down at Gereshk to refuel. Calling up *Crowbar*, the air traffic control radar unit at Bastion, Baz asked for the call-sign for the *Widow* at Gereshk in charge of air ops. But *Crowbar*'s services were in such heavy demand that by the time the reply came back to them fuel supplies were critical.

Ugly Five Zero now only had enough juice to make it back to Bastion, the nearest Allied base. The flight plan was adjusted again. The three aircraft would continue south to Camp Bastion, drop off the casualties and the prisoners, refuel and then move on to the pick-up at 'Lash', as Laskhar Gar had been nicknamed by the British troops.

The three aircraft pushed onwards towards Camp Bastion, trimming their air speed to maximise endurance. As they did so, Baz caught sight of a shadowed mass on the far side of the British base. He eyed it nervously, the darkness building to around three thousand feet and its boiling mass extending to ground level, blocking out all light. Even though they were still some ten kilometres out, Baz could see that his was no normal cloud formation: it was a giant sandstorm.

Baz and Tim conferred with the Chinook pilots, and an attempt was made to fly around the storm. But it was to no avail: the storm was just too large, the aircraft too short on fuel. They watched aghast as the dark mass engulfed the far watchtowers, and then the entire British base disappeared from view. *Ugly Five Zero* put a call through to *Crowbar*, only to learn that wind speed was at twenty-two knots and rising, while visibility was dropping fast. Soon it was down to a hundred metres, well below the limit under which helicopters were not supposed to fly.

Glancing out of the Apache's cockpit, all Baz could see below was the brown waste of the desert rolling towards the horizon. They were three aircraft, so perhaps a dozen airmen in all, and each would be armed with an SA80 carbine. They had their grab bags, containing spare magazines and ammo, grenades and a little water. Even so, there was no way on earth that he wanted to put down on the hostile Afghan desert. There was nothing for it: they would have to try for Bastion.

'We sent the Chinooks on ahead, going for Bastion to try to get there in time,' remarks Baz. 'We decided to sit three miles out and prepare for a GPS approach flying on instruments only. But we would be doing so in visibility of a hundred metres or less, dangerously low on fuel and with the wind driving us off the proper approach.'

Baz and Tim watched as the two Chinooks carrying the wounded soldiers headed into the storm. The giant twin-rotor aircraft were dwarfed by the shadowed mass bearing down on them. For a second it reared before the pair of Chinooks like the wall of a dark and angry tsunami. And then they simply disappeared, swallowed whole in to

Predator: Captain Baz Hunter in the Apache cockpit. The helmet-mounted display is clipped to the right side of his helmet, placing the monocle screen – the mechanism that slaves the 30mm cannon to the pilot's line of sight – in front of his right eye. The tinted daytime visor reflects his arm as he takes the photo.

Apache front-seater's view of his rear-seater, using his pilot's mirror. The mirror is set in the top left of the cockpit and is used for communicating via hand signals if normal comms breaks down, as it did with flight *Ugly* during Op Wasir.

A 662 Squadron Apache during training at Gila Bend, part of the vast
Barry M. Goldwater Range, Arizona.

The rearming point for Apache live firing exercises at Gila Bend. Ground crews wait
to load Hellfire missiles on to the Apaches of 662 Squadron.

Always outnumbered, never outgunned. Captain Baz Hunter danger-close to an Apache's M230 30mm automatic cannon.

Not a rogue. Captain Baz Hunter's Apache unleashes a Hellfire missile during live firing training at Gila Bend, Arizona.

Armed and dangerous: an Apache with rotors spinning on the flight line, photographed from a second Apache's 30mm cannon.

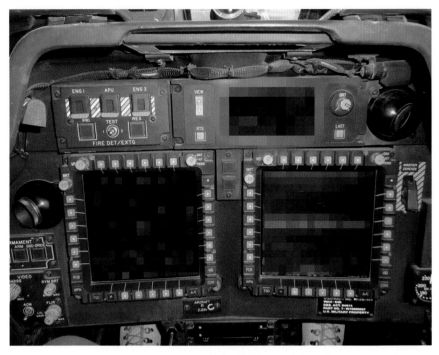

The Apache rear-seater's instrument panel. The screen on the pilot's right displays an infrared image, detecting hotspots as potential targets, while that on the left displays navigational information.

Nothing is impossible. View from the rear seat of an Apache heading fast and low up a valley in the Kajaki Mountains.

Steve James with the array of ordnance available to the Apaches on deployment in Afghanistan: 30mm cannon rounds, CRV7 2.7-inch rockets and Hellfire missiles.

Under each of the Apache's stub wings nineteen CRV7 rockets can be carried in the cylindrical pod, and four Hellfire missiles mounted on rails.

Shark attack: classic graffiti added to a Hellfire missile after Apaches engaged the 'Taliban Navy' on the Helmand River.

A pair of semi-automatic laser-guided Hellfires loaded onto the stub wings of an Apache.

Soldier first: the sixteen aircrew of 662 Squadron, Army Air Corps, who together crewed four flights, each of two Apaches.

Captain Tim Porter, Captain Baz Hunter and WO1 Steve James about to board a Hercules C-130 transport aircraft at Camp Bastion.

Steve James with Apache call-sign *Ugly Five One*.

Sign situated at the entry point to the Camp Bastion Apache flight line.

Home sweet home: ranks of tents and a walkway of Rolla-Trac plastic matting at Camp Bastion, with a line of earth-filled Hesco walling to the left.

View of the Camp Bastion flight line from the runway, the Apaches separated by concrete blast walls.

Joint Helicopter Force (Afghanistan) Forward, more commonly known as the Ops Room – the nerve centre of 662 Squadron's operations.

Accommodation tent with sleeping pods at Camp Bastion.

Dust devil: sandstorms kicked up over Helmand within minutes, making flying conditions atrocious. This one, at Camp Bastion, is a mere baby.

the roiling belly of its darkness. It was time for *Ugly Five Zero* to follow them.

From five kilometres out Baz lined up the aircraft on where his instruments indicated the base had to be and set the flight computer to run in on the GPS coordinates. Flicking on the forward-looking infrared, he prayed that it would give them at least some limited look-down capability for they would be lost without it on the final stages of the approach.

As the wall of darkness loomed ahead, Baz tried to make contact with the pair of Chinooks but the only response was a hollow void of echoing, wailing static – the screaming voice of the sandstorm. Either the Chinooks had gone down in the storm or radio contact had been lost due to the terrible atmospheric conditions.

As they neared the storm it began to take on an animal form, fingers of wind-blown sand reaching up thousands of feet from the desert floor, their tops curling like vicious talons stretched towards the approaching aircraft. The mass was darker at its base where the wind sucked and tore at the sands, lighter at its tumbling peak where shafts of sunlight rent the blackness.

For an instant the lone Apache fell into the shadow of the wall of sand and then the storm was upon them. The calm progress of the flight was broken as the wind grabbed and shook the aircraft like some angry giant throwing a toy around. The storm screamed and wailed, its voice deafening even in the soundproofed cockpit, sand-grains blasting in a blinding wave against the cockpit glass.

Baz wrestled with the controls, feeding in the power and the rotor pitch to fight the angry winds and pedalling with his feet on the yaw controls. Tim searched the darkness below for the barest hint of the flight line. But not a thing could be seen down there – not even the faintest suggestion of land.

The Apache runway was lit by low-luminance bulbs as a precaution against enemy attacks at night. Even in good visibility it could be difficult to spot. In conditions such as these it was impossible. As his left eye scanned the goldfish bowl of wind-blown sand that had become his world, his right checked the monocle screen of his HMD, checking on the airspeed, altitude and artificial horizon indicators.

Flicking his eyes downwards he checked the electronic flight page of the computer, scanning the image on the forward-looking infrared, but nothing seemed to indicate where the landing strip might be.

As the Apache was sucked in to the centre of the storm the wind speed increased in force until the crosswind was so fierce that Baz was fighting to maintain any sense of a course. Checking the FLIR again, a pattern of glowing dots seemed to emerge, which might just indicate the outline of the runway. Baz conferred with Tim and they decided that the screen was showing them an image of the flight line – the two hangars to one side visible as a blocky mass adjacent to the glowing points of light.

Both pilots tried to commit that image to memory, and its location in relation to their aircraft. They powered down the FLIR and stowed the lens in the nose pod to stop it being broken apart by the sandblasted storm. Flying on instruments and memory only, the Apache made its final approach to what Baz hoped – and prayed – was the flight line.

Suddenly the deserted tracks and walkways of Camp Bastion loomed out of the darkness. They had overshot the helicopter landing site, and were about to put down right on the ammunition compound. Yanking up the collective, Baz pulled the aircraft out of its descent and turned in the direction of where he guessed the flight line had to be. Breaking clear of their initial approach he hover-taxiied the aircraft over to the Apache base, breathing a massive sign of relief as they touched down on the runway.

'It was a close call,' Baz remarks. 'That sand storm seemed to have the devil himself inside it. It was thousands of feet high and really, really thick. The training paid off and we got down safely, but it was truly frightening . . . and hard. It was the toughest flying I have ever done in my twenty-five years of flying . . . Luckily, visibility picked up after we landed and Steve and Alex made a safe recovery and got into Bastion okay behind us.'

An hour after touching down the two Apaches got their second call-out of Op Kulang. It was to return to the Task Force Fury LZ, again with two Chinooks in tow. Thankfully they would be doing so under cover of darkness, which should reduce the missile threat. On the flight up to Kajaki Sofle the weather was atrocious. The aircraft were buffeted by fierce storms as they pushed ahead, the cockpit like a fish bowl blasted by sand. They flew the fifty-mile route at high altitude in an attempt to avoid the worst of the weather and relied on their radar systems to hold formation with the other aircraft.

On the approach to the LZ the pair of Chinooks dropped down to low level to try to find some visual markers to guide them in. As commander of JHF (A), John Bryant, the squadron's Commanding Officer, had joined the crew in one of the Chinook's jump seats. As they groped their way ahead in the darkness and poor visibility they encountered telegraph poles and wires dotted across the land-scape. The lead helicopter skipped over them, narrowly missing two sets.

As it landed on the LZ the crew discovered a third set of wires right under the aircraft. The Chinook had to make a careful take-off in order to cut the wires now wrapped around its undercarriage and leave it free to set a course for Camp Bastion.

Flight *Ugly* were sitting in a sand bubble at five thousand feet, using the FLIR to keep watch over the landing zone. It was like looking down a telescope filled with mud.

'We were flying in weather the likes of which we'd never expe-rienced before,' Baz remarks. 'Just trying to follow the lights of the aircraft in front, the visibility at minimum, the threat of wires all over the place – let alone the enemy – and then the Chinooks taking off again with telegraph wires wrapped around their wheels.'

Flight *Ugly* made it back to base a little before dawn. As they touched down they hoped for a few hours' rest prior to the next mission. Yet in spite of their exhaustion they were glad they had remained in Bastion, rejecting their scheduled rotation at Kandahar.

There was now a personal issue facing the four flight *Ugly* airmen and all of the soldiers at Camp Bastion. Owing to the death of the British soldier on the downed US Chinook an Operation Minimise had been declared – a shutting down of all personal communications between British troops and home. This was so that the MOD could deliver the news of the death to the deceased's family before it made its way into the newspapers.

However, the fact that a helicopter had been shot down during operations over Helmand was big news. Already the basic facts had leaked into the British press. No one knew for sure the type of helicopter that had gone down, or which country was operating it, or the nature of the mission, or the number of casualties. But there was ample speculation that it might be a British aircraft, as British forces were leading operations in Helmand.

The airmen could just imagine the impact that news and the lack of clarification would be having on their families back home. Might it be an Apache that had been shot down? Might it be a British Apache? And might it be an Apache of 662 Squadron? And if so, which aircrew had been flying it? There was a compelling desire among the airmen to phone or email to put the minds of their wives and children, and wider families, at rest.

'Op Minimise was in force,' remarks Steve, 'At that point we couldn't get entry into the booths. It was so the MOD could inform the families and be the first to give the bad news. It might be frustrating for us – it can last for half a day, or three days, or even more – as we couldn't call home during that time. It must have worried families back in the UK, not getting a call. But we all agreed that it was the right thing to do.'

Communications security at Camp Bastion was not taken lightly. All soldiers had to hand in mobile phones before entering theatre. The enemy had been known to monitor mobile calls and subsequently phone the number of a soldier's family in order to threaten them. If any soldier was caught with a mobile at Bastion they would be returned to unit – sent back in disgrace to their parent regiment in the UK.

The network that enabled phone calls home was a satellite-based system, and it had the characteristic two-second delay between the caller speaking and the listener hearing the words. At the start of each and every call there was a recorded message warning that it was an insecure means of communication. Before deployment all soldiers had been cautioned about the types of things they should refrain from saying over the phone. All up-and-coming operations were briefed on a need-to-know basis only, but even so the base was known to have its weaknesses.

Scores of Afghan civilians were employed at Bastion, largely on construction work, serving food or cleaning. A small number had been found to have questionable loyalties. Afghan workers had been caught smuggling documents out of the base, documents that they had scavenged from the bins. There was also the notorious problem of dickers – locals hanging around Camp Bastion with mobile phones and making warning calls to the enemy, telling which route an aircraft or land convoy might be taking as it left the base.

As Steve would often remark, 'You can buy an Afghan, but you can never own him.'

As the men of 662 Squadron waited impatiently for Op Minimise to be lifted, further intelligence came in regarding the shooting down of call-sign *Flipper*. The dead British soldier was named as twenty-eight-year-old Corporal Mike Gilyeat of the Royal Military Police, who had been seconded to the British Army's Combat Camera Team. He was the fifty-first British soldier to be killed in Afghanistan since UK forces deployed to Helmand in 2006.

The following morning the Op Minimise was finally lifted. Corporal Mike Gilyeat's death had been communicated to his family and his name was shortly to be released to the press. Baz went to make a call to his wife Tracy. The reaction made him realise just what his family had been going through over the last forty-eight hours. Tracy was overjoyed just to hear his voice. Once she was over the relief she asked her husband the obvious question: was everything okay?

How could he communicate over a horribly echoing phone line and several thousand miles that he'd just lived through the worst flying conditions of his entire career, twice been targeted by enemy ground weapons and had a Chinook shot down in his area of operations? And that was just in the last twenty-four hours. Who but a fellow pilot could understand what it felt like when the HIDAS went off and the machine did its defensive stuff as a howling projectile of death flying at 2000 kph chased down the aircraft's hot exhausts?

All Baz found himself able to say was: 'Love, I've had an interesting few days. I'll tell you all about it when I get home.'

Tracy went on to tell him her news, including that she'd found a new gardener to tidy up the lawn while Baz was away.

'Don't worry,' she teased. 'He's older than you are and not half as good-looking.'

Baz's daughter Jenny then came on the line. Before he could even ask her how she was, Jenny was telling him just how young and fit the new gardener was. Baz smiled. *Thanks, Jen.* She always did know how best to wind up her father.

For the next three days Op Kulang was ongoing. British and US forces linked up on the eastern side of the Upper Sangin Valley, clearing the enemy from that region. Small but stubborn pockets of resistance were encountered but most fighters were retreating north to the relative safety of their redoubt at Musa Qaleh.

Flight *Ugly* were back on Duty Ops and they were tasked with escorting a pair of Dutch Chinooks on a resupply mission. Again they were heading in to support the 82nd Airborne troops of Task Force Fury, although by now the threat of ground fire had been all but eliminated.

The Dutch pilots proved to have a wicked sense of humour. The pair of Chinooks were call-sign *Beavis* and *Butthead*. One had a female pilot, a tall and willowy blonde. Shortly after take-off the female pilot headed out across the desert terrain, the aircraft's bulging under-slung net trailing cargo across the landscape. Papers could be seen blowing in the wind and Tim was worried that it might be soldiers' mail, or even classified material. He alerted the woman pilot to the fact that her aircraft was throwing long white streamers across the desert.

She laughed: 'Uh-oh . . . No toilet roll for the troops now! Only butt plugs!'

The flight remained in constant action for the rest of that day, clocking up 7.25 hours' flight time mostly on Chinook escort duties. On the way back from their last resupply run the aircrew overheard a *Widow* call-sign requesting air support. Just north of Sangin a group of enemy had been engaged in an area nicknamed Three Trees, where they had been spotted with an unidentified long-barrelled weapon.

Ugly Five Zero put a call through to the Bastion Ops Room to request a release from their escort duty to go to the *Widow*'s aid. Chief of Staff Ian McIvor cleared them for five minutes over the target, with a warning that they either had to 'get firing or get home!'

Tim made the call to the *Widow*.

'*Widow Seven One*, this is *Ugly Five Zero* and *Ugly Five One*. Inbound to your position three minutes, standard loads. How can we help?'

'*Ugly, Widow Seven One*. Search along the canal bank nearest to the location of Three Trees. Troops in contact have killed a number of EF and we expect them back in that area to pick up their dead. This might be an opportunity to kill some more. There's a long-barrelled gun with the EF but we can't identify the type.'

'Roger that.'

It was a regular pattern of the Taliban in combat that they rarely left the bodies of the fallen on the battlefield. As the two Apaches swept into the position identified by *Widow Seven One* he came on the air again, warning the aircrew to look out for a motorcycle on the canal's west bank that was suspected to be a dicker.

In the back of each of the aircrew's mind was the thought that the long-barrelled gun could be a surface-to-air missile launcher. If that motorcyclist was indeed a dicker, he might spot the inbound Apaches and call through details to the missile operator, warning him of flight *Ugly*'s line of approach and to prepare to fire.

'We quickly spotted the motorcyclist with the naked eye,' remarks Baz. 'As both call-signs got the sensors on him we followed his rapid movement south for about three miles. He was clearly wise to our presence. He rode like Evel Knievel, his 50cc Afghan motorcycle at full pelt. We noticed him stop at a junction that was slightly hidden from above by trees, but we could clearly see him talking on his radio. His age, the motorcycle and the radio, linked to the previous sighting of him in the area of the contact, confirmed to us that he was indeed Taliban and probably a local spotter.'

As the Apaches slaved their 30mm cannons to the lone target, *Widow Seven One* sought permission for flight *Ugly* to open fire. The response came back that as no weapon was visible they were not to engage. The aircrew accepted the decision and passed the target coordinates to an American F-15 on station near by. If the lone motorcyclist did anything suspicious, or showed a weapon, they left the US pilot in no doubt to take him out.

'Perhaps command was right not to allow the engagement on this occasion,' remarks Baz. 'After all, the guy on the motorbike might just have been an innocent bloke out for a sunny afternoon bike ride along the canal, perhaps collecting shrapnel for his son's collection, the radio actually a mobile phone and him making a call to his wife that he would shortly be home for lunch, and the speed of his riding perhaps a response to the irate wife telling him he was late and that his dinner was in the dog! Or maybe he was just the luckiest Taliban dicker in the whole valley.'

By day twenty of 662 Squadron's deployment, Op Kulang was pretty much at an end. Freed up from the punishing routine of ferrying arms to the US troops of Task Force Fury, flight *Ugly* were tasked with a resupply mission to the Brigade Recce Force (BRF). The BRF are modelled on the Long Range Desert Group (LRDG) of the Second World War, the renowned forerunners of the SAS who were commanded by the maverick, but brilliant, David Stirling.

For weeks on end the Brigade Recce Force had been out in the open deserts of Helmand, operating behind enemy lines gathering intelligence and hitting their supply lines. After sixty-odd days on the move in the Afghan deserts the men of the BRF were a wild-looking bunch, all bearded and wearing a motley assortment of battered clothing. They were also running desperately short of ammo and food.

Having escorted the Chinooks in to drop their supplies, Baz and Tim wished the men of the BRF luck. When might they next get a chance for a wash and a shave back at Bastion, the pilots asked? The BRF *Widow* replied that they had an extraction date some time between the next two days and the next month. This was followed by lots of banter, including the Apache aircrew inviting the *Widow* for burgers and DVDs if he ever made it back to civilisation again.

On their return to Bastion the four airmen were crashed out to respond to what was initially described as troops in contact at FOB Robinson with a T2 casualty. The Apaches were airborne ahead of the casevac Chinook, and on approach to the landing zone the T2 casualty was reported as an Afghan civilian.

But his body was swabbed for any traces of explosives and it turned out that he was covered in gunfire residues that could only have come from operating a weapon. He was now a wounded prisoner of war and a careful eye would have to be kept on him during the return flight to Camp Bastion.

Back on terra firma that evening, the airmen grabbed a few hours' desperately needed rest. The tempo of operations during Op Kulang had been intense, yet for that very reason it had also been a deeply rewarding experience for the airmen of *Ugly Five One* and *Ugly Five Zero*. Any fears that they might have been left on the sidelines were now very much behind them.

They also felt a growing sense of the moral superiority of their own mission, as opposed to that of the forces that they were fighting. Before sleep Baz wrote his combat diary:

On arrival at Bastion Hospital we knew the wounded Afghan prisoner of war would be treated humanely and exactly the same as our own troops. This does not always sit well with us or the other soldiers. Although he would be treated in accordance with the Geneva Convention, the Taliban would have no regard for fair treatment and if taken prisoner the only thing we would expect is a cruel death. However, we are not the same as these people and we must always remain humane and seize the moral high ground.

Having said that, on the flight back the Chinook radioed us that the combat medic in the back treating the prisoner had upgraded the casualty priority to a T1. We reckoned this was because a soldier in the back had his boot on the prisoner's windpipe . . .

Although it wasn't true, at least it made us laugh.

12
OPERATION GASHEY

Day 22

The day started horribly early for flight *Ugly*. The four airmen were called from their beds in the dead hours of darkness to take over VHR duty from crews who had been up all night flying ops. It was approaching the hottest time of the year and Steve was dog tired. He'd had an unusually bad night of it, tossing and turning and sweating in the suffocating closeness. Their kit and accommodation was starting to fall apart, which only served to increase the irritation factor of the lack of sleep and being constantly on the go.

During Op Kulang the daylight hours had been spent flying missions, in briefings for missions or prepping the aircraft for missions and waiting for the 'go' on the flight line. The night hours had been burned prosecuting the toughest operations – shepherding in the resupply Chinooks at low level. Sleep had been snatched – an hour here, an hour there – and none of the pilots had really had the chance to catch up. They were all running a sleep deficit and Steve's was doubtless the worst as he was a famously light sleeper in any case.

'You can't really sleep during the day,' Steve remarks. 'So if you're up all night you grab an hour whenever you can. On VHR you have a real bed with a mattress, and in the other tent its camp beds . . . But the intensity of missions and the lack of sleep was really starting to get to us by now.'

With fatigue levels rising it became harder to chill out and relax. Small things began to bug and annoy. The toilets were squat metal boxes that lay in the full heat of the sun. A couple of days back Steve had set out for a crap with a good book in hand. He'd been looking forward to a few minutes away from the rest of the aircrew. But he'd sat down only to realise that the metal toilet seat had heated up to be red-hot. With a yelp he'd jumped up and hit his head on the roof. There was to be no relaxing read for him that day, just some uncomfortable burns to deal with instead.

He didn't need this. He really did not. The only way to get over it was with humour. Steve returned to his fellow aircrew and regaled them with the tale of his toilet experience. He warned them about the burning-hot seat: he'd been sweating so much in the metal cubicle that he'd been losing weight both ends. It had truly been a RES – a real emotional shit. It seemed trivial, somehow, when viewed in the greater scheme of things – the past twenty frenetic days of missions – but the other units at Bastion had all been provided with air-conditioned toilets so a RES was a thing of the past.

'Going for a crap commonly became know as a RES,' Steve remarks, 'as opposed to a NES – a non-emotional one. The best place for a NES was Kandahar, where the toilets were normal, everyday ones with air-conditioning. Such a difference from Bastion, and such a pleasure!'

With the intensity and the sensory overload, one hour's flying in an Apache equates to many, many hours of 'normal' activity – say driving a car, or working at a computer terminal. In combat conditions, when the fear dynamic and the tension of the hunt for an elusive enemy are factored in, that equation increases several times over.

'You never get enough down time to get past the fatigue,' remarks Baz. 'We were in theatre for a hundred days without a break . . . As time went on little niggling things suddenly became big issues. "Mate, we haven't slept for three days" was a constant refrain. You found yourself bitching with the other flights; I noticed how it was creeping in slowly over the tour, with more and more arguments and heated discussions.

'At one stage with me it almost came to fists with another pilot.

Our flight was getting a lot of missions and we were getting a lot of banter and stick, and it just started to be personal. At the end of the day you go and have a run or lift some weights and try to work it all out of your system. Because I run a lot slower than the others, for obvious reasons, I had a lot more time to think it all through!'

On that morning the airmen of flight *Ugly* tried to shake the sleep out of their heads as they headed down to the Ops Room. They settled in for the first briefing of their VHR duty, little knowing what that day would hold for them. Going into the Upper Sangin Valley had been akin to poking a big stick into a hornet's nest. Intelligence reports from all areas suggested that the enemy response to Op Kulang was going to be both high profile and dirty.

Scores of Foreign Taliban were moving into Helmand via the enemy's forwards mounting base at Garmsir. These were well-experienced fighters – part of an international brigade of Islamist mujahidin – with a greater technical know-how and tactical sophistication than the indigenous Afghan and Pakistani fighters. Among their number were suicide bombers who were infiltrating towns and villages as far north as Gereshk.

So far there had been no suicide attacks in Helmand and few across the wider Afghan war zone, but all of that looked set to change. Op Kulang had truly upped the stakes: it had driven the enemy out of one of their supposedly impregnable strongholds yet it had also been a gift to them. At last they had achieved their oft-stated aim of shooting down a coalition aircraft. The downing of *Flipper* was hailed as a major victory by the enemy.

'The mujahidin of the Islamic state downed a Chinook helicopter that belonged to the NATO occupiers yesterday, using a new anti-aircraft weapon,' a Taliban spokesman proclaimed. He also claimed that sixty enemy soldiers had been killed in the aircraft.

The fact that a Chinook is incapable of carrying sixty soldiers appeared lost on him, as was the fact that in reality only seven men had died on the aircraft. But, regardless of the numbers of dead, the shooting-down of call-sign *Flipper* remained a rallying point for the enemy, and a powerful recruiting tool to attract foreign fighters to the war.

'We realised that enemy tactics were about to change,' remarks Steve. 'And that the stakes were going up, up, up.'

No sooner had that early-morning briefing finished than the flight were scrambled to respond to troops in contact (TIC) to the north of Sangin. Trouble was flaring up again in the Upper Sangin Valley. *Greenpeace Flight* were already providing close air support to a unit of British soldiers there, and flight *Ugly* were tasked to go in and relieve their fellow Apache aircrews over the battlefield.

In twenty minutes the aircraft were airborne and heading northwards towards the battle zone. As Baz worked out the quickest route to the location of the TIC, a call came in over the radio. A second firefight had flared up just north of Gereshk and flight *Ugly* were ordered to reroute to that one.

At first light the Worcesters and Foresters had pushed a probing patrol into the Upper Gereshk Valley. The vanguard had been hit by a massive barrage of mortars, RPGs and machine gun fire. There was already a T1 casualty and one British soldier was dead. Corporal Paul 'Sandy' Sandford had been killed in action during the first minutes of the battle, just outside the mud-walled village of Mulla Abdur Rahim Kalay.

Baz plotted a course to this new location, way to the south and in the opposite direction from Sangin, and the pair of Apaches did a swift about-turn. As the two aircraft neared the battleground the Joint Terminal Attack Controller (JTAC) on the ground, call-sign *Widow Seven Nine*, could be heard talking to a pair of British Harrier jets that were inbound to his location. The tension in the *Widow*'s voice was clear as he tried to make himself heard over the pounding of explosions in the background.

The two Harriers, *Recoil Four One* and *Recoil Four Two*, were passed the coordinates of an enemy mortar unit. But as the Harriers went in to attack they were forced to abort their bombing run. The Taliban had set up their mortar tubes in the midst of a crowd of women and children, knowing full well that the British warplanes would be unable to attack for fear of killing civilians. It was a tactic that was not unheard of in Helmand, and it was to become all the more common as the day wore on.

As the Apache aircrew listened in on the radio chatter they could feel the tension levels and the frustration of both the Harrier aircrew and the *Widow*. They pushed their aircraft to maximum flight speed in an effort to get over the battlefield to assist the troops on the ground. Yet one of the Apaches was about to suffer a serious malfunction, the first in a series of such problems that would occur that day.

'The patrol was under very effective enemy mortar fire,' Baz remarks. '*Widow Seven Nine* was talking to a Harrier. He was asking the Harrier to stand by for further coordinates to attack. But as we neared the village for some reason all our encrypted communications dropped out and we lost contact with the *Widow*. Try as we might we had no joy.'

Ugly Five Zero had lost all its secure communications facilities, without which it was unable to communicate with troops on the ground, other aircraft or headquarters. Baz and Tim had no choice but to split from their wing and head back to Bastion.

'Alex and Steve remained on station as we returned to Bastion,' Baz remarks. 'We made the call to the ops tent that we had major comms failure, asking the signaller to meet us on the flight line. So we're sitting there with rotors turning and we've got two guys running up and connecting the fuel lines. We shut down the one engine nearest to the fuelling point; at the same time the signaller has dashed up to the flight line in the Land Rover to reload the crypto and Steve and Alex are telling us that it's kicking off big time out there.'

As *Ugly Five Zero* had turned away from the battlefield *Ugly Five One* received a call from an inbound Chinook. It was heading in to pick up the wounded, plus the British soldier killed in action. But there was no secure landing zone from which to carry out the casevac as the British troops were pinned down under heavy mortar fire.

Ugly Five One would have to find and kill the enemy mortar teams before they could clear the Chinook in to land. Steve and Alex saw the soldiers on the ground put out smoke grenades to identify a potential LZ. But as the ground troops tried to secure it

enemy forces firing from the far side of the village were hitting
them with increasingly accurate mortar fire. One man was dead
and there were now two wounded, and there was every chance that
more would die if those mortars weren't taken out.

C Company, of the 1st Battalion, Worcestershire and
Sherwood Foresters, together with a Czech unit, had launched
that morning's operation from start lines in the open desert. The
ground troops consisted of three mobile platoons driving
armoured Vikings and WMIKs, the open-topped Land Rovers
armed with heavy and light machine guns. The Company was
spread over a kilometre, with the lead elements now on the western side of the village and the rear established at an Afghan
National Army post to the south.

Widow Seven Nine was located with a command element in the
desert to the west of Rahim Kalay, with good eyes on the village.
The command position was protected by a team operating the
Javelin hand-held anti-tank missile. It also had a weapons-locating
radar (WLR), a portable system that can provide a ten-figure grid
reference of enemy mortar firing points to within approximately
one hundred metres.

Advancing towards the mud-walled compounds of Rahim Kalay,
the lead troops had been expecting little resistance. The first mortar
barrage had come like a bolt from the blue. Pinned down in the
open desert the troops had taken casualties as enemy RPG rounds
and machine gun fire had added to the mayhem.

Using the WLR, the ground troops had identified three enemy
mortar-firing positions. All were several kilometres distant and out
of sight on the far side of the village. With mortar rounds falling
ever closer to the British troops it was clear that the enemy had
spotters situated forwards and calling in their fire, either in the village or the woodland to the south.

This had all the signs of being of a well-planned ambush, with
British forces caught in the apex of three 81mm mortar teams. Not
only that, but those mortar teams were putting down accurate and
rapid fire. It seemed likely that it was a Chechen or Iranian crew as
the local Taliban were rarely such proficient mortar operators. In

which case the ground troops were up against a bunch of the Foreign Taliban – those that intelligence reports had suggested were moving into Helmand.

The Taliban's 81mm mortar units are resupplied with ammunition via Pakistan and Iran so there was no reason to believe that they would be short of rounds. The enemy were also skilful at improvising weapons platforms by welding mortar tubes or heavy machine guns to truck beds: this could be a mobile mortar unit, using the vehicle to change their firing points.

As the British Army also uses the 81mm mortar the soldiers on the ground were well aware of the destructive power of the weapons being used against them. An 81mm round would make mincemeat out of a Land Rover, and a direct hit on a Viking would be pretty terminal. Likewise, a Chinook hit by an 81mm shell would be finished. An 81mm mortar team was embedded with the Worcesters and Foresters and they were itching to fire a counter-barrage, if only the enemy firing positions could be nailed down.

From their orbit high above the village Steve and Alex could clearly see the mortar rounds landing and exploding beneath them, little puffs of cotton wool appearing all around the British troops' location. At ground level they knew that those cotton wool puffs were deadly and had already claimed lives. Sounding remarkably calm, *Widow Seven Nine* put up the first of the coordinates of the enemy mortar positions to *Ugly Five One*.

'*Ugly Five One*, this is *Widow Seven Nine*. We are under sustained mortar fire . . . *Ugly* we have a first grid we wish you to look at. Grid is 1849285749. Suspected mortar base plate.'

'Grid 1849285749. Roger that.'

Alex, *Ugly Five One*'s front-seater and gunner, scribbled the sequence of numbers onto a notepad strapped to his right leg. He proceeded to punch the coordinates into the palm-sized keyboard just to the side of his left knee. The video lens in the nose pod immediately slaved to that location. There was no need for Steve to alter the aircraft's orbit: to do so might alert the enemy to their interest and intent. The 127-times magnification was more than sufficient to provide a close-up picture of the target area.

But all that the camera revealed was a mud-walled compound with a bunch of raggedy children playing in the dust. A group of women, presumably their mothers, clustered to one side in the shade of a spreading tree. If this was the correct location the enemy mortar team had either just moved on or they had hidden themselves well. Two further sets of coordinates were passed up to *Ugly Five One*, and on each occasion the location turned out to be an apparently peaceful village setting. There was no way in which Alex and Steve could engage any of the targets.

'It was hugely frustrating,' Steve remarks. 'We looked over the grid square and found a large compound full of people milling around, only to discover it was a load of women and children. If those grids were correct it was very, very cunning – a really sly tactic of the enemy. We'd push out four or five kilometres, keeping eyes on and trying to lure them out: it was like a game of cat and mouse. We were feeling total frustration.'

All three firing points were in low ground on the far side of the village. Steve decided to move the Apache into an orbit over those positions. Maybe its very presence would silence the enemy mortars, giving the ground troops a chance to find some cover and allow the Chinook to go in. Sure enough, once the Apache moved overhead a mortar point all fire from there would cease. But as soon as it moved on to the next location ten rounds would be fired in quick succession from the one they had just left.

'They would stop and hide,' Steve remarks. 'Then, once we'd gone, they'd come out and start the fight again. Ten minutes after we left a grid the ground troops would get a load of mortar rounds down on them from exactly that location . . . This had been going on for what seemed like an age. And it was then that we decided to fire the warning bursts into the desert to the side of the compounds to tell them we knew they were there.'

Lining up the 30mm cannon on a hundred-metre offset from the first compound, *Ugly Five One* fired a ten-round burst into the desert to one side of the buildings. Even at that distance the rounds exploding would be like a jackhammer next to your head. The women and children were quick to clear the area. Moving on to the other two coordinates, *Ugly Five One* did a repeat performance, with exactly the same results.

It was now that Steve and Alex really felt the loss of their wing aircraft: ideally, one Apache would remain on station over the mortar firing points while the other shepherded in the Chinook to land. As it was, *Ugly Five One* broke away from its orbit to lead the Chinook, call-sign *Morphine Three One*, into the LZ.

Unfortunately, the Apaches were unable to speak directly to the Chinook pilots as the big helicopter's secure comms radio wasn't enabled for aircraft-to-aircraft calls. Instead, they had to communicate through the loadmaster, who was ensconced in the aircraft's echoing hold.

'*Morphine Three One*, this is *Ugly*. You're cleared to go in to the LZ.'

Chinook loadmaster, shouting to make himself heard: '*Ugly*, *Morphine Three One*. Say again – say again slowly.'

'*Morphine – Three – One –* this – is – *Ugly* – you – are – cleared – to – go – in.'

'Okay, happy with that. Going in now.'

The Chinook flew in at tree-top height in an effort to hide its approach from the mortar spotters until the very last moment. But there were obstacles in the way of a low level pass that Steve could see from a height, and the Chinook aircrew might blunder into. He talked the Chinook around them and into the landing zone, which was out in the desert to the west of the village.

'Turn right thirty degrees, there's telegraph wires to your left, plus an enemy position on the far side . . . Break left! Break left! Incoming RPG!'

Amid the confusion and chaos of the battle, the Chinook put down on the wrong LZ. The casualties were located some distance away and either they would have to be moved across to the aircraft, or it to them. The four casualties were manhandled into the open-topped WMIK Land Rovers and bussed across to the waiting aircraft. It took ten agonising minutes to get the wounded over to the Chinook, during which time it sat with its rotors spinning, kicking up a thick screen of dust.

As the British troops rushed the wounded soldiers up the rear ramp of the aircraft mortar rounds started slamming into the sands all around them. With the casualties finally on board the Chinook lifted off, turning hard and banking away from the village and the danger zone. *Ugly Five One* shadowed it all the way out into the far desert and safety, whereupon the Chinook set a course for Camp Bastion.

Meanwhile, *Ugly Five Zero* was inbound over the battlefield. Tim made contact with *Widow Seven Nine*, asking where his presence would most be useful. The *Widow* responded that they were still being hit by the enemy mortars, and that one or other of the Apaches needed to get some rounds down on the enemy to silence their guns. At the same time Baz was getting a sitrep (situation report) from Steve and Alex.

'The *Widow* feared that his failure to direct the air cover – us – on to target was causing the ground troops to get hit,' Baz remarks. 'We've been on the ground in our careers – we've served as soldiers – so we care about the troops on the ground. But we're in the air with *Ugly Five One*, starting the hunt once more, when the crypto just falls out again . . . Tim and I try and stay on location and work via Steve – but we have to speak to the *Widow*, to Bastion, to the fast air – and it isn't working. Finally I tell Tim we have to go back. We have to go back and change the aircraft.'

Baz and Tim's aircraft had suffered its second secure comms failure of the morning. What made matters infinitely worse was that *Ugly Five One* was now running dangerously short of fuel. Both aircraft would have to break off the contact, leaving British troops pinned down under a devastating mortar barrage and with no air cover.

Tim made the call to *Widow Seven Nine* that both Apaches were returning to base. To all four Apache airmen it felt as if they were abandoning their fellow soldiers in their hour of need. All Tim could do was give his word that flight *Ugly* would return to the battle over Rahim Kalay just as soon as they were able.

Widow Seven Nine's response was only to be expected: he was incredulous, and pissed as hell.

'It's always the bloody same. I'm sick and tired of ground troops being left forgotten on the ground . . . I know its not you guys' fault but I've lost one man, the mortars are still coming in and you lot are pissing off to Bastion!'

The atmosphere on board the two aircraft was tense and frustrated as they headed back towards Camp Bastion. Baz had Steve relay a message to the Ops Room that his aircraft was unserviceable, and that he needed a replacement bombed-up and fuelled-up and ready on the flight line as soon as he came in to land. It was a ten-minute haul from Rahim Kalay to Bastion, which gave the groundies and REME technicians ten minutes to get that replacement Apache air-ready.

As the call went out from the Ops Room to the flight line that *Ugly Five Zero* was inbound for a complete aircraft change eight blokes sprinted for the airstrip, pulling on their protective overalls as they ran. It was a race against time and each one of them knew that British lives depended on them getting that aircraft armed, fuelled and ready to go in record time.

At the same time, the four airmen of flight *Ugly* were having to argue their case for a return to Rahim Kalay. To their commanders in the Ops Room it seemed like a bad use of flight hours, especially as all they had done so far was fire a few warning rounds at an elusive and largely invisible enemy. It was at times like these that the men gave silent thanks that they had Ian McIvor to fight their corner for them.

'We were thinking, we're not going to get released again.' remarks Baz. 'We were thinking, what are we doing here if we're not being used? Or if we can't respond to what the guys on the ground ask of us? We updated the Ops Room constantly during the flight back in as the contact was ongoing at Rahim Kalay, and eventually we were cleared to take the new aircraft and prepare to go.'

The two Apaches ran into Bastion at high speed. The aircraft were dumped on the hot airstrip and within seconds the ground crew were up on the stub wings of *Ugly Five Zero*, the cockpit was thrown open and Baz and Tim were handing out their grab bags, their carbines and their ammo.

'It was just like a Formula One pit team,' Baz remarks. 'We were out of that cockpit, calling for the groundies to give us an update on the new aircraft. We sprinted over to the one allocated to us, which had just flown in from Kandahar Airfield. But all it was armed with was three hundred rounds of 30mm so we start bawling out the Ground Crew Commander for the lack of weaponry and yelling at the groundies to go Hellfire-heavy as the fastest way to get us armed.

'As we strapped into the cockpit both ground crews were working on our aircraft to get us up again. They physically ran over the Hellfires, pushing a six-wheeled carry trolley, and it was forty degrees plus out there, with each missile weighing a hundred pounds. Then there's twenty-four rockets slotted into the pods, we're firing up engines, punching in laser codes, checking comms, getting the HIDAS up and running, inputting grids of the enemy positions, getting the radar up . . . And we're ready to get airborne in five minutes flat – record time.'

Fortunately, *Ugly Five Zero*'s front-seater, Tim, had remembered to grab the data card from the malfunctioning aircraft. On this was mapped the whole of the Helmand operational area, with up-to-the-minute information added that very morning. Once that was slotted into the replacement aircraft's flight computer they were more then ready to set a course back to the battlefield.

'Alex and Tim, as young computer whizzes, are far better at this sort of stuff than the old boys who fly the aircraft,' remarks Baz. 'By the end of the changeover the groundies had done such an excellent job that we were praising them. We've got four radios in the cockpit and we can tune in on any one. We're listening in on the battle at Rahim Kalay, we're briefing Chief of Staff so that he can justify us going out and we're ecstatic with relief when we're finally cleared to get airborne again and go help those guys on the ground.'

Ten minutes later *Ugly Five Zero* and *Ugly Five One* rocked up over Rahim Kalay. They requested an update from *Widow Seven Nine*. Little had changed on the ground; if anything, the situation had worsened. The Company had been under accurate mortar fire for the past four hours, they were pinned down and unable to move. They wanted those mortars neutralised so they could advance from the desert to clear the village.

The western edge of the village consisted of a series of compounds set on higher ground, each of which was surrounded by a thick mud wall. A rutted track led into the centre of the village before dividing in two. The upper branch led north-east, through the built up areas. The lower track led south, crossing a bridge over a shallow canal of brownish water. On the far side of the bridge lay several patches of low woodland, with fields dotted in between.

If the British forces could fight their way through to that fork in the road they could either move further into the village or head southwards out of the built-up area and into open farmland, depending on the level of enemy resistance.

Once again *Widow Seven Nine* sent up the coordinates of the most active mortar grid. It was situated on the far bank of the canal, and the aircrew of *Ugly Five Zero* could clearly see smoke in the vicinity of the grid with the naked eye. Could this be an enemy mortar team, caught in the open and in the process of firing? The video camera slaved to the grid reference and instantly five males became visible in the smoky haze. Finally it looked like *Ugly Five Zero* had nailed them.

But as the 30mm cannon swung around to fire the five men bent to tend the soil at their feet, the hooked blades of mattocks clutched in their earthy hands. It suddenly became clear what the men were doing. This was no mortar team: they were farmers, burning off the old crops in their fields and digging fire breaks as they went.

'Phew! If ever there was one, that was a close shave,' remarks Baz. 'Thank God for our systems and the speed with which we can move over the battlefield. In this instance our ability to do rapid positive identifications had saved lives.'

Back on the ground there was the *whoomph* of incoming mortars and another barrage fell among the British positions. The grid for the enemy mortar battery had changed again, and when the Apaches locked their video lenses to the target area what they found was . . . yet another group of apparently innocent women and children. Where the hell were the enemy hiding themselves and firing from? This was becoming like a bad joke, and something was going to have to give if the impasse was to be broken.

'We were only checking the obvious firing points,' remarks Steve. 'We had to start thinking like ground troops, like the enemy. It's so easy to look but not see; if you've got no experience of fighting on the ground you're not able to find the right places to look. We had to think: where would I be if I were trying to kill those British troops, and how would I act? Once we'd done that we could search accordingly and maybe start finding them.'

It was time to go back to the most basic precept of the Corps – soldier first. It was time to tune in that soldier's sixth sense, the instinct that a hunter has for the location and behaviour of his prey.

'You don't know you're doing it, it's a basic instinct,' Baz remarks. 'Sensing fear with your instinct; sensing someone's desire to hide . . . Tune it in and you can tell by the gait of a person on the move if they're a man, a woman, a child or whatever. An enemy fighter is purposeful, fast, circumspect; another time you see a group of three and there's a dog out front; a child playing with the dog; a woman with her head down. And you've been cleared to fire but your instinct tells you that those are innocent people.'

A further salvo of mortars pounded the British positions, and this time the grid coordinates were put up to the Apaches within forty-five seconds of the rounds having been fired. The flight was overhead the grid a minute after that last round had landed. The area was to the north-east of the village. It consisted of a series of wooded ditches with two larger patches of woodland, each about five hundred metres square. The area was dotted with a maze of small compounds, and it was just the sort of place where the Apache airmen would have placed their mortar, had they been hitting the British positions.

Because of the rate of fire from this location, *Widow Seven Nine* had asked for anybody within the grid who fitted the target profile to be hit. Ground forces had also spotted a series of puffs of smoke coming up from the area of the grid. Enemy mortar units were known to use smoke signals to communicate with their spotters, in order to hone the accuracy of their fire. The puffs of smoke had certainly looked suspicious: a series seemed to go up every two minutes after a mortar had fired.

The British mortar team had sighted their 81mm guns on the position of the smoke-signaller and were preparing to fire. Next time there was a puff of smoke apparently synchronised with an enemy mortar barrage, a counter-barrage of British mortars was going to rain down on that position. They were determined to counter-attack, even if the target remained elusive.

As *Ugly Five Zero* moved into a hover over the smoke-signaller's compound all they could see was an old boy crouched over a cooking fire, preparing a late breakfast. As he bent over the hearth he took a small plank of wood and began fanning the flames, a puff of smoke belching out from the fireplace. At that moment there was a call from the JTAC on the ground: '*Ugly*, *Widow Seven Nine*. Mortars are engaging now.'

Tim alerted *Widow Seven Nine* to what they could see: '*Widow Seven Nine*, this is *Ugly*. Do not fire. Repeat, do not fire. It's just some old bloke cooking his breakfast.'

But as *Widow Seven Nine* warned, the mortar rounds were already in the air, and the flight *Ugly* Apaches had to move out of the airspace for their own safety.

All of a sudden the aircrew could see the silent puffs of mortars landing all around the compound below them. And then they realised that each of those mortars was tracing a high arc and slicing through the air in which the Apaches were flying. What goes up must come down, the pilots told themselves as they peeled off from their orbit and rapidly got clear of the airspace.

The mortar rounds fell wide and the old man making his breakfast remained oblivious to the destructive power that his cooking had attracted. As for the Apache aircrew, they could understand the ground troops' desire to meet fire with fire. It only served to fuel the sense of disappointment and failure that the four airmen were feeling at not finding and nailing the enemy mortar teams.

The game of cat and mouse continued. Four more times mortars were fired from a clearly visible grid, but when the aircrew checked it out only women and children could be seen. There was no way that the weapons-locating radar could be repeatedly getting the grids wrong. The *Ugly* airmen could only conclude that the mortar teams were firing off ten rounds then collapsing their mortar tube and hiding in the compounds. As for the women and children, they were apparently willingly playing their part as cover, knowing that British forces wouldn't open fire on them.

While the grids couldn't be treated as legitimate targets, warning shots could be fired danger-close to each, sending a clear message to the civilians: stop doing what you're doing or we will attack. The pair of Apaches returned to one of the most active grids. With video cameras zoomed in, a group of five men was spotted sitting under a tree. That was most likely the mortar team. But to their left were some children playing in a lane, and to the right a woman was washing clothes and a few cattle nuzzling at some bales of hay. It looked, to all intents and purposes, like a normal Afghan village scene but this position had repeatedly been identified as a mortar firing point.

'We knew the Taliban had a tactic of firing rounds then moving the mortar under cover, laying down their weapons and mixing with the locals,' Baz remarks. 'Although the Taliban do use human shields to camouflage their activities this did not warrant killing innocents. We decided that firing at this point would be inappropriate and the *Widow* agreed. We decided we would give the civilians a warning and a chance to clear away from the area.'

Selecting a target offset by fifty metres, *Ugly Five One* fired a ten-round burst of 30mm cannon shells. At such close range the explosions had the desired effect: the women and children rapidly moved away from the compound and made themselves scarce. The flight repeated this process at two further firing points, walking the rounds closer and closer to the grid reference. In each case the civilians fled the scene and the rate of mortar fire reduced to a trickle.

By the time the last warning rounds had been fired the enemy mortar batteries had fallen silent. It was time for the ground troops to move into the village.

Widow Seven Nine radioed the Apaches that his men were on the move. They would advance into the built-up area and take the track north-east through the village. The Czech team would take the other branch of the track, across the canal and into the wood line. In that way they would dominate the territory in its entirety. They needed top cover, with eyes in each of the compounds that the patrol would be passing. The pair of Apaches set up in wheel formation with an excellent view of the entire village.

As Baz scanned the terrain below him his soldier's sixth sense suddenly kicked in. Towards the far end of the village the track was clogged with people moving into the open desert. As he watched, women, children and old folk were streaming out of compounds and heading in that direction. This was a classic indicator that combat was imminent and that the whole of the village was under the control of the enemy.

Women, children and the elderly had been ordered to stay put as long as they could provide human shields to the enemy mortar units. Now that game was over, they were being moved out en masse so that the real fighting could begin. It was looking more and more as if the whole of Rahim Kalay village was on a war footing. Not only that, but the enemy appeared to be ready and prepared for a long, and tactically astute, battle – a battle that had already claimed one British life.

Tim relayed the information to *Widow Seven Nine*. He rapidly reached the same conclusion as the Apache pilots. The enemy were up to something and the ground troops could easily be advancing into a well-planned and well-resourced ambush. The troops were ordered to halt their advance and consolidate their positions.

Scanning the compounds below, Baz and Tim could see that each and every one of them was devoid of human life. Rahim Kalay had suddenly become a ghost town. It was ominous, and Baz felt his hackles rising. No doubt about it, a hidden enemy were preparing for battle down there. At the same time he felt a grudging admiration for an enemy who could orchestrate such civilian–military manoeuvres with apparent speed and ease.

But if the compounds were deserted, where were the enemy fighters and how would the Apaches flush them out? Putting his mindset into that of the enemy, Baz tried to imagine how he would have prepared his forces to repel the British troops and drive them out of the village. He scanned the track leading in towards the village centre. It was the obvious route of advance, and that would be the focus of his defence.

He spotted a white vehicle lying at the very apex of the fork in the road. It immediately struck him as being not right somehow. What was it? Why was a vehicle parked by the roadside alarming him?

The answer came in a flash: the vehicle had been left in a way that no Afghan would ever have parked it. It wasn't close enough to anyone's compound to signify who was the vehicle's owner and, more importantly, it was parked in the full sun. It was barely mid morning but already it would be like a furnace inside that vehicle.

Perhaps it was abandoned, Baz reasoned. But with the video camera on full zoom it became clear that there was no way that this was a derelict vehicle. It was a smart white Toyota-type estate car parked beside the canal, its bodywork reflected in the dull brown surface of the water.

The vehicle was situated at a bottleneck, where the track was funnelled between the canal on one side and a high mud wall on the other. Any soldier advancing along that road would be forced to walk or drive right past the vehicle, which was all but blocking the way. It was the perfect setting for a vehicle-borne improvised explosive device (VBIED) – or, in layman's terms, a car bomb.

If that innocent-looking white estate car was packed with explosives, around which had been placed nails and bolts and other scrap metal, the consequences of it detonating amid the advancing British soldiers didn't bear thinking about. All it would take was a watcher with a mobile phone, the call from which would trigger the fuse, and an almighty explosion would tear into the vanguard of the British troops.

Baz had seen at first hand the effect of such devices during his time in Northern Ireland. They were crude and basic weapons, but highly effective at killing men on the ground. Tim punched the coordinates of the vehicle into the flight computer. He and Baz shared their suspicions with Steve and Alex in the sister aircraft. All four airmen had a feeling that they'd soon be hitting that vehicle with a Hellfire or two.

But first they needed to flush the enemy fighters out of hiding. A British Harrier had joined them overhead, and with that aircraft's assistance a plan was put in place to fox the enemy.

'We could see no enemy fighters, but something was wrong,' remarks Steve. 'It was obvious that the Taliban would not attempt to fight while we were overhead, so we decided to play a ruse. The plan was to move out to the desert to the west of the village as if leaving the area. We contacted the Harrier in the overhead, and asked him to use his sniper pod to check for any movement in the compound adjacent to the white estate car, just as soon as we had vacated the area.'

Having shared the plan with *Widow Seven Nine*, the two Apaches turned west and headed away from Rahim Kalay until the village was lost in the haze of the horizon. Once they were out of sight they dropped down to tree-top level and did an about-turn. As they powered back in towards the village the Harrier pilot came up over the net. Sure enough, figures had emerged in the compound next to the white vehicle.

There were four of them, and they were all males of fighting age.

13

THE BATTLE FOR RAHIM KALAY

Slaving their surveillance pods to the coordinates provided by the Harrier, the Apaches thundered in to take a closer look, all weapons locked to the target and the 30mm cannons primed to fire on twenty-round bursts.

Hugging the contours of the ground, the aircraft hid their presence until the very last moment. A kilometre out from the village, the pair of Apaches power-climbed to altitude. As they did so, their video cameras caught a figure out in the open. A male dressed in black robes and turban was moving across the compound's main courtyard towards the western wall – the vantage point that overlooked the British soldiers' route of advance into the village.

As the figure neared the wall he spotted the incoming Apaches. He looked momentarily skywards and the anger and consternation on his face was clearly visible. The enemy had thought the cursed mosquitoes had gone – yet here they were back again!

The black-robed figure moved to the cover of the wall, from where he seemed to peer through it in the direction of the British troops. Many of the village's mud-walled compounds looked like something from *The Arabian Nights*. For centuries Afghanistan has been a country at war, and the ancient mud-walled complexes had been built for defensive purposes. The walls were about the height of a man, with spyholes at regular intervals.

It was through one of these that the black-robed figure was now peering. Some five metres to the left of the lone figure something could be seen leaning against the wall: it was a straight, regular object wrapped in a thick blanket.

'Anywhere else in the world and this could have been ignored,' remarks Steve. 'But you don't ignore anything in Afghanistan. This was possibly a weapons bundle. We continued to watch the figure as we relayed everything we could see to the *Widow* call-sign . . . By now we were under increasing pressure to return to Bastion. We told Chief of Staff what we could see: that we thought we were observing an ambush site, and that the *Widow* was requesting us to stay on task. Ian gave us another ten minutes.'

The Apache pilots would now have to make their decisions quickly. The black-robed figure moved along the wall and as the airmen tracked him he joined up with two other men. Until now they had been hidden in a slough of shade. Beside them were similar oblong bundles wrapped in blankets. The two men were wearing white, giving this the appearance of a classic Taliban set-up: a black-robed commander with his two white-robed minions.

The Apache pilots discussed what they could see. If the British troops advanced along the track into the village they would be directly in the line of fire of these figures. There were only three visible, but how many more were hiding down there? The compound consisted of a dozen or more domed-roof buildings set amid a complex of interconnected courtyards. A small army could be concealed down there. If the British troops took the southern branch of the track, so avoiding the compound, they would still have to pass by the white estate car – the suspect car bomb.

'It was obvious to us that this was an excellent ambush position,' remarks Steve. 'If our troops had decided to go down this track they would have taken heavy casualties. If they had chosen the route to cross the river they would have had to pass the car, which we now suspected was a bomb. This was a textbook ambush and we believed that we had found some Taliban.'

Ugly Five Zero radioed *Widow Seven Nine*, giving a full description of what they could see and asking for permission to open fire. As they waited for clearance a fat male emerged from a building and joined the others. He glanced through the spyhole in the wall and turned to talk to the three men beside him, making hand signals in the direction of the British troops.

The aircrew talked among themselves. Perhaps 'Fatty' was a double glazing salesman, they joked. He had parked his car in haste as he was late for an appointment with a customer, hence it not being left in the shade. He was now checking the spyholes in the wall so that he could price up a set of bespoke windows. And they were haggling over the price he would charge for the job.

The humour was dark, but it was necessary. It was the only way to relieve the tension in the cockpits as they prepared to attack. Once again flight *Ugly* were poised to open fire on what could still conceivably be an unarmed group of men. *Widow Seven Nine* gave the clearance to attack. Tim gave a quick battle order, deciding to fire warning shots: 'Just in case it was a double glazing survey,' the aircrew quipped.

From the chin turret of *Ugly Five Zero* the 30mm gun barked. A tongue of white flame shot out from the Apache's cannon as spent shell casings rained down onto the buildings below. There were a couple of seconds' delay and then the rounds tore into the hard-beaten surface of the dirt track some seventy-five metres in front of the western wall of the compound.

The figures inside didn't so much as move a muscle. A second warning burst was fired, this time the rounds impacting barely thirty metres from the thick mud wall. Only one of the figures reacted: he turned away from the peephole, put his arms behind his back as if he was on a leisurely stroll and moved down the wall to the next spyhole.

'It was just so surreal,' remarks Steve. 'It's impossible to comprehend how they reacted, especially as they'd just had 30mm rounds land right nearby. I know what I'd have been doing if I was getting shot at like that . . .'

The whole scenario was eerily reminiscent of earlier engagements – when they had hit the enemy mortar crew in the well, and the figures on the river island beach. Then, as now, the enemy fighters had ignored the pair of aircraft, as if by doing so they might cease to exist. The four airmen were now as certain as they could be that this was a well-prepared enemy ambush, and that these were the vanguard of a larger force that was linked to the mortar units.

Both aircraft opened fire on target, their sights set on narrow-field view to minimise the risk of missing. Two twenty-round bursts tore into the position, the 30mm shells exploding on and around the western wall, throwing up gouts of mud and shrapnel. Figures came running out of the dust storm, abandoning their blanket-bundles in their haste to get out of the killing ground. The aircrew tracked the runners with their weapons sights as they crossed the twenty-five yards of open ground and linked up with another two figures.

The figures paused momentarily to brush the dust and debris from their robes, and as they did so the Apaches hit them again. Four sprinted for cover but there was nothing left of the fat man or the black-robed commander. Both had been vaporised by the heavy-calibre explosive rounds. The survivors split up, running in opposite directions. The guns of the Apaches tracked them, firing twenty-round bursts that chased the figures across the compound, gouts of dirt and shrapnel exploding at their heels.

'Both aircraft were firing at the same time, the rounds exploding on target,' Steve remarks. 'The Taliban were running for their lives, leaving the weapon bundles in their haste. The cannon followed them, rounds smashing into the ground and the buildings. We could see chickens going wild and a small pig broke free from its tether and ran. Boy could it run, sensing a chance for freedom as it left the compound, headed up the track and made off into the open desert. The Taliban were not so lucky.'

The four survivors had made for the cover of two domed-roof buildings situated along the northern wall of the compound. From two kilometres out *Ugly Five Zero* and *Ugly Five One* lined up the aircraft for a Hellfire strike. At the same time they slaved their 30mm cannons to the target coordinates, knowing that any 'leakers' – survivors of the missile strike – would run from the buildings as soon as they were hit.

Keeping their lasers on the centre of each target, Tim and Alex, the Apache gunners, pulled the triggers of their left-hand pistol grip controls. There was an instantaneous flash of flame in front of the cockpits as each Hellfire fired, followed by the shimmering veil of heat haze thrown out by the missiles' rocket motors.

Four seconds later there was a needle flash of black in the top of the aircraft's video screens as the missiles streaked through the frame and hit. Two almighty explosions rent the air, throwing plumes of smoke and debris high into the sky. As the dust cleared a gaping black hole in each of the roofs showed where the Hellfires had hit. Leakers streamed out of the buildings and all of a sudden the compound was alive, figures rushing about in apparent disarray. And for the first time since hitting the compound weapons could clearly be seen.

'Men were running everywhere, with us shooting as soon as we spotted them,' Baz remarks. 'This was fast and furious as we circled above trying to be aware of our wing so as to not to crash. We got closer and closer and Tim started screaming "Azimuth! Azimuth!" meaning I had got the aircraft so close over the compound that he couldn't get the gun to bear on target. So I had to start pushing firmly on the pedals and spinning the aircraft in a tight circle so he could get on target and keep firing.'

A figure came running out of a large building in the southern end of the compound, heading for the gate and a smaller structure on the far side. This would later turn out to be one of the compound's arms dumps. He clutched an AK-47 assault rifle in one hand. *Ugly Five Zero* targeted him with a ten-round burst, the rounds smashing into the ground all around him. He fell to the dusty earth, but an instant later he was up and running once more and made it into the small building alive.

Ugly Five Zero hit the building's roof, the 30mm cannon blasting holes in the domed mud structure. The rounds drove the fighter out again and he reappeared, sprinting for the gateway. He ran through the entranceway and a second figure was spotted squatting in the sliver of shade beneath the arch, an AK-47 clutched between his knees. As *Ugly Five One* prepared to hit them both with a twenty-round burst, Steve spotted movement in the bottom right-hand corner of the video frame. It was a donkey tethered to a stake, and so unable to make itself scarce as the pig had done a few minutes earlier.

'I yelled to Alex to hold his fire,' Steve remarks. 'The donkey was a big, floppy-eared beast and more than likely innocent. We decided we couldn't fire as the donkey would've been slaughtered. How would we live with ourselves if we had killed the donkey? We may be many things, but we are not Donkey Killers!'

The pair of Apaches were flying tight orbits directly above the compound. All doubts that this was an enemy position were now long gone. The only remaining uncertainties were precisely how many enemy were down there, and what exactly they might be armed with.

A figure broke cover carrying a PKM, the Russian equivalent of the general-purpose machine gun. The PKM is a 7.62mm weapon capable of firing 650 rounds a minute and accurate up to a thousand metres. It is a highly effective light anti-aircraft weapon, and it was crucial that the runner be taken out. The enemy fighter sprinted past the floppy-eared donkey and the aircrew held their fire.

He headed out of the gate and along the southern wall of the compound, *Ugly Five One* tracking him as he ran. He went to raise his weapon but the aircrew were too quick: the 30mm cannon spat fire, a twenty-round burst slamming into the earth all around the target. The figure disappeared in a cloud of dust laced with razor-sharp shrapnel.

As the dust cleared the enemy fighter was spotted rising to his knees and crawling towards a small crescent-shaped patch of shadow at the base of the wall. As *Ugly Five One* prepared to hit him again his arm shot out and grabbed his machine gun, then he rolled into the area of the shadow, disappearing completely.

There was no way in which that twenty-round burst could have missed him, of that the aircrew were certain. Either his heart was running on pure adrenalin or the Taliban fighters were drugged to the eyeballs with amphetamines, which wasn't unknown from previous battles. With his system pumped up on massive amounts of speed, a wounded man could keep fighting until his body was literally blown apart or his lifeblood had drained into the baking sand.

Where had the wounded fighter disappeared to?, Steve and Alex wondered. Zooming in the video camera to its maximum, they took a long hard look at that crescent-shaped patch of shadow. It was the entrance to a cave or a tunnel, which by the looks of things had to run beneath the whole of the enemy compound. As the aircrew panned the camera along the base of that wall a series of four similar openings were visible, each half-hidden by a sprawl of straw. The enemy position appeared to be honeycombed with tunnels: the mystery of where the enemy fighters had been hiding had been solved. They had been underground.

As *Ugly Five One*'s aircrew scrutinised the cave entrances for targets the pilots of *Ugly Five Zero* spotted a figure running out of a building in the main compound. Baz flicked the gunnery controls to manual, the 30mm cannon instantly slaving to the crosshair sight of his HMD and hence to his line of sight. He glanced at the target, selected 1200 metres range and pulled the trigger. He fired off three twenty-round bursts, the earth exploding at the feet of the fighter as he ran and then tumbled to the ground.

To the right of the fallen enemy fighter two more came charging out of cover, one armed with an AK-47 and one with a PKM. They sprinted through the gate, vaulted over a short hedgerow and went barrelling down towards the canal barely thirty feet below them. They hit the water, charging in up to their chests, making for the cover of the tree line on the far side. As the bridge over the canal would have made a far easier and quicker route across, this reinforced the aircrew's suspicion that the white car was booby-trapped, and perhaps the approach to the bridge itself also mined.

If those two fighters got into the trees with the machine gun they could cause the Apaches some problems, not to mention the troops on the ground.

'An adrenalin rush took them across the river,' Baz remarks. 'You're so focused on the enemy that nothing else matters at that moment. It's like tunnel vision, there's no fear at that point: the hunt is on. Steve and Alex went straight to engage, immediately opening up with their 30mm cannon, the rounds exploding in the canal and surrounding banks, water pluming upwards. At exactly the same time we hit them from the opposite direction. The whole scene seemed to play out in slow motion. Only one of them escaped from the fire; we could see a body floating downstream.'

The lone survivor sprinted for cover as *Ugly Five One* tracked him, its cannon spitting fire. Somehow he made it into the wood line, which meant that there was potentially a live PKM gunner in there that they needed to find and kill. Both attack helicopters turned their fire on the dense woodland, plastering it with sustained bursts of 30mm cannon fire. They could see with the naked eye individual rounds slamming into tree trunks and branches, the explosions throwing out chunks of shrapnel that ripped through the foliage.

As the 30mm rounds hit, a series of sudden, sharp explosions rippled through the shadows beneath the trees. Whatever had been the PKM gunner's motive for fleeing in to the wood line, it looked as if there were stores of ammunition in there – ammo that was being ignited by *Ugly Five One*'s cannon fire.

The woodland was set 150 yards back from the bridge over the canal. Between the woods and the bridge was nothing but open farmland. It was a perfect location for a secondary ambush site: the first in the compound to hit the British troops as they moved into the village, the second in the woods to hit them again as they retreated across the bridge, making for the safety of the open countryside.

Ugly Five Zero moved northwards again, hunting among the smoking debris of the main compound for further enemy fighters. As it did so *Ugly Five One* flew out into the open desert to the east to set up for a rocket attack. Flying in from three kilometres, Steve put the aircraft into a shallow dive so that it was heading directly at the woodland. If there were PKM gunners still alive in there he was flying right down their gun barrels.

The one drawback of the 2.7-inch rockets is that they cannot be independently targeted: instead, the aircraft's line-of-flight directs the trajectory of the rockets as they are unleashed. The main concern for Steve and Alex was how wide the spread of the deadly tungsten darts might be, and to thus maintain a flight profile that would avoid hitting friendly forces.

As *Ugly Five One* hit the two kilometres to target mark, it fired. There was a belch of smoke from the pods beneath the stub wings and four flechette-armed rockets sped away. At that distance the 320 tungsten darts fired out in a funnel of death large enough to saturate the entire wood line. They tore in towards target at a speed in excess of Mach 1, the darts making a high-pitched howling noise as if an express train was screaming down a narrow tunnel. It had to be terrifying to be on the receiving end of such an attack.

From their position orbiting above the enemy compound, Baz and Tim could actually see the darts strike. They punctured tree trunks and punched their way through branches, shards of wood spitting skywards as if a giant chainsaw was chewing up the tree line. After that first strike, *Ugly Five One* banked around hard and lined up again, a further four rockets sending their eighty flechettes tearing into the cover of the woodland.

'The flechette rocket strike was the first time we'd fired them in anger,' remarks Steve. 'We were hugely concerned about friendly fire; they do Mach 1 and it was a flat, level shot so we knew it could go for miles. I spoke to *Widow Seven Nine* on the ground and got the friendly troop coordinates, and they shaped our attack heading. The attack approach had to hit the wood and the caves while avoiding friendly forces.'

Ugly Five Zero put a call through to *Widow Seven Nine* with an update on the action so far. The pair of Apaches had been in the battle for one hour and one minute, although to the pilots it felt as if barely five minutes had gone by. The tunnel vision of combat was all-consuming, the battle scenes flashing past in slow-motion clarity, yet oddly seeming to last no time at all.

A further call was put through to the Ops Room at Camp Bastion to reassure the Chief of Staff that flight *Ugly* was doing good out there as they burned up the air hours in the skies above Rahim Kalay.

Not surprisingly, the ground troops were itching to get into the fight. All that *Widow Seven Nine* was waiting for was the word from the Apaches, and they would be up and at the enemy positions. Baz figured they needed to kill more enemy fighters and their assets before they could give the British soldiers the word to go. First on his list was the white estate car, whose coordinates he had stored in the aircraft's flight computer.

So far every aspect of the aircrew's analysis of the battlefield – every instinct and hunch and suspicion – had proven correct. He had no doubt that the white estate car was an enemy vehicle parked in a position to kill and maim British troops as they moved into the village.

From four kilometres out *Ugly Five Zero* ran in towards the target, a Hellfire primed. As Baz flew the aircraft front-seater Tim stroked the targeting mouse on his right-hand pistol grip control, keeping the hot point of the laser dead centre on the body of the vehicle. At two kilometres' distance he switched the targeting to image auto tracker (IAT) – a system that holds the sights on target no matter what the movement – and fired.

There was a fierce bloom of heat in front of the cockpit as the Hellfire sped away, and for an instant the IAT lost its lock, the shimmering haze in front of the nose pod obscuring the view. But as the heat haze cleared the IAT recovered its lock, the Hellfire plummeting earthwards and striking the roof of the white estate car. The high-explosive armour-piercing warhead tore into the vehicle, the blast ripping it apart and sending chunks of metal cart-wheeling into the air.

A split-second later there was a ripple of further explosions as whatever explosive charge had been contained in the vehicle det-onated. As *Ugly Five Zero* turned away from the target all that was left of the white estate was a twisted heap of warped metal in a seething mass of flames.

The two Apaches returned to their orbit above the compound. The enemy had been hit hard in what had been a series of sophis-ticated, well-planned ambush positions. Two buildings in the compound had been Hellfired and destroyed. The woodland had been strafed with 30mm cannon fire and raked with 640 flechette darts. And the white estate car-bomb was no more. How many scores of enemy fighters had been put out of action – either killed or badly wounded – the aircrew didn't like to hazard a guess, but it had to be a considerable number. It had been a nasty turnaround for an enemy force that had been expecting to ambush and kill a large number of British troops.

But there were two things that still worried the Apache aircrew: one, a large, 300 foot by 100 foot building in the southern corner of the compound; and two, the tunnels and caves that must run below it. Repeated strikes with the 30mm cannon had set fires burning inside the large building but it had by no means been cleared or made safe. The aircrew had seen scores of enemy fighters take refuge inside it and many could still be alive in there.

As for the tunnel system, there was no weapon that the Apaches carried which could penetrate several feet of sun-baked Afghan earth to neutralise that threat. The Hellfire was essentially an anti-armour weapon and the very size of the building, plus the depth of the tunnels, put both targets way out of its league. It was time to call in the big guns. A US Air Force F-15 was approaching the restricted operating zone above the Rahim Kalay battlefield.

Ugly Five Zero made the call: '*Dude One Seven*, this is *Ugly*, do you read me?'

'*Ugly*, this is *Dude One Seven*, good copy. What can I do for ya?'

'What's your ordnance status, *Dude*?'

'I got four five hundred-pounders, and a pair of thousand-pound JDAMs. What's the target, *Ugly*.'

'The target's a large building at the southern corner of an enemy compound that we've been hitting. You see that plume of black smoke? That's the vehicle we Hellfired. The target building is four hundred yards to the north-east of that smoke. It's three hundred feet, by a hundred feet.'

'Visual the column of smoke; visual the enemy compound.'

'Right, I'm lasing the target building now. Confirm you see my laser spot.'

'Good spot.'

'Okay, we need to flatten that building. What weapon d'you suggest, *Dude*?'

'Something that size . . . A thousand-pound JDAM. Gotta be.'

'Roger that. *Dude*. We will lase the target for you when ready.'

'Okay, ready: spot on, *Ugly*.'

'Spot on: we're lasing the target for you now, *Dude*.'

'Okay, good spot. I'm starting my run in now.'

With the code of *Ugly Five Zero*'s laser entered into the F-15's flight computer, the pilot could programme his bombs to home in on the Apache's laser beam. The 'hot point' of the laser – the point at which it bounced back from the target – would be the lock-on point for the JDAM.

As the F-15 made its run in to target, *Ugly Five Zero* sought final clearance from *Widow Seven Nine* for the airstrike. This was in case British soldiers had advanced into the area without the Apache aircrew realising it and were now in the vicinity of the compound. With *Widow Seven Nine*'s clearance given, the airstrike was on.

The *Dude* call-sign announced that his bomb was on its way. The wait seemed like an age, although in reality it was just seconds before a black wheelie bin-sized shape arrowed through the air above Rahim Kalay and punched into the target building. There was a massive crumpling impact as walls and roofs blew outwards, and the entire building seemed to lift slightly before collapsing in on itself. The debris tumbled back to earth, the smoke clearing slowly, and not a wall was left standing. A massive crater had been scoured out of the earth where the building had once been.

Steve and Alex radioed their flight leader, Tim, to alert him to the fact that they were 'Winchester' – out of ammunition. They had no 30mm rounds remaining, no 2.7-inch rockets left and only one Hellfire still on its rack. Fuel supplies were also running low, with each aircraft having no more than ten minutes remaining before they would be forced to return to Bastion.

The four airmen reckoned that the enemy threat had been massively reduced, if not neutralised, although the tunnel system remained a worry. There could still be scores of enemy fighters hiding down there. Either way, they would shortly have to head for home. Before doing so, *Ugly Five One* radioed Camp Bastion, asking for a replacement Apache flight to be held on standby in case the British ground troops required further air support. Then it was time for a last call to *Widow Seven Nine*.

'*Widow Seven Nine*, this is *Ugly*. We're Winchester ammo and approaching bingo fuel. We need to return to Bastion. The position seems clear of EF but watch out for the tunnel system under the compound and the wood line to the south. As indicated, we reckon that's the EF's second ambush position, in the cover of the tree line.'

The wood line into which the PKM gunner had fled remained an unknown to flight *Ugly*. While one enemy fighter had gone into the tree line and none had come out again, that didn't mean that they had killed all enemy positioned in there. If it was a secondary ambush position enemy forces would be well dug in, and some might have survived the cannon fire and flechettes that had pounded the tree line.

'*Ugly*, this is *Widow Seven Nine* . . . I can't thank you guys enough for what you did today.'

'No problem. We've one favour to ask, *Widow Seven Nine*: can you guys check what damage those flechettes did to target? We've never used them before, and we're kind of curious.'

'Roger that, *Ugly*. Not a problem.'

'Right, we're out of here. We've asked Bastion to keep a replacement flight on standby in case you need them. Good hunting, *Widow*. Stay safe.'

'You too, *Ugly*. You guys should know you saved a lot of lives down here today . . . We lost one guy KIA, but there'd have been a whole lot more killed and wounded if . . .'

Widow Seven Nine was understandably emotional as he said farewell to the aircrew. As Baz listened in he could feel the adrenalin draining out of his system and he found himself becoming all choked up. He leaned forwards and flipped the radio to a different frequency. He couldn't take any more of that from *Widow Seven Nine*, or he'd be weeping all the way back the flight line. It was time to put a call through to base.

'Hello Bastion, this is *Ugly Five Zero*. Winchester, low on fuel, returning to base.'

It was a ten-minute flight back to Camp Bastion. As the flight *Ugly* aircrew dismounted the four men turned to each other and shook hands. They were on the ground and safe, and they knew that they had done a fine job out there in the skies over Rahim Kalay. As they headed for the waiting Land Rover a couple of the groundies could be seen stripped to the waist and sunning themselves around the back of the hangars.

'That's the surreal thing about Afghanistan,' Baz remarks. 'One minute you could be engaging the enemy in a major contact, the next you're taxiing in to the Apache bay and you see people turning themselves over for an even tan.'

Things were about to get even more surreal. On the short drive to the Ops Room for the debrief, flight *Ugly*'s Land Rover was waved down by a member of the Royal Military Police, who patrol and police Camp Bastion. Steve wound down the window.

'Excuse me, sir, but I noticed that you're not wearing your seat belt.'

Steve shook his head in disbelief. 'You what?'

'Your seat belt, sir. It needs to be worn.'

'Listen, mate, twenty kilometres up the road there are British soldiers losing their lives . . . And this is what you're worried about?'

'I'm only doing my job, sir,' the RMP replied. 'At all times . . .'

Steve gunned the engine. He supposed the RMP did have a job to do, and much of what they did was necessary, but rather them than him any day. It was almost as bad as the time when the RMPs had tried to book them for speeding. The flight had been flagged down during a VHR call-out, with Steve and Baz driving the Land Rover hell-for-leather for the flight line. Finally a deal had been reached: Apache aircrews on call-outs would not be pulled over for speeding if they drove with their hazard lights flashing.

As the four airmen strode into the ops tent the buzz seemed to be all about the battle for Rahim Kalay. Heading straight into the debrief, the aircrews played their gun tapes and talked through the whole, epic engagement. As they had no ideas of numbers of enemy killed all the pilots could do was an estimate based upon what they had seen during the battle: eight dead was their best guess.

To the OC, Jules Franks, they made a special request: they wanted a big thank you said to the ground crews as it had been a real team effort. No doubt about it, it was the groundies getting them airborne again so quickly halfway through the battle that had helped save British lives.

After the debrief the flight *Ugly* aircrew went to grab a late lunch. Nothing much had changed in the canteen. It was a choice of the same three sandwich fillings as always – coronation chicken, spicy beef or fresh prawn. As Steve sat munching on his baguette he found himself wondering where on earth they got fresh prawns in the middle of the Afghan desert.

'We're looking around thinking: this is surreal,' Steve remarks. 'People here have no idea what we've just been through . . . We kill the enemy in our own particular way, just like the troops on the ground, and it is up close and personal for us just as it is for them . . . After lunch it was back to the tent to watch a DVD of *Starsky and Hutch*. But we couldn't phone home, 'cause there was an Op Minimise on due to the British soldier killed that morning in Rahim Kalay.'

Lying on his bunk that night, Baz Hunter realised just how exhausted he was feeling: 'We were dog tired. We'd been in hours of continuous combat, which equates to so many hours of any normal activity . . . It's not just a physical fatigue, its an emotional fatigue, 'cause you're up and down all the time . . . Rahim Kalay was one hour of extreme violence, and the next you're having a laugh and a baguette. Ground troops would have a more gradual let down whereas ten minutes after battle we're on this surreal, weird trip back at Bastion. Sometimes I wake up and think, did all that ever really happen?'

The following morning there was a second, more detailed debrief on the Rahim Kalay battle, and this one was for all the Apache air-crews to attend. In fact the groundies, the REME fitters, the combat medics and the Chinook aircrews were also in attendance.

It was already clear that Rahim Kalay had been the single biggest engagement for 662 Squadron to date. A very significant number of enemy fighters had been killed. More importantly, over the space of several hours, flight *Ugly* had prevented a British force from advancing into what would have been a murderous ambush, saving untold numbers of lives.

On the flight back to Bastion, Steve and *Widow Seven Nine* had exchanged email addresses. The *Widow* turned out to be one Sergeant Paul 'Bommer' Grahame of the Light Dragoons. He'd been seconded to the Worcesters and Foresters.

This is what he had to say about the part the air operations played in the battle for Rahim Kalay:

'What sticks in my mind about this operation is how diligent the *Ugly* call signs were – having pointed out the suspicious vehicle, the weapons, the observation points in the compound walls, the cave complexes and generally having a bad feeling about the troops moving forward into a possible ambush . . . The Taliban had many hidden ambush positions which were only cleared when the Apaches came in and denied them, so disrupting ambush plans.

'With over seventy-five Taliban (minimum) in the compound and surrounding area, the operation could quite easily have been the biggest loss of British life . . . There are a lot of soldiers, myself included, that owe their lives to the aircrew involved in that day . . . This operation lasted for only sixty hours but it was to become the most important and memorable event in the whole of the 146 days of our tour.'

The British ground troops had advanced into Rahim Kalay and proceeded to hold a *shura* – a traditional council – with the village elders, one of whom was something of a Taliban himself. The elders had confirmed the numbers of dead and injured: forty-eight enemy fighters were confirmed killed, with a further forty-five unaccounted for. As for the wounded, it was likely that their numbers would far outweigh the number of fighters killed.

The village elders revealed that at least one of the mortar teams operating in Rahim Kalay had consisted of Chechen fighters, and scores of those killed that day had been the so-called Foreign Taliban. Few if any of the fighters in the village had actually been Afghans, let alone come from Rahim Kalay.

Shortly after the fighting was over, a Harrier had been tasked with taking an aerial photograph of the battlefield. From that alone, the devastation wreaked across the enemy position was clear. Two smaller buildings to the north of the compound had neat, Hellfire holes punched in their roofs. And to the south, the large building had been reduced to a heap of rubble by the thousand-pound JDAM.

'The ground troops had been dying to get in there,' remarks Baz. 'When they did they were amazed and shocked at the level of destruction; there were craters all over and the once-beautiful village was like a ghost town. Bodies were all over the place, bits of people, discarded weapons . . . The ground troops realised that they never wanted to be on the receiving end of that – of what the Apaches, coupled with the fast air, could do.'

As the British troops had funnelled out across the village they had discovered a series of well-prepared ambush sites. In the poppy fields to either side of the main enemy compound there was a series of trench systems with underground bunkers. The bunkers were roofed over with stout tree trunks covered in earth and camouflaged with heaps of dry poppy stalks. They were all but invisible from the air. Their sides were reinforced by makeshift sandbags made out of old flour sacks stuffed full of earth.

As for the cave entrances beneath the compound, they were so small as to be barely accessible to a fully grown man. It would have been very easy to have missed them from the air. After the main enemy compound, the woodland across the river provided a secondary ambush position. It included dug trenches, with vegetation cleared to provide interlocking arcs of fire, and ammunition dumps interspersed down the tree line.

Wider Allied intelligence reports had revealed that enemy units were training to use surface-to-air missiles in Iran with the elite Iranian Republican Guard. And Chechens were being brought into Helmand to act as mobile mortar training teams. Prior to the battle for Rahim Kalay, Taliban leader Mullah Bashir had announced that Arab, Chechen and Uzbek fighters were moving in to support the 'jihad'. The money used to pay all of these fighters – Iranians, Chechens, Uzbeks and Arabs – was coming from the booming opium trade.

Afghanistan is the world's foremost supplier of opium, which is refined into the heroin sold on the streets of the UK, mainland Europe, the USA and elsewhere. As British forces had advanced into Rahim Kalay they had been doing so through fields of opium poppies. And it was those fanatical Chechen, Arab and Uzbek fighters – those reinforcements heralded by Mullah Bashir – that had been hit hard in the battle.

Following the Apache airstrikes over Rahim Kalay village, intelligence revealed the enemy shouting and screaming. Enemy commanders had been yelling at their troops to attack the 'mosquitoes', only to get the following response: 'We will attack, but I am the only one left alive!'

The effect of the 30mm cannon fire, coupled with the flechette rockets, had been devastating. The enemy fighter who had dropped his PKM machine gun then picked it up again and dived into the entrance to the tunnels had died almost immediately after making it in there. British ground troops found him with two 30mm holes in his chest. He had died of his injuries, and it was only adrenalin that had allowed him to climb into the cave.

Scores of dead fighters were found in the compound and the cave system that ran beneath it. The caves had been explored and they were found to be stuffed full of arms and ammunition. There was a labyrinth of tunnels leading to numerous entrances dotted around the compound, which explained how the enemy had been able to move around so effectively without being seen.

The remains of the white estate car had also been examined by British troops: the boot was found to have been stuffed full of rocket-propelled grenades, and traces of C3 plastic explosives were also found in the vehicle. As suspected, it had been one gigantic explosive device – a car bomb par excellence.

The Czech unit had advanced into the wood line across the river from the enemy compound. There they discovered nine dead enemy fighters plus arms dumps with many thousands of rounds. Much of the spare ammo was stored in the trees, allowing fighters to reach up and rapidly reload. There were also sleeping bags and food and water supplies, indicating that enemy forces had been lying in wait for some time.

At first the Czechs were unable to tell how the enemy had been killed. It wasn't until they discovered the small puncture wounds of flechette darts that the means of death was realised.

Rahim Kalay would turn out to be the single biggest defeat that the Taliban had suffered in the Green Zone, with the destruction of at least two mortar-based plate teams, scores of machine gun and RPG teams, and at least two complete cells of Taliban, including many foreign fighters. It was also the biggest single engagement to date for the Apaches in Afghanistan.

For the men of 662 Squadron it was also the day upon which four aircrew had saved the lives of scores of British soldiers, and in the process killed dozens of enemy fighters in a classic action against the enemy.

It will be remembered by the airmen of *Ugly Five One* and *Ugly Five Zero* as the day upon which their flight truly came of age. The men of flight *Ugly* named that day's battle Rahim Kalay Day.

14

PEACE LIKE A RIVER

Days 23–28

Flight *Ugly* was rotated back through Kandahar Airfield for three days' downtime. For once they really did feel that they deserved it. There was almost a demob happy atmosphere among the *Ugly* aircrew: they felt as if Rahim Kalay had been their one big hit, that they were unlikely to see such action again during the remainder of their tour.

In the luxury of the base the four men hit the alcohol-free beer and oddly they started feeling pissed after the first few cans. It had to be wishful thinking, they told themselves. Op Minimise had been declared over so Steve was able to put a call through to his fiancée Tracey. It was the first opportunity to speak with her in several days, during which time they had carried out numerous ops, culminating in Rahim Kalay.

'Hello, love, it's me,' he told her. 'It's been a busy few days, but all's fine . . . How's it going back home?'

The relief in Tracey's voice gave Steve just a hint of what it must be like to be the wife of a Corps pilot, or any British soldier serving on the front line. He'd called late in the week, and Tracey had been dreading the arrival of the weekend. There was nothing – not one single thing in the world – that was worse than trying to brave it through a weekend home alone, not knowing if your loved one was okay.

'You try to do the normal things that get you through the days and nights,' Tracey remarks. 'But all the while you're longing for

Monday morning to come and for work to fill up your days again. It's a rollercoaster, from the lowest depression to the height of joy – and the tears again – when your man's just called.'

Tracey told Steve that one of his relatives was coming to visit that weekend. Brian Fusilier was an Army recruiter, and Steve never missed a chance to rag him. Being infantry, Brian always tried to steer the most promising recruits in that direction, but anyone with half a brain would join the Army Air Corps, Steve reckoned. Still, it was good to know that Tracey would have some company for the weekend.

'All week you're constantly praying that everything's all right,' Tracey remarks. 'You're scanning the news, dreading switching it on yet dreading missing anything. You dread that heart-stopping moment when Afghanistan comes on, then the worry and tears when you hear bad news, and the relief and joy when you realise its not your man – followed by the guilt for feeling happy that its not him but someone else's much-loved husband, brother or son.'

The first parcel Tracey sent out to Steve in theatre had become something of a standing joke between them. Knowing of Steve's sweet tooth, she'd parcelled up a load of chocolate. The only problem was that by the time it had reached Bastion it had melted in the heat into a gooey mess.

Upon hearing of flight *Ugly*'s health kick – the daily gym-swim-run and no fry-ups – Tracey had paid a visit to her local wholefood store and purchased a basket full of nuts, seeds and dried fruits. This she had parcelled up and posted out to her man, eagerly awaiting his excited reaction when he got it.

Steve had just received the parcel at Bastion. As soon as he'd opened it and the rest of the flight had clocked its contents they had ripped the piss out of him mercilessly.

'Nice parcel, love,' he told Tracey over the echoing phone line. 'Thing is, I'm not a bloody parrot, so don't send me any more birdseed!'

Back in Bastion on Duty Ops, Steve caught a ride on a Chinook north towards Sangin and Gereshk in the company of 662

Squadron's OC, Jules Franks. The OC was attending a ground briefing on a forthcoming operation and was to give the Apache input. Steve knew that either the Rahim Kalay *Widow* or some of the ground troops from the Rahim Kalay battle would be present at FOB Price, just south of Gereshk. He wanted to do a debrief with them to see what the Apache pilots could learn from the ground troop's perspective and vice versa.

Once the Chinook had touched down at FOB Price, Steve met up with the Rahim Kalay crew and there were handshakes all round. As they went to get a brew Steve remarked on how tough it must have been, being on the ground at Rahim Kalay and getting shot at, RPG'd and mortared the whole time.

One of the young soldiers turned to Steve: 'Mate, maybe you didn't notice, but as soon as you lot turned up they stopped shooting at us and turned their guns on you. Those airburst RPGs are nasty, as is their 12.7mm. I wouldn't want to be you lot if I was paid.'

Steve and the ground troops were just getting down to business when all hell broke loose in the platoon house. A Land Rover with blown-out tyres, shattered windows and a smashed-up front came barrelling in through the gate. A British patrol had been hit in an explosion on the outskirts of Gereshk, and had taken casualties.

On the Chinook ride back to Bastion combat medics were working on the wounded, stringing up drips from the aircraft's hold and bandaging up wounds. It was a sobering moment for Steve as he saw at first hand what the ground troops were being put through and what the casevac teams were doing on a daily basis across Helmand.

More intelligence was filtering in to Camp Bastion in the aftermath of Rahim Kalay and it was clear that the defeat had hurt the enemy badly. After the battle, tractors and trailers had been used to take the dead and injured enemy fighters away. Those killed had been slated to reinforce enemy numbers around Gereshk and Sangin. They'd lost several top commanders plus a fortified headquarters base with a sophisticated cave system. They'd also lost key weapons systems, arms dumps and their expert foreign fighters.

Mullah Barich, one of the enemy's senior commanders, had just given a speech in the Tribal Areas (the lawless lands straddling the Afghanistan-Pakistan border), outlining how badly their war effort had been hit. The jihad was faltering, he had said. They needed two thousand fresh volunteers to take the fight to the 'infidel enemy'.

There were even reports that the Taliban high command was splintering. Recriminations were flying over the Rahim Kalay defeat and the killing of several top commanders. That, coupled with the earlier losses in the Upper Sangin Valley, had dented the credibility of the leadership.

To the north-east of Rahim Kalay lies the settlement of Haydarabad. With Rahim Kalay having fallen, this was now the enemy's main stronghold on the supply route from the Tribal Areas into Helmand. Haydarabad was known to Allied intelligence as a major Taliban base and a perceived safe haven for them. After the deaths of commanders at Rahim Kalay a new leader, one Mullah Janan, had been promoted to be the new Taliban commander of the Haydarabad region.

Mullah Janan declared his immediate aim as being the recon-quest of Rahim Kalay. He called for battle casualty replacements, and British intelligence had picked up groups of 150 fresh fighters filtering in to reinforce Haydarabad. He had also called for his fighters to avenge the defeat at Rahim Kalay by seeking out and destroying an Apache – *a cursed mosquito* – at all costs.

Meanwhile, and despite the recent bombing, the whole of the Sangin area was calmer. The Sangin town market was open and doing a roaring trade, while the Sangin Valley was quietening. Electricity had even been restored to some of the larger towns.

At the Camp Bastion Apache base life went on pretty much as normal, with call-outs to casevacs for small-scale hit and run attacks on the ground. As the Duty Ops flight, the *Ugly* aircrew were getting nothing.

On day twenty-seven of their deployment, the four airmen rotated on to Deliberate Ops. Enemy fighters had been re-infiltrating the Upper Sangin Valley, using the Helmand River as a route into the hinterland. They were trying to re-establish control over the local population.

In the aftermath of Op Kulang, FOB Fox had been established to the north-east of Sangin as a permanent base. Situated on the eastern bank of the Helmand River, it was put there to dominate the region. The enemy were hitting FOB Fox in sporadic attacks, just to show that they hadn't gone away.

There were further intelligence reports of surface-to-air missiles being smuggled into Helmand along with missile-operating teams who had been trained in Iran. After the shooting down of call-sign *Flipper*, enemy forces were desperate to hit another high-value target as a propaganda victory to boost recruitment.

Groups of enemy fighters were reported to be heading south from Musa Qaleh into the Upper Sangin Valley, and the Apache aircrews were warned to keep a careful eye on movements via the river. In particular, a barge was apparently on the move, carrying some thirty fighters, hundreds of RPG rounds and dozens of 'long tubular devices' that could be SAMs.

Baz had always wanted to own a river barge. Perhaps it was because the slow and easy way of life on the canals would be the perfect antidote to flying and fighting the Apache. Pottering along the waterways and pulling in at the odd pub for a pint of real ale was his idea of the sweet life. Sadly, his wife and daughter had never seemed so taken with the idea.

But in recent months his daughter had secured a place at university and now he saw his chance. Rather than the expense of renting her a flat, he would buy her a canal boat to moor near the campus. This was his Trojan horse, and he never stopped talking to the other lads about it. He was going to buy her a dream boat that after her three years' study would be his, of course.

As the flight *Ugly* airmen were briefed on the barge on the River Helmand they ripped the piss out of Baz mercilessly. Intelligence reports had pegged it as a simple flat-bottomed boat, but was it clinker-built or iron-hulled? Was it a Thames barge or a regular narrowboat? Was it horse-drawn or diesel-engined? Was it called Barry's Barge, by any chance? And did it have pretty potted plants on the roof, a wood-burning stove and a brass ship's wheel?

*

Rotated on to VHR duty, flight *Ugly* were given a resupply escort mission into Sangin. But as they approached Sangin town they were alerted to a troops in contact that was right in their flight path. Troops at FOB Fox had come under attack from groups of enemy fighters on the river. Bastion gave flight *Ugly* five minutes to break from its scheduled mission and check it out.

As *Ugly* headed into the Green Zone they contacted the *Widow* on the ground. A flotilla of craft was out on the river and from within their number sporadic fire was being put down on FOB Fox. Some of the boats were clearly civilian so the ground troops were unable to return effective fire. The enemy were up to their old tricks again: using women and children as human shields, this time to mask a river-borne assault.

The pair of Apaches popped up over the river at the very location of the attack. They spotted several craft directly below them.

'We went down to take a look and suddenly there's a load of boats mid-river in front of us,' Steve remarks. 'The main craft was a twenty-foot barge, six feet wide, crammed full of blokes and with an aft section covered. We knew immediately it was a resupply as we could see all sorts of weapons stowed in the back. A rope had been strung between the river banks to haul the boat across . . . We could see the rope-puller starting to panic and there was clear shock on the faces of the blokes as they realised we were in the air. The rope-man stood up in alarm, got hit by the rope and fell into the river.'

The attack on FOB Fox was a diversionary tactic to keep the ground troops busy as this reinforcement boat pulled itself quietly across the river. The question was, how many more might there be? *Ugly Five One* took the lead as *Ugly Five Zero* adopted a wider orbit over the river, searching for further enemy craft. But before it could begin to find and kill any, *Ugly Five Zero* was called off task to escort a Chinook on an urgent flight into Sangin.

That left the lone Apache, Steve and Alex's *Ugly Five One*, to deal with the enemy forces that had been spotted on the river.

'We decided to put warning shots into the river,' Steve remarks. 'They really started to panic then, paddling with their hands and with everything they had. They lost the rope, people were diving into the river and suddenly the barge was accelerating downstream and spinning out of control. There's two blokes left on board and the boat shoots off downstream. We see another, larger boat parked up on the riverbank with a crowd of enemy fighters around it. We're cleared to engage, so in we go to attack.'

This second boat was using the same rope-crossing, which was how enemy commanders were ferrying their reinforcements into battle. As the first rounds of 30mm cannon fire hit the boat, splintered wood exploded from the impact, the enemy fighters diving for cover. Coming around again, *Ugly Five One* set up in an attacking run and unleashed a Hellfire.

In the heat of things the pilots hadn't set up properly and they rushed the attack. The missile missed the boat and slammed into the riverbank, cutting the mooring rope in two. Slowly at first, but with increasing speed as it was pulled into the current, boat number two was swept downstream. Turning after it, *Ugly Five One* pounded the craft with cannon fire, the 30mm rounds blowing it to pieces.

'We decided to give the two guys on the first boat a chance to escape,' Steve remarks. 'They'd been warned off, we had taken them out of the battle and they might have learned a lesson to remain out of it. But that just goes to show that we don't kill unless we have to . . . Word went out the next day from the District Commissioner: if you don't use the designated river crossings, you're a target. But that didn't stop the piss-taking back at base: all you lot ever seem to do is shoot up the Taliban Navy!'

Flight *Ugly* came off their VHR duty and spent the next few days on downtime at Kandahar Airfield, followed by a stint on Duty Ops. There was the odd call out to a TIC, or casevac flight or convoy escort duty, but nothing much to write home about.

In mid June Steve had to return to the UK for five days as his interview for his commission as an Army Air Corps officer was due. Reluctant though he was to leave, Steve felt, as did the rest of flight *Ugly*, that they'd had the best of their time in the Afghan theatre. Steve's absence called for a rejigging of the aircrews, as flight *Ugly* needed a fourth man for its forthcoming Deliberate Ops and

VHR duties. They ended up getting Staff Sergeant Colin Norton, who would take Steve's place in *Ugly Five One* alongside Alex.

Colin Norton normally flew as the OC's back-seater on *Super Six* flight and he was a highly experienced Apache operator. Like Baz and Steve, he had come up through the ranks. He was tall for an Apache pilot – the cramped cockpit favoured short-arses like Steve – at around five foot eleven, with a messy shock of reddish hair. He had the reputation of being a maverick in the Corps – and that's in an outfit that was replete with mavericks. He had reached the stage in his career where he was known for speaking his mind. He had a very British, offbeat sense of humour and was known for pulling the sort of pranks that many would find incomprehensible.

Colin joined flight *Ugly* as they rotated on to Deliberate Ops. The duty had its normal ups and downs in terms of Chinook incident reaction team duties – mostly escorting the big, twin-rotor helicopters on casevac missions. During downtime Baz, Tim and Alex tried to introduce their new flight member to some of the flight's esteemed traditions. Jogging around the base just wasn't Colin's thing so they tried the gym. But pumping iron with old lumps of engine block didn't light his candle either.

Colin promptly informed the other flight members what a waste of time it all was. He, Colin, was going to challenge them all – Steve included, when he made it back to theatre – to a muscle-building competition. The wager was this: that he would have the largest biceps of any of them by the end of the tour. The other flight members rose to the challenge, redoubling their efforts in the gym. But they were amazed to see Colin doing absolutely nothing to get himself in shape. At the same time he exuded a quiet confidence in his own abilities that was ever so slightly unnerving. How on earth was Colin going to beat them, they all were wondering.

The answer became clear a couple of days later, when Colin arrived with a large plastic shopping bag from the NAAFI stores. He emptied its contents on to his bunk and held up a giant tub of Muscle Man Muscle Builder Powder, complete with a semi-naked and rippling-muscled bodybuilder on the front. He proceeded to inform the others that this was his secret weapon. But what Colin seemed to have missed was that you had to exercise, as well as drink the stuff, in order to make it work.

'Colin thought you just took the stuff and became massive,' remarks Baz. 'After a week he gave up for the following reasons: the cost of the tubs of powder was threatening to bankrupt him, plus the fact that the only muscle growth he was experiencing was in his fingers when they were exercised opening the tin!'

Colin Norton was an excellent pilot, but he was also one of a kind. The men of flight *Ugly* embraced their new team member for the simple reason that he had them cracked up laughing with his unpredictable, oddball ways.

The flight were next rotated on to VHR duty. The aircrew were approaching their fortieth day in theatre. After the rush of the Rahim Kalay battle there was still the odd piece of action but they seemed to be getting fewer and further in between. Or perhaps the aircrew were just becoming immune to the sort of drama that on day one of operations would have lit them up. Perhaps it was all just becoming routine.

An Apache had recently been in the air and taken a burst of 12.7mm rounds through the rotor blades – most likely from a Soviet-era DShK 'Dushka' heavy machine gun. The Dushka is the Russian equivalent of the .50-calibre Browning heavy machine gun used by British and American forces. It was used extensively by the Soviet military when they were waging war in Afghanistan. A lot of Dushkas fell into the hands of the Afghan mujahidin back then, and the weapon was now ubiquitous in Afghanistan.

The Apache's rotor blades are designed to take a hit from a 12.7mm round or larger and remain intact. Each blade is constructed from four separate spars, consisting of steel boxes reinforced with fibreglass tubing. In theory, a direct hit from a heavy-calibre high-explosive round might take out one of the spars, but the others would remain intact.

It was a relief to see that in practice the Apache had taken those 12.7mm rounds and remained in the air long enough to make it back to Bastion. But it was also a reminder to the aircrew that however much the action may have seemed to have dulled, the enemy were still out there and itching to bring down a British or Allied helicopter.

On the first night of their rotation the four airmen were lying in bed in the VHR tent and trying to sleep in the suffocating heat when they were jerked into wakefulness by the ringing of the field telephone. It was 0100 hours, and by now the crew were totally conditioned to the rigours of VHR duty. By the second ring they were already out of bed and pulling their boots on. It was a three-ring call-out, signifying an Apache-led mission, and the men sprinted for the ops tent and the flight line.

A Lynx Mk 7 helicopter had run into serious trouble while on a mission south of Bastion. Flying over the Green Zone, the air-craft's main transmission had malfunctioned. Oil pressure was falling fast and the temperature was rising. At worst, the main transmission had taken a round and was pissing out oil. At best, either a seal had gone or the gauge was simply faulty. But with the crew having no way of checking they had to presume the worst: a holed gearbox spurting out oil into the night air and a main trans-mission that was about to seize solid.

The Apache has grease-lubricated gearboxes and ballistic-toler-ant drive shafts, all of which are designed to run for some thirty minutes if drained dry of oil. In contrast, once the Lynx has lost its oil it is only a short time before the transmission will overheat, seize and shatter. If that happened the aircrew faced an emergency land-ing in the open desert or the Green Zone, depending on where exactly they were when the system died on them.

Neither was a pleasant option, which was why flight *Ugly* were waiting on the flight line with their rotors spinning.

'The Lynx pilot appeared calm on the radio as he updated HQ,' Baz remarks. 'The atmosphere in that cockpit, while professional, was clearly tense, the three men knowing the risks involved in the options they had open to them, each of which was fraught with danger. The Green Zone would involve landing blind and at night in the heart of enemy territory. It would not be long before the Taliban would become aware that an aircraft had landed, and not long after they would attempt an attack.

'Landing in the desert was the only option if they had to put down. This would keep them away from the enemy, but the dangers of landing in the Afghan desert are well known to all pilots. The lack of references and the darkness make it difficult to see, even with night vision goggles, and then there was the talcum powder dust that would envelop the aircraft in the final thirty feet, hiding obstacles and the undulating ground below. Get the landing wrong and you would be doing the enemy's job for them.'

The third option open to the Lynx aircrew was to try to nurse the aircraft back to Camp Bastion. All British helicopter pilots train on simulators and during exercises for such an eventuality. The pilot put the Lynx into a shallow descent while at the same time trying to get away from the Green Zone. The door gunner sorted out the aircraft's hold, gathering up the aircrew's grab bags and water supplies in case they had to put down and escape and evade. He checked the door gun, preparing to disconnect it from its mount, and gathered up the boxes of ammo.

Finally the Lynx pilot radioed through that he had made the decision to try for Bastion. The flight *Ugly* aircrews were on the flight line, strapped in and with the engines spooling, ready to launch and support the Lynx at a moment's notice. They might be called upon to provide top cover, being the eyes and ears searching for the enemy. Or in the worst-case scenario they might have to go in to extract the aircrew and shoot up the Lynx to deny it to the enemy.

As the four airmen sat there on the flight line memories of the Jugroom Fort incident were running through their minds, as were the procedures to lift a downed aircrew out of danger that they had practised during Kush Dragon. Baz, Tim, Alex and Colin were glued to their radios as they listened in to the Lynx pilot nursing his aircraft across the darkened Afghan airspace.

After a horribly tense twenty minutes they finally spotted the Lynx limping over the security wall and putting down on the safety of the runway. The men of flight *Ugly* powered down their engines. As they did so Baz reminded the others to include on their CVs the fact that they could rouse themselves instantly from a deep sleep and be fully dressed, should they ever want to leave the Corps and join the fire brigade.

The flight *Ugly* airmen met up with the Lynx aircrew in the ops tent. The banter began immediately.

'Hey, *Billy Bunter* Flight, transmission problems my arse! More like you couldn't stay up due to the extra doughnut you ate for tea.'

'Yeah, whatever, dickheads. The reason we flew home is that we'd rather chance crashing than be extracted by you lot.'

The Lynx had made it back to base unharmed, which only served to strengthen the Apache aircrew's conviction that the real action was over. In fact, nothing could be further from the truth. Some twenty-four hours later the four airmen would find themselves on the receiving end of a murderous barrage of ground fire and in danger of being shot down.

15

OPERATION WASIR

Day 49

In theory, Operation Wasir was to have little to do with the British forces. It was an American mission in territory dominated by joint US–Afghan National Army operations. It involved a push by a ground convoy into an area to the far north-west of the Helmand River valley – the remote and rugged Bagrahn region.

Bagrahn was seen as being a backstop to the Taliban's hold on Musa Qaleh, the last significant town in Helmand still under enemy control. The aim of Op Wasir was to push into the rugged mountains that run all the way into neighbouring Oruzgan Province, denying territory to enemy forces and flushing out any high-value targets that had their bases there.

Flight *Ugly* were back on VHR duty and the call to scramble came very early in the morning. The mission was briefed as being a troops in contact (TIC) taking place to the far north-west of Helmand, in territory dominated by US operations. American and Afghan forces were taking accurate and sustained fire from the southern side of Wasir town. Their convoy had been crossing a large wadi – a seasonal riverbed – when it was ambushed. Flight *Ugly* were to escort in a Chinook to casevac American and Afghan wounded.

The Bagrahn region was way out of the normal territory of 662 Squadron. After a long haul north from Bastion flight *Ugly* arrived over the battlefield, only to discover that it was all but impossible to communicate with the US forces on the ground. They could see two distinct groups of US vehicles, mainly Humvees and light armoured personnel carriers, pinned down on the northern edge of the wadi. But when they tried to make radio contact with the *Widow* all the pilots could hear over the airwaves was deafening static. They were suffering some kind of radio malfunction that made communications all but impossible, both with the ground forces and each other.

'The instant we arrived we had major problems communicating with the Yanks,' Baz remarks. 'Whatever the problem with the radios was, it was like World War Three had broken out inside our helmets. It was so bad that we had to shout to each other in the cockpit to make ourselves heard. We resorted to using the mirror in the front cockpit, performing hand signals and using facial expression to communicate with each other.'

Every Apache has a mirror set in the top left hand corner of the front-seater's cockpit, which is just like a rear-view mirror in a car. It is put there for the very reasons that Baz and Tim were using it now – in case comms breaks down between the two pilots. Via the mirror Tim could signal to Baz and vice versa.

By yelling into their helmet mikes the aircrew of *Ugly Five Zero* finally managed to contact the Joint Terminal Attack Controller (JTAC) with the US convoy. Even over the noise they could hear the crack and thump of gunfire as the American soldiers returned fire with their .50-calibre heavy machines guns, Minimi SAW light machine guns and M–16 assault rifles.

The American JTAC, call-sign *Mayhem Six Six*, gave a hurried update on the convoy's situation: they were taking heavy fire from an area just to the south of Wasir town. The convoy had been split and there was about a kilometre separating the front and rear elements. The main body of enemy fire was coming from positions some four hundred metres to their front.

All of a sudden, as the aircrew were trying to get an accurate fix on the targets, an F-15 dropped from the sky between the two orbiting Apaches. It unleashed a five hundred-pound bomb directly below them, the shock waves of the blast rocketing around the aircraft. A narrowly avoided midair collision with an F-15 was bad enough. The follow up shockwaves of the bombstrike an instant later were doubly worrying, especially as there had been not a word of warning from *Mayhem Six Six*, or the F-15 pilot.

'That was one close call,' remarks Baz. 'There was a hell of a lot of swearing in the cockpit as we made best speed and departed to what we considered was a safe distance to the south. Tim was really annoyed: he got on the radio asking what the hell was going on, and whether or not *Mayhem Six Six* was indeed a qualified JTAC. "Sir, I'm just trying to do the best I damn well can," was the stressed reply he got from *Mayhem Six Six*.

'As *Mayhem Six Six* spoke we got an indication of the pressure he was under. We heard the bullets whizzing past his headset and the responding thud of his heavy weapons in response. The American convoy was under very heavy small-arms fire and was having extreme difficulty in locating the enemy's firing points. *Mayhem Six Six* was clearly crapping himself, his comms peppered with "goddamn this" and "goddamn that"!'

It was hardly surprising that the American JTAC was worried. From the bird's-eye view of the Apaches the intensity of the fire-fight was clear. Lines of fiery tracer could be seen burning their way across the wadi as enemy forces in good cover pounded the US convoy. The enemy had sited their ambush well, with US forces exposed on the rocky high ground to the north side of the dry riverbed. The American soldiers were responding with a wall of fire from their Humvee-mounted .50-calibre heavy machine guns.

Yet it didn't appear to be having much of an effect: enemy forces just kept on putting down a barrage of accurate fire in return. Without some significant airstrikes to quieten the enemy the US forces were in real trouble. Already, there was one Afghan National Army soldier killed and half a dozen wounded American troops down there. There was an urgent need to get the Chinook in on its casevac mission.

'At about this time we finally got contact from the F-15 pilot,' remarks Baz. 'He informed us that he was setting up for a strafing run of 20mm cannon fire on the southern part of the village. Tim ordered him to stop and explained that the action was unnecessary:

we were in a better position to observe and deliver point weapons on any enemy positions. The F–15 broke off and headed back to Bagram. At least we all felt a little safer that way.'

The pair of Apaches set up in wheel formation above the battlefield and proceeded to identify targets. *Mayhem Six Six* pointed out a greenhouse-like building at the southern edge of the village as the anchor for all subsequent talk-ons. It looked like the sort of thing one might buy from a garden centre, but at least it was a distinctive marker. *Mayhem Six Six* talked the Apaches on to enemy forces situated in a small mud-walled compound to the east of the greenhouse and cleared the aircraft to open fire.

The compound was surrounded by dense woodland and flight *Ugly* decided to saturate the area with 30mm cannon fire. Both aircraft opened up, pumping in repeated twenty-round bursts that exploded among the mud walls and the tree line. But the high-explosive rounds appeared to have little effect. The enemy kept putting down a fierce barrage of fire, only now it was aimed at the pair of attack helicopters orbiting above.

As lines of tracer arced skywards, sparking around the two aircraft, they pulled back and prepared for a different line of attack.

'The surprising thing for us was that the enemy had not been put off by our presence,' Baz remarks. 'We guessed this was probably due to the fact that they had not seen British Apaches in action before . . . We established with the JTAC that all his troops were positioned along the northern rim of the wadi . . . We would have to set up and use the flechette rockets as that was the only way in which we could be sure of saturating the area and giving us some chance of hitting a well-concealed enemy. It was crucial that we got the Chinook in to pick up the casualties and the dead ANA soldier.'

With the aircraft running out to some seven kilometres from target, Tim issued a quick battle order to Alex, the gunner of *Ugly Five One*.

'Rockets; shooter, shooter; my lead, fire at two km; me break left you break right, target greenhouse.'

This meant that the aircraft would fly in tandem to a position

Skull and crossbones: Chinthe Lines is the Apache and Chinook helicopter landing strip at Camp Bastion. The Chinthe is a mythical creature, half lion, half griffin, from which the First Air Commandos of the Burma Campaign – one of the forebears of the Army Air Corps – took their name.

Vae Viso – woe to he who is seen. A mural on a blast wall at the Apache flight line, listing those who served with 664 Squadron, Army Air Corps, the Apache squadron that preceded 662 Squadron's deployment.

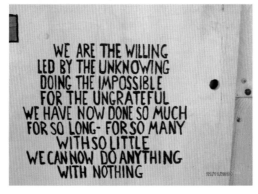

Toilet humour: graffiti on the inside of one of the Camp Bastion lavatories, at the Apache end of the base.

A 662 Squadron Apache
returning from a mission as the
sun sets over Camp Bastion.

British Apache on an escort
mission over Helmand,
photographed from a Chinook
door-gunner's position.

A lone Apache at sunset,
Camp Bastion.

Brown-out: a Chinook prepares for a difficult landing at its Camp Bastion base, the twin rotors kicking up a fierce dust storm.

Combat medics. They regularly braved enemy fire to casevac the wounded in Chinooks, with the 662 Squadron Apaches providing an armed escort.

A Chinook with under-slung ammunition and equipment flies in to re-supply troops in Op Kulang, during which both Chinooks and Apache escorts were targeted by surface-to-air missiles.

The four aircrew of flight *Ugly*. Left to right: Captain Baz Hunter, Captain Alex Wagner, Captain Tim Porter and WO1 Steve James. Each carries a shortened SA80 carbine.

Decoy flares over Helmand. Such was the intensity of combat during summer 2007 that Apaches went 'Winchester' – all ammunition expended. Firing flares was the last resort to keep the enemy's heads down.

Mission accomplished: an Apache of 662 Squadron lands at the Camp Bastion helicopter landing strip after completing a successful sortie.

View from an Apache cockpit of the Green Zone, the vegetated area that follows the course of the Helmand River. The Green Zone is bordered by harsh deserts and mountains, and is home to the province's civilian inhabitants, as well as the enemy.

Soldiers from the 2nd Battalion, The Mercian Regiment (Worcesters and Foresters) advance into Rahim Kalay, passing the wreckage of the white estate car that was Hellfired by Apache *Ugly Five Zero*. To the right of the picture is the enemy fortress positioned on the high ground.

Labyrinth: the enemy position at Rahim Kalay, showing the man-sized entrances to the network of tunnels and caves that ran beneath the stronghold.

Opium den: hidden enemy sniper positions were dotted around the main stronghold at Rahim Kalay. The roof is camouflaged by dried poppy stalks, and in the background British soliders patrol through poppy fields.

All that remains: ruins of the enemy stronghold at Rahim Kalay after being hit by the flight *Ugly* Apaches and a US Air Force F-15, call-sign *Dude*.

The wreck of the white Toyota estate car beside the canal at Rahim Kalay after the Hellfire strike. The car was a massive vehicle-borne improvised explosive device – or, in layman's terms, a car bomb.

Super bug: a dusty, battle-worn Apache on the flight line at Camp Bastion. The red blanks are to keep sand and dirt out of the exhaust ports.

Working under harsh conditions to keep the aircraft airborne, fitters from the Royal Electrical and Mechanical Engineers (REME) carry out essential Apache maintenance.

Ground crew reloading the 30mm cannon. It takes real precision to ensure the feeder mechanism keeps running smoothly and the gun doesn't jam.

We will remember them. The flight *Ugly* aircrew at the Camp Bastion memorial to those who gave their lives while serving in Afghanistan.

Rahim Kalay photographs on pages 13 and 14 courtesy of Paul Grahame. All other photographs courtesy of Army Air Corps pilots and ground crew.

two kilometres out from target, whereupon they would fire flechette rockets on *Ugly Five Zero's* lead then break in opposite directions having done so. As the aircraft turned towards Wasir town and began their run in, all four airmen knew that they would be flying down the enemy's gun barrels on this attack. For Baz and Tim this would be their first time firing flechette rockets in anger, which upped the tension in their cockpit still further.

'If the speed or direction of flight of the dart was just a degree or so out you could easily send the flechettes off target and towards friendly troops,' remarks Baz. 'At this time we were also unsure of what the exact spread of the cone of darts was.'

Barely four hundred metres separated friendly forces from the enemy and the aircrew were using a weapon that would shred and kill anything inside an area the size of a football field. Get it slightly wrong and the flechettes would fall short, killing a lot of American troops.

At five kilometres out both aircrews selected the CO-OP method of firing, which meant that the front-seater held his sight and laser on target while the rear-seater placed the aircraft in a shallow dive, flying directly on to the enemy. As usual, Baz found himself faced with several different tasks all at once: he was flying the aircraft, keeping a lookout for the enemy tracer fire and keeping a check on the other Apache's position while trying to line up the rocket steering cursor using the tiny screen in front of his right eye. It was quite a set of skills to master.

'Running in I was trying to remember all the tips that I had been given in the simulator by Dave and Ben, the weapons officers,' Baz remarks. 'However, this was not the simulator and things were very different . . . The slightest gust of wind, the slightest movement of the sight as Tim tried to keep it on target and that would affect the steering cursor, making my task even harder. And then there was the constant noise in the headsets, which was causing major problems for us in the cockpit.'

As they neared the two-kilometre firing point Baz realised that he was in trouble. He couldn't hold close enough to the course to guarantee a strike on target and *Ugly Five Zero* was forced to abort.

As he pushed his aircraft into a tight left-hand turn he noticed the dirty brown billow of smoke from *Ugly Five One*'s stub wings. Alex and Colin had fired.

'I couldn't get it right and had to abort,' Baz remarks. 'This is dangerous, as the enemy would be expecting a similar attack profile the second time around and would be better prepared to fire back at us. The training in the simulator and even the aircraft predeployment on exercises was not realistic enough to prepare us for the type of battle situation we now found ourselves in. Then we weren't flying through a wall of enemy fire and we didn't have the screaming battle noise, which was almost making the task undoable.'

Ugly Five One had unleashed a salvo of four. Seconds after firing the casings of the 2.7-inch rockets disintegrated, a charge blasting out 320 flechette darts that hammered into the southern end of Wasir town. As Baz brought *Ugly Five Zero* around for a second launch attempt the level of fire coming up at them had lessened noticeably. *Ugly Five One*'s strike had been right on target, and already the enemy resistance was weakened.

On this attack run Tim slaved the rocket sights to the coordinates of the target, making that one less thing for the aircrew to deal with. Four rockets were fired and as *Ugly Five Zero* peeled away Baz watched the arrow-sharp projectiles screaming towards target. He felt confident that they'd been bang on aim. As the flechettes hit the rate of enemy fire fell away to nothing, confirming that they had found their mark.

Ugly Five One radioed the Chinook, clearing it in to do the casevac mission. A site had been secured to the north of the wadi and the two Apaches hustled the big helicopter into the LZ. As it put down in a cloud of dust the rear ramp lowered to receive the wounded and the dead. The casualties were loaded in a matter of seconds and the two Apaches over-flew the aircraft as it made for the open desert. Once it was out of danger flight *Ugly* turned back to the battlefield.

A radio call from *Mayhem Six Six* confirmed that enemy forces around the area of the greenhouse had been silenced, the fire from that area dropping almost to zero. However, the US convoy was now being targeted from the north and it looked as if enemy fighters had outflanked them, so as to hit them from the rear.

As the Apaches moved in to investigate the aircrew received a call from Joint Helicopter Force (JHF) command in Kandahar. Flight *Ugly* was to break contact and return to base as their casevac escort mission was now complete.

In response, the aircrew sent an urgent update regarding the battle, pointing out that *Mahem Six Six* was desperate for their assistance. After receiving that tactical update and realising the seriousness of the situation on the ground, the commander at Kandahar approved *Ugly Five Zero* and *Ugly Five One* to stay in the air over the battlefield until other air assets arrived.

At the Camp Bastion Ops Room 662 Squadron's key command and control personnel were already fending off queries from above in order to cover the flight as they remained on station. The next few minutes over target would prove to be time well spent.

The two Apaches moved further north, hunting for the enemy force that had infiltrated into the wooded high ground behind the US convoy. As they did so, Baz felt his heart miss a beat. He'd spotted the distinctive dirty white smoke plume of an RPG being fired from out of the woods below them. As it streaked upwards towards his aircraft he threw the Apache into a series of violent evasive manoeuvres, while screaming out a warning at Tim.

'RPG – ten o'clock! RPG – ten o'clock!'

'I can't hear you! I can't hear!' Tim was mouthing a reply.

Baz pulled full power to get them out of the RPG's kill zone. With his left hand heaving on the collective lever, his right playing the cyclic, and both feet dancing on the foot pedals, he threw the aircraft into a searing turn, the horizon going vertical as he headed away from the trajectory of the RPG's 2.5-kilo warhead.

The greatest strength of the RPG is its crude simplicity. He'd seen the RPG firing and the lazy smoke-trail groping its way towards them; he knew that a grenade set on airburst was heading right for them.

To his rear left and above Baz saw the blinding flash of the RPG exploding, followed an instant later by a rapidly expanding blast wave tearing outwards, shards of shrapnel spinning off fiery trails behind them. The shockwave slammed into the speeding aircraft and in the Apache's wake there was left a smear of black on the bright blue of the Afghan sky – the signature of the exploding RPG warhead.

As Baz righted the aircraft a second and a third RPG fired from what had to be a battery of RPG gunners down in the tree line. As the rounds barrelled skywards he realised they were heading for his wing aircraft, *Ugly Five One*. Baz fixed the RPG gunner's position with his right eye and screamed to Tim that he was slaving the 30mm cannon to his eye line. Catching the sense of what he meant, if not the words, Tim gave a thumbs-up.

An instant later Baz flicked up the guard and jerked the trigger on his left pistol grip control column. From its chin turret *Ugly Five Zero*'s cannon spat out a long burst of white fire. The howling interference on the comms system drowned out the chuntering of the cannon below them as it churned out a twenty-round burst. Seconds later the 30mm cannon fire tore into the wood line, trees splintering and braches being blasted apart.

Ugly Five Zero's cannon fired again and again. As the high-explosive shells found their target a series of secondary explosions rippled through the darkened foliage, dozens of RPG rounds exploding in a sea of fire.

It was a mighty fine thing to see, Baz found himself thinking, before turning to check if *Ugly Five One* had escaped the RPG strikes unscathed:

'By now Alex and Colin were also in the thick of the action, firing cannon rounds at enemy firing points. But the racket caused by the radio malfunction was so bad it had completely fatigued us and it made the task before us extremely difficult.'

The flight went into search and destroy mode: this was the full-on kill-or-be-killed of combat. It seemed as if the enemy were getting a sense of what they were up against with the pair of British Apaches. The four aircrew combed the woodlands below them for targets but no more enemy fighters could be seen. For now, at least, they had gone to ground.

A white pickup was spotted in a compound to the north of the tree line. Was this the vehicle the enemy RPG gunners had used to get into the wooded high ground? To one side of the parked vehicle was a dense slough of tangled trees. Lying abandoned beside it were a series of telltale Taliban blankets – those that they would have used to cover their weapons as they moved about the battlefield. *Ugly Five Zero* and *Ugly Five One* turned on that wood line and pounded it with repeated bursts of 30mm cannon fire.

As the savage onslaught tore apart the position *Ugly Five Zero* received a call from *Mayhem Six Six*: the attack to the convoy's rear was dying down to nothing. As far as he could tell, the enemy force had been defeated. The two Apaches went into orbit above the American convoy, waiting to see if any further threat should emerge. As they did so there was a call from the Bastion Ops Room requesting a briefing on the battle. *Geek Flight* were being stood up to replace flight *Ugly* over the battered US convoy.

Flight *Ugly* were approaching bingo fuel and would soon have to pull out of the battle. Then a suspicious movement caught their eye. In the distance a motorbike could be seen approaching the US convoy's position, two-up with both riders males of fighting age. The enemy commonly used motorbikes for communications, command and control, and even to get reinforcements into battle quickly.

Ugly Five Zero homed in on the motorcycle, shadowing its movements, but it quickly did an about-turn and moved away to the north-east at speed, heading in the opposite direction from the battle.

'We followed their journey very closely but felt they must have been aware of us,' remarks Baz. 'After looking around for a while they simply moved out of town and into the open desert – which was a good move on their part!'

As flight *Ugly* bade farewell to *Mayhem Six Six* the American soldier's gratitude was clear for all to hear, as was the comparative calm that had descended over the US positions. No longer was the whine of incoming rounds or the thump of machine gun fire audible above the radio chatter.

The aircrew left the battlefield with *Mayhem Six Six*'s words of thanks ringing in their ears. Each aircraft had fired off eight flechette-armed rockets, so 1280 darts in all. Plus each had used up two hundred rounds of their three hundred-round 30mm magazines. It wasn't quite a Rahim Kalay, but it was the heaviest contact the men had been in outside of that epic battle.

During the long flight back to Bastion Op Wasir was handed over to US fast air and *Geek Flight* were stood down. For now, at least, the battle was pretty much over. On landing, the four airmen dismounted on to the flight line and proceeded to do their post-mission handshake. While Colin Norton did manage to take the proffered hands his bemused expression said it all: what the hell are we doing this for?

'We did the traditional flight thing and shook hands,' Baz remarks. 'I think Colin thought this a strange thing to do and mentioned it to some of the others in the squadron. The reason we always did this was to quietly say to each other, well done guys, good job. But, more importantly – glad we all made it back alive. Other flights may have thought we were celebrating what we had done . . . How wrong they were.'

On turning away from their aircraft the aircrew noticed that the groundies were all wearing smart new T-shirts. They must have got them printed up and sent out from home.

Over a cartoon of an Apache were the words ALWAYS OUTNUM-BERED, NEVER OUTGUNNED.

16
OPERATION TUFAAN

Days 59–70

Some two weeks later things were pretty much back to normal for flight *Ugly*. Colin Norton had returned to his regular place on the OC's flight and old Panda Eyes, Steve, was back in the hot seat in *Ugly Five One*. With his unconventional ways, Colin had made a good contribution to the dynamic of the flight. But it was good to have the *Ugly* fellowship back together again.

Steve wouldn't hear whether he'd got his officer's commission for several months, but that didn't stop Baz, Tim and Alex ripping the piss. At every opportunity it was Sir this and Sir that. Steve was sad to have missed out on Op Wasir. He was glad to be back with his flight and on VHR duty, and to be tasked with a series of Chinook escort missions in to the southern enemy stronghold of Garmsir.

Garmsir was the Taliban's proving ground, and it constituted the most fiercely fought-over terrain in all Helmand. Its cratered, pockmarked surface resembled a First World War battlefield, and only enemy fighters were to be found there. The Taliban were hell-bent on keeping control of this territory, especially after their recent losses. Defeats in and around Sangin town; in the Upper Sangin Valley and around Kajaki; in the Upper and Lower Gereshk Valleys; and particularly Rahim Kalay had hit them hard.

The Chinooks were on resupply and casevac missions, and each flight was an excuse for the enemy to attack.

'On each trip into Garmsir we were in the thick of it,' remarks

Baz. 'All the time we were putting down fire to support the Chinooks and taking fire in return. It was a daily series of fire-fights – Garmsir being the testing ground for the enemy's new combatants. They'd open up with everything they had as the Chinooks went in, and our job was to keep their heads down.'

The aircrews of 662 Squadron were on their sixtieth day of continuous operations by now and exhaustion was beginning to take hold – though none of the pilots liked to admit it. Falling asleep or losing control while flying and fighting an Apache was far more dangerous than dropping off at the wheel of the car back home in the UK. One moment's slipped concentration could be fatal, with the risk of a mid-air collision, falling out of the sky or killing friendly forces or innocent civilians only ever a heartbeat away.

'On one of those night ops down at Garmsir there was tracer going everywhere, but for some reason I couldn't see a thing,' remarks Baz. 'It was like I was blind. I was screaming at Tim and he was screaming back at me. All of a sudden I realised that I had my daytime visor down and that's why I couldn't see. As soon as I slipped the visor up I could see the tracer kicking off everywhere . . . I knew then that I was getting tired.'

The Apache pilot's daytime visor is heavily tinted to cope with the harsh sunlight at altitude.

It was during these Garmsir missions that Baz reached a major milestone in his career: he completed his 4000th flying hour. Most pilots pass out of the military with 2000 to 2500 hours, so this was a massive amount of flying by anyone's reckoning. In normal circumstances every pilot receives a bottle of champagne for each 1000 hours completed and there would be a celebratory piss-up.

But there was no alcohol to be had in Bastion and they couldn't exactly pop down to the local boozer. Instead, Baz was grabbed by his three fellow airmen and roped to a chair. They proceeded to chuck water over the veteran airman, sand and flour him and generally torture him – just to show that the achievement hadn't gone unnoticed by his buddies. And to cap it all they tried to force-feed him several British Army sausage rolls.

*

Each successive call-out was becoming slightly more irksome than the last, largely due to the fatigue. It was the intense heat of the summer and the Chinooks were increasingly being called out to do casevacs for the Brigade Recce Force (BRF). The BRF were operating in the high mountains towards the Pakistani border, seeking to cut off enemy supply lines. But at remote altitude and lacking in water, the elite soldiers kept going down with heat exhaustion. The higher the altitude the more difficult the flying conditions for the Chinooks and their Apache escorts, and the more demanding each of these casevac missions would prove.

In mid July British forces launched a premeditated operation: an air assault on a small town to the east of Garmsir. British vehicles kept getting hit by makeshift roadside bombs that were killing British soldiers. The air assault was to hit the location where intelligence indicated a bomb-making factory was situated. The assault force was briefed and prepped in Sangin, then flown out in Chinooks in a pre-dawn raid so that enemy forces would have no forewarning of the attack. The role of the Apaches was to provide top cover as the troop-carrying helicopters went in.

The raid was a resounding success, uncovering a veritable bomb-making production line: this was where the improvised explosive devices (IEDs) were being assembled. An enemy fighter was captured red-handed, setting off on his motorbike on a mine-laying expedition. Incredibly, he had his five-year-old son riding pillion as cover for what he was really up to. If that motorcycle had been spotted from an Apache no pilot would ever have suspected the rider of being an enemy fighter on a mine-laying mission.

The problem facing the British ground forces that had captured the father and son team was this: what were they to do with the mine-layer's son? At five years old they could hardly arrest him or hold him as a prisoner of war. The only solution was to send him home to his mother, but presumably she had to be in on the act as well. It made the mind boggle.

This one event typified the type of dilemmas that the Apache pilots – and wider British forces – faced on a daily basis in Afghanistan. In a situation such as the father and son team the Apache pilots would be damned if they did and damned if they didn't. If they did shoot they would have killed an innocent child and would have faced prosecution as a result. If they didn't shoot they would have allowed more British soldiers to get hit by IEDs. With their every action recorded on the aircraft's gun tape there would be no escaping a legal case if an Apache pilot did mess up in any way.

The capture of the father and son team signified something wider to the men of flight *Ugly*. It defined the mindset of the enemy, symbolising the lengths to which they would go in order to kill British troops. What British soldier, or member of the wider ISAF coalition, would have deliberately taken his five-year-old son into battle in order to disguise what he was up to, when by so doing he was clearly putting that child's life in harm's way?

What lay behind it? Was it blind fanaticism? Was it a form of cowardice? Was it the ultimate in guile? Or was it simply an indication of how even small children were being dragged into the jihad? Either way, it was disheartening and extremely difficult to defend against or to deter. A new generation of jihadists were being bred and trained and conditioned for battle even as the war was being fought in Afghanistan.

Three days after the incident of the mine-layer's son a real buzz of excitement went around the Apache base at Chinthe Lines. After days on end of scrappy missions there was at last something major for the aircrews to get their teeth into – Operation Leg Tufaan. Op Tufaan was a follow-up to the battle for Rahim Kalay, in which British ground forces planned to launch a major push into the Upper Gereshk Valley, and would last for three days.

The men of flight *Ugly* reckoned that Op Tufaan should, by rights, be their mission as it had all been started by the Rahim Kalay battle. The aircrew of the other flights disagreed. As far as they were concerned, Baz, Tim, Steve and Alex had had more than their fair share of the action, what with their recent engagement during Op Wasir and their epic action over Rahim Kalay.

As bad luck would have it, flight *Ugly* were on Duty Ops during Op Tufaan and they were forced to sit out the entire mission. At one stage the four airmen were stood-to to fly, but fast jets took over and they were stood down. Op Tufaan was spearheaded by 662

Squadron's *Super Six* flight, with the OC, Jules Franks, getting into the heat of battle. Some ninety-five enemy fighters would be killed during Op Tufaan, with hundreds more injured and put out of action.

Sitting watching the Apaches of *Super Six* flight bombing up and refuelling on the flight line was hugely frustrating for the four aircrew of flight *Ugly*. They consoled themselves with the thought that Op Tufaan was a very different type of engagement from the Rahim Kalay battle. The action during Op Tufaan was spread out over several days, with scores of aircraft involved. The air battle wasn't in any sense dominated by the Apaches, as Rahim Kalay's had been. In short, the flight still believed that they had fought the Squadron's fiercest battle to date on Rahim Kalay Day.

'The other flights had a busy period; we didn't,' remarks Baz. 'We were on Duty Ops and it was a real low point as we were getting no action . . . Op Tufaan was huge, and the attrition rate of the enemy was massive, so much so that they started to doubt the integrity of their own commanders. Of those ninety-odd enemy fighters killed, eighty or more were foreign – Pakistanis, Arabs and Chechens. The kill rate of the enemy was thirty on day one, forty the next day; fifteen were killed by an Apache just in the one shot alone.'

That 'one shot alone' had been pulled off by Colin Norton, just recently returned to *Super Six* flight after his stint with flight *Ugly*. Scores of enemy fighters had tried to escape the vice of Op Tufaan by mingling with the civilian population and moving east across the Helmand River valley towards safety. But in order to do so they had to cross the Helmand River. Colin had been returning from a mission escorting a Chinook back into Bastion when they'd received a call from ground troops.

'Apache, Apache, this is *Widow Six One*. Do you have any weapons on board and are you able to engage?'

Colin's aircraft was fully bombed up as there had been no action so far during the flight. The *Widow* alerted Colin, plus his front-seater Jules Franks, to some fifteen to twenty enemy fighters who had just crossed the Helmand River and were heading for the safety of the foothills. GPS coordinates for the unit of enemy fighters were passed up to the aircraft and fed into the flight computer. The nose pod slaved to the target immediately, the video camera picking up an image of a group of men moving away from the exposed banks of the river and into the shadows of a cliff face.

Colin's aircraft was moving fast up the Helmand River, some three kilometres out from the target. As the OC, Jules Franks, went to engage with 30mm cannon fire the auto-targeting system failed. Luckily Colin had just glanced out of the cockpit to his right front and spotted movement. He could just make out the figures against the cliff.

Confirming with the OC that he had the target visual, Colin actioned the gun and slaved it to his HMD, placed the crosshair sight directly on the target, set the range to 1200 metres and opened fire with a ten-round burst. It fell a hundred metres short of target, exploding in gouts of white water on the far side of the river.

Moving his right eye a hundred metres beyond the target to adjust the aim he fired again, this time selecting a twenty-round burst. The rounds hit dead on, tearing into the rock and exploding in a sheet of orange flame. It was around dusk and the darkness under the cliff face was lit a ghostly red. Colin continued to pound the enemy position with twenty-round bursts. By the time he had finished firing he'd loosed off 120 30mm rounds, transforming the cliff face into a wall of fire.

The engagement had taken no more than thirty seconds. By now Colin's aircraft was five hundred metres from the enemy position. As it passed overhead both pilots could see the total devastation that lay below them. It left little to the imagination. Colin had proven that when the auto-targeting systems of the Apache failed, manual shooting via the helmet-mounted display could be effective and deadly.

Later a Predator UAV would fly over the target coordinates and the images recorded by the aircraft would show a blasted landscape littered with body parts.

'No doubt about it, Colin's was the shot of the campaign,' remarks Baz. 'HMD shooting is like throwing a brick and seeing where it lands. It was a shot from approaching two kilometres away and he did it with split-second, instinctive timing. The enemy wouldn't even have known where the shots were coming from, or who was shooting at them.'

Colin Norton's ace shot had been but one in a series of punishing hits delivered to the enemy during Op Tufaan. What had really turned the tables on enemy forces in the Upper Gereshk Valley had been the probing patrols by ground troops. These had provoked enemy forces into battle. Rather than melting away in the face of a superior force and living to fight another day, the enemy had chosen to stand and fight and to give no quarter. Many had died trying.

In the aftermath of Op Tufaan British intelligence reports picked up on an air of paranoia among the enemy as so many of their fighters, and their top commanders, had been killed.

'It felt as if the enemy were on the run, almost,' remarks Baz. 'They were getting out of the area at night and running like hell to Musa Qaleh, their last stronghold. The Danish MOGs were out in the hills, as were the Brigade Recce Force, trying to cut them off wherever possible. They had been hammered by fast air, Apaches, infantry and everything. After first being hit in Rahim Kalay, and now Op Tufaan, in a sense it was a rout.'

In briefings the flight *Ugly* airmen learned that enemy forces were now feeling shocked and threatened. There was a noticeable absence of enemy fighters in the Gereshk and the Upper Gereshk Valley. Their forces were retreating in small groups, heading for the comparative safety of the mountainous areas to the east of the Helmand River. Groups of enemy were trapped in those mountains, and running low on food and ammunition, while some were attempting to filter into the town of Haydarabad.

That last location, Haydarabad, was now the focus of British attention in the Upper Gereshk Valley. After Rahim Kalay and Op Tufaan enemy forces had retreated to their last stronghold – Haydarabad. If they could be defeated there the rout of the enemy in the Upper Gereshk Valley would be complete. The Helmand River Valley would then be clear of enemy safe havens for 90 per cent of its length. Only Musa Qaleh in the far north, and some bases in the extreme south around Garmsir, would remain.

All British intelligence indicators suggested that the enemy were reeling from their defeats and that Haydarabad was ripe for the picking. Wasting no time, British forces put in place plans for

Operation Chakush – the Pashtun word for hammer. Op Chakush would be a massive ground and airborne offensive designed to drive all enemy forces out of Haydarabad.

In preparation for Op Chakush a scale model of the Helmand River valley was put together in one of the hangars at the Apache end of Camp Bastion. With that model serving as a visual aid, rehearsal orders confirmation (ROC) briefings were held with the Apache and Chinook pilots, together with the Royal Anglians and the Worcesters and Foresters, the main troops spearheading Op Chakush on the ground.

A ground convoy would drive up overnight to start lines in the desert to the east of Haydarabad. In a dawn airborne assault Chinooks would drop troops on to the bridges that led across a network of canals and into the town itself. Once these were secure the ground convoy would push east into Haydarabad, clearing the town street by street. A series of cut-off groups would be dropped in positions to the west of Haydarabad so that retreating enemy forces would run into their guns.

Op Chakush was scheduled to last for three hours from the moment that the first bridges were secured. Once the town was clear the objective would have been reached.

Unfortunately, and as with Op Tufaan, flight *Ugly* were scheduled to be on Duty Ops on the day of Op Chakush. As the plans stood, the four airmen would be lucky to get the odd escort duty taking in a Chinook on a resupply job or a casevac. They were convinced that they were destined to sit out this battle too. Rahim Kalay had been their Big One and the war was pretty much over for them.

'*Geek Flight* was leading on Op Chakush, with us left in a covering role,' Baz remarks. 'We really thought we were going to get forgotten again and we were really depressed at this stage. I felt certain we were complete for the whole tour, and that Rahim Kalay would remain our big engagement.'

How wrong the events of the next two days would prove the *Ugly* airmen to be.

17

OPERATION CHAKUSH

Days 69–70

Op Chakush was an early start for all four flights of 662 Squadron, Army Air Corps. At 0200 hours the sixteen pilots (fifteen men and one woman) roused themselves from their beds and headed for the flight line. Eight aircraft squatted on the tarmac awaiting their next mission. In the harsh light cast by the Camp Bastion flood-lights their dark, ghostly forms conveyed a barely suppressed animal lethality.

Turbines wailed and rotors started to turn, slowly at first but with increasing speed. Two by two the aircraft taxiied to the refu-elling area, and with fuel lines attached they drank greedily, taking on the maximum avtur (aviation turbine fuel) that each could carry. Small shadows flitted among the darkened forms as the groundies tended the aircraft's every need. In the glare of the floodlights their blue-grey exhaust showed as a white cloud enveloping all, like the breath of a pack of hunters preparing to stalk their prey.

By this stage – day sixty-nine of 662 Squadron's deployment – the elite Apache aviators were so fatigued and ops so stressed that crews were being shaped around mission requirements rather than any duty roster. While officially on the dog days of Duty Ops, flight *Ugly* had been roped into Op Chakush. As *Geek Flight* got to spearhead the combat assault over Haydarabad, they had been tasked with shepherding in a Chinook carrying troops in to an LZ.

'We thought ours would be a bone escort duty,' remarks Baz. 'We flew up in complete darkness and as we approached the battle area we could already see a massive firefight underway. It was like a proper full-on war movie was playing out below us as the artillery barrage went in prior to the assault. And we could see massive return fire coming from the enemy positions as they woke up to the attack.'

The pair of Apaches shepherded the lone Chinook into its destination. *Ugly Five Zero* took up orbit over the LZ while *Ugly Five One* shadowed the twin-rotor aircraft in to land. The big helicopter descended in a cloud of dust, sinking into the gloom of the darkened terrain. All of a sudden there was a burst of fire on the ridgeline above and the fiery-white trail of an RPG sliced the darkness. The enemy had been lying in wait for the assault force, and as was so often the case they seemed to have forewarning of the attack.

The Chinook was now almost completely lost in the blindness of a rotor-blown dust storm and it had little room for manoeuvre. As the aircrew of *Ugly Five One* yelled out a warning to the Chinook's aircrew a second and a third RPG fired.

'Break left! Break left! Incoming RPGs! Incoming RPGs!'

Up above the battlefield Baz threw *Ugly Five Zero* into a sharp right-hand turn. As he did so Tim fixed the enemy position with his pilot night vision sensor, transforming the darkness of the ridge into the unworldly luminous green glow of infrared daylight. The enemy were clustered along the contours of the ridge on the far side of the canal, in the cover of dense woodland.

The Chinook was down on the deck now, rear ramp lowering and already disgorging troops. More RPGs fired, the rounds burning through the darkness and bracketing the landing zone, the fiery blasts peppering the armoured underside of the Chinook with shrapnel. As the RPG operators had fired, so *Ugly Five Zero* had fixed their positions, locking the gun sight to the blinding white glow of the rockets igniting.

Ugly Five Zero's 30mm cannon spat a stab of angry fire, repeated twenty-round bursts raking the tree line, the explosions of the shells clearly visible in the woodland's velvety darkness. As *Ugly Five One* spun her cannon around to join in the attack the tree line was pounded into a mess of splintered branches and shattered trunks. The exploding 30mm rounds spewed fire and jagged steel into every living thing. For now, at least, the RPG gunners on the ridgeline had fallen silent.

The last of the soldiers piled off the Chinook into all-round defensive positions. Barely three minutes after it had landed the Chinook was airborne again and heading low and fast away from the LZ. It was now up to the ground troops to move forwards and secure the bridge in front of them. The main British attack convoy was lying out in the darkness to the east. On receiving the signal that the bridge was clear they would cross the canal and advance into Haydarabad, the enemy's last stronghold in the Upper Gereshk Valley.

With the Chinook safely out of harm's way, flight *Ugly* turned northwards and set a course for Camp Bastion. They would be back on the ground by 0700 hours, just in time for breakfast. By midday Op Chakush would be done and dusted, all having gone to plan, and that would be flight *Ugly*'s first and only action of the whole battle.

'We escorted the Chinook back to base and by eight o'clock we were having our second breakfast of the day,' remarks Baz. 'That's it, we thought: we're going home soon. That was our last action. As we ate that breakfast a depression set in . . . But the enemy dug in and fought to the last, and our troops hit real trouble.'

Three hours into Op Chakush and the town of Haydarabad should have been in British hands. But the assault was going more slowly than planned. In some cases the bridges across the canals had yet to be secured, preventing the ground convoy moving forward to join the attack. Each bridge across the dog-legged canal system was overlooked either by a compound or wooded high ground, and in these areas of cover the enemy had set their ambush positions.

The enemy appeared to have learned the lessons of Rahim Kalay and Op Tufaan, and had refined their tactics accordingly. They had mined the major approach routes to the town, they had booby-trapped buildings and they had sniper and mortar units targeting British troops before they could reach the cover of the built-up areas. In Haydarabad itself every building had been set up as a kill zone. As the enemy fell back from their positions they would lure the British troops into what was intended to be a death trap.

The enemy also had robust contingency plans in place: as their forces fell back they would filter into the high ground surrounding the town and move behind the British lines, coming in to strike from the rear. In doing so they would maximise the natural advantages that they had in their knowledge of the local terrain and their ability to move on foot in small units.

During the whole of that first day of Op Chakush, *Geek Flight* and *Greenpeace Flight* were seeing action, doing repeated combat runs into the battlefield. Meanwhile the men of flight *Ugly* were resigned to the fact that they were surplus to requirements. They tried their best to take it easy and to ignore the Apaches buzzing in and out of Camp Bastion.

That night, while on a Chinook resupply mission, *Greenpeace Flight* got into a massive firefight. Suddenly Baz, Tim, Steve and Alex were dragged out of their beds. Tim and Alex made for the Ops Room where they were briefed to do a relief in place – a live takeover from *Greenpeace Flight* in the thick of combat.

Out on the flight line Baz and Steve fired up the aircraft, waiting for their front-seaters to join them. As they did so they were wondering what the mission might be, as Op Chakush should have been over long ago.

'*Greenpeace Flight* was running low on fuel so we took off and pitched up over the battlefield,' remarks Steve. 'Amazingly our ground troops were still not across all of the bridges. So that vital first objective of the first hour of the assault had not yet been secured in the first twenty-four hours! Ground troops were stuck at this one bridge in particular and were being hit from several compounds on the far side. It was complete chaos, when we got there.'

In an effort to make sense out of that chaos, flight *Ugly* contacted the Widow Tactical Operations Centre, a clearing house for all ground troops requiring close air support. Where were their aircraft needed most?, the aircrew inquired. Troops were in contact in all areas, they were told. *All areas.* Eventually flight *Ugly* was split, each

Apache going to the assistance of a particular group in trouble and each being given a particular *Widow* call-sign with whom to liaise.

Ugly Five Zero was assigned to *Widow Six Eight*, whose troops were pinned down on the wrong side of the canal and were unable to secure the bridge in front of them. As the Apache set up in orbit over the epicentre of the battle a Toyota pickup was spotted pulling into the cover of some bushes on the far side of the waterway. It was in the vicinity of a blocky, mud-walled fortress that had the high ground and a commanding view of the battlefield. It was from here that enemy forces were hitting British ground troops.

The white Toyota had all the signs of being an enemy resupply vehicle. As Tim and Baz scanned the area Baz noticed a tree line leading from the car into the courtyard of the fortress. All of a sudden figures started emerging from the end of that tree line and hurrying into the shelter of the fort. They were using the trees as cover to move forwards from the vehicle.

Several of the figures had the unmistakable forms of rucksacks on their backs, with the tail fins of RPG rounds sticking out of their open tops. In the interior of the compound a massive bearded figure in the black robes of a Taliban commander could be seen, legs planted firmly on the ground, his gaze fixed on the British troops below. All the time he was speaking into a hand-held radio.

Baz had seen more than enough and he rolled the aircraft in to attack. The 30mm cannon sparked and roared, the lone Apache blasting the courtyard with bursts of fire, the rounds cutting down figures as they ran for cover. Those first twenty-round bursts had killed, or scattered, the fighters in the open, but more would be hiding in the cover of the thick mud walls. *Ugly Five Zero* pounded the fortress with burst after angry burst of 30mm, but in spite of the repeated attack runs the massive mud walls appeared immune to the heavy-calibre rounds.

Indeed, the fortress seemed substantial enough for its occupants to survive an attack using flechette rockets. The massive walls might prove impervious to a strike with 320 five-inch tungsten darts, and that was a risk the *Ugly Five Zero* aircrew were unwilling to take. Instead they lined up for a Hellfire attack. From two kilometres out the Apache fired, the missile streaking in towards target along the beam of the aircraft's laser.

It impacted in the middle of the fortress, punching an almighty hole in the outer wall and ripping it apart inside, the explosion throwing debris high into the air. With the thickest walls breached, Baz and Tim launched a second mopping-up attack. From four kilometres out *Ugly Five Zero* prepared to fire off a salvo of flechette-armed rockets in order to saturate the area and kill any fighters left alive in there.

Four rockets fired out from the aircraft's wing pods in a burst of dirty smoke and flame. After streaking through the air for a kilometre the rockets' secondary charge detonated, releasing the 320 flechette darts. Each five-millimetre wide shaft of tungsten had a tiny set of tail fins at the rear to ensure that it ran true, tapering to a fine, needle-sharp point at the front. That flechette strike silenced the last of the enemy fighters in the ruins of the fortress building.

Barely had that salvo done its work when *Ugly Five Zero* received a call from another group of ground troops. They were pinned down by an enemy force on the far side of the canal and taking heavy fire. *Ugly Five Zero* responded to the call-out, moving towards the coordinates of the contact, all the while the *Widow* briefing them on the enemy positions that needed to be hit. As the *Widow* spoke into his helmet-mounted radio the noise of incoming rounds and of the British troops returning fire was deafening, and he was having to scream to make himself heard.

'*Widow Six Eight* was effing and blinding as it was pretty heavy down there,' Baz remarks. 'We lined up and launched a Hellfire at the enemy position, a compound on the far side of the river. It fired out okay but then shot off at a wild tangent to the right . . . and suddenly we realised we had a rogue missile. Tim and I were doing the countdown to impact but there was nothing; no bang, no explosion, nothing. There was total silence in the cockpit and we were thinking: oh shit, that missile's shot off in the direction of our own forces and we're going to end up hitting our own men.'

The Hellfire's guidance system had malfunctioned, and the danger was that it might suddenly come back to life as the rogue missile hunted across the darkened skies. British ground troops use lasers to guide in airstrikes, and any number of *Widow* call-signs might be doing just that on the battlefield below. If that rogue Hellfire found one of those lasers and locked on the consequences didn't bear thinking about.

Suddenly there was a burst of static and a new *Widow* call-sign came up over the net.

'*Ugly*, this is *Widow Seven Nine*. I've got friendly troops asking did you just Hellfire their position? They've been targeted by something big. They're asking: did you fire?'

Widow Seven Nine was none other than their old friend from the Rahim Kalay battle, Sergeant Paul 'Bommer' Grahame. He had gone in with the main ground convoy at the start of Op Chakush as the JTAC embedded with a unit of the Royal Anglians.

'*Widow Seven Nine*, this is *Ugly*. Affirmative: that was us with a rogue Hellfire. Is anyone . . .'

'Not to worry, *Ugly*. It hit fifty metres from their position but they were in the Viking at the time so they're all okay.'

The 'danger-close' distance for a Hellfire strike – the distance at which friendly forces are considered safe from the blast – is five hundred metres, so that rogue missile had impacted at a tenth of that distance. Had they not been in a Viking armoured vehicle there could well have been British casualties.

It was a sobering moment for Baz and Tim, especially as *Widow Six Eight* was asking for another Hellfire strike on the original target. The two airmen's greatest fear was that the whole batch of Hellfires they were carrying might be faulty.

'*Widow Six Eight*, this is *Ugly*. You sure you want us to do this?'

'Too damn right! We're taking heavy enemy fire. Hit that bloody compound with all you got, *Ugly*.'

'Roger that. Starting our attacking run now.'

Widow Seven Nine then came up on the air.

'*Ugly*, if you *are* putting in another Hellfire just give us time to get our bleeding heads down!'

'Roger that. Take cover guys, 'cause we're fifteen seconds to target.'

As they lined up the aircraft on the enemy compound and pulled the trigger, Baz and Tim held their breath and said a small prayer. Thankfully this Hellfire ran good and true, faithfully tracking the laser beam to its point of impact on the mud-walled compound. That first strike blasted the main building apart, after which *Ugly Five Zero* hit the position with repeated bursts of 30mm cannon fire. Under the cover of the Apache's fearsome attack the ground troops moved forwards to take the bridge.

The bridge lay on a ninety-degree bend of the canal. To one side of the canal, the enemy compound had been pretty much taken out of the battle. But as the Royal Anglians moved onto the exposed approach an RPG fired out of the tree line on the high ground facing the enemy compound. It barrelled across the open sky, smashing into the riverbank in front of the British troops and exploding in a murderous burst of shrapnel and flame.

Then, up on the ridgeline, a heavy machine gun opened up, raking the British positions. Before the RPG gunner had a chance to reload, *Ugly Five Zero* slaved the 30mm cannon to the muzzle flash of the machine gun and opened fire. The blasts tore into the enemy gunners as *Ugly Five Zero* pounded their position with repeated bursts of cannon rounds. British troops were out in the open and getting hit hard; the Apache aircrew were determined to protect them.

Finally the Apache's gun fell silent. But the instant it did so the RPG gunner popped up from a hidden position and unleashed another grenade. Even before the warhead had hit, *Ugly Five Zero* targeted him with a further twenty-round burst of 30mm, the rounds seeming to impact all around the enemy RPG gunner's position. But once the fire had ceased he was up and aiming again, and a third RPG was loosed off at the British soldiers below.

'We did two 30mm runs and each time he was down in the cover of this deep irrigation trench, so he survived both passes,' Baz remarks. 'So we decided to give him a personal Hellfire. It was the first time we'd ever used a missile to take someone out – and it finished him. Finally, the guy went down.'

As the aircrew of *Ugly Five Zero* were finishing off the enemy positioned on that ridgeline, *Ugly Five One's* aircrew were themselves busy. Steve and Alex's aircraft had been engaged forwards of their wing as the leading edge of the British assault force moved into the outskirts of Haydarabad.

Holding station above the British vanguard, *Ugly Five One* was putting down a fierce barrage of 30mm cannon fire, keeping the enemy's heads down so as to enable the Royal Anglians to creep forwards. The larger pockets of resistance were saturated with flechette rocket strikes, or where the buildings were too substantial for the tungsten darts, Steve and Alex were hitting them with Hellfires.

As the British troops pushed in to clear the first compounds Steve and Alex could see groups of enemy fighters hurrying back through the dark streets to take up prepared positions. The British ground forces were going to have to fight tooth and nail for every inch of territory gained in this town.

'Our blokes were moving into the first compounds,' Steve remarks. 'But the enemy were clearly smarter now: they were falling back and regrouping when they knew that they had to, so living to fight on and to come back at our ground troops.'

By now the two Apaches of flight *Ugly* were approaching bingo fuel. They were forced to break off from the battle and set a course for base. Both aircraft were all but out of ammo: *Ugly Five Zero* had fired off a total of five Hellfires (one rogue), thirty-two flechette rockets and 240 rounds of 30mm. *Ugly Five One* had managed six Hellfires, twenty-eight flechette rockets, and 270 rounds of 30mm.

On the way back to Camp Bastion the aircrew were ordered to refuel and re-arm their aircraft at the flight line and return directly to the battlefield. Some twenty-four hours after Op Chakush had begun the fight for Haydarabad was as ferocious and brutal as it had been at its very start. An operation initially slated to last for three hours had now gone on for more than eight times that number and the battle remained far from over.

With 662 Squadron's deployment scheduled to end shortly, replacement Apache pilots were already arriving in Kandahar. One of those, Bruce Alford, was immediately tasked to rush a replacement Apache forwards to Camp Bastion. Baz noticed him standing to one side of the flight line, watching in open-mouthed amazement as the Apaches thundered in.

'Bruce arrived in theatre and was immediately tasked to ferry an Apache forwards,' Baz remarks. 'It was flown out fully armed up with a resupply of weapons. When he arrived he just stood rooted to the flight line, watching all the aircraft going in and out bombed-up – like it was a scene from a Vietnam movie or something.'

Back on the ground there was no time for a debrief. The flight bombed up, going Hellfire-heavy as there were likely to be a lot of compounds that needed clearing in Haydarabad. As the two aircraft took off and headed east they were warned to keep eyes on the Helmand River in case there were any resupplies of enemy fighters and weaponry on the water.

British forces were now pushing further into Haydarabad. But the enemy launched a counter-attack against the soldiers holding the bridges over the canal. They were trying to cut off supply lines to the British troops advancing into Haydarabad. It was an audacious move, and enemy forces had to be stopped at all costs. If the land supply lines were cut, and casevac and resupply flights had to go right into the cauldron of Haydarabad, the chances of losing one or more helicopters were high.

The two Apaches set up in wheel formation over the canal system, searching for enemy positions or forces on the move. Each time they found any sign of the enemy they hit them hard with 30mm cannon fire, flechette rockets or the full might of the Hellfires. By the time that this, their third mission, came to an end the four airmen had spent five hours in full combat.

Back at Bastion there was to be no respite. Flight *Ugly* had been moved on to full VHR status, as had every other flight in 662 Squadron. As the battle for Haydarabad raged a firefight kicked off down at Garmsir. In the dead hours of darkness the four exhausted airmen had to escort a Chinook on a casevac mission. The three aircraft rocked up over Garmsir well after midnight and began to shepherd the Chinook into the LZ.

'The casualty was picked up from the middle of nowhere,' Baz remarks. 'We were knackered, totally chin-strapped by now . . . We'd done six and a quarter hours of flying, most of it in combat, and we'd not had time for a single debrief, let alone any rest. We finally managed to hit the sack, only to be woken again at five. Our first mission of the day was to escort a Chinook on a resupply of ammo and kit to the Brigade Recce Force, who had established cut-off lines on the far side of Haydarabad. Thankfully it was a fairly quiet op and we routed back to Bastion dreaming of breakfast and some kip.'

But as the two aircraft neared base the exhausted aircrew learned they were going to have nothing of the sort. They were ordered to refuel and re-bomb on the flight line. With sunrise the fighting at Haydarabad had restarted with a vengeance. Back over the battle-field once more, the airmen were put in contact with three *Widows*, each of whom required urgent close air support. More worryingly, battles were being fought at the same positions as the day before, with enemy forces counter-attacking against the bridgeheads.

As the four airmen scanned the ground below them it all looked very familiar: they were fighting over the very same ground as they had done twice before. Suddenly the aircrew of *Ugly Five Zero* spotted a row of feet sticking out of one side of a hedge below them. The footwear was a mix of sandals and trainers, with the odd pair of army boots thrown in – a typical Taliban assortment. Slaving the 30mm cannon to the tree line, *Ugly Five Zero* opened up, pounding the position with a murderously accurate burst of fire.

There was little time or space to think much any more. The only way for the aircrew to deal with the fatigue levels, plus hour upon hour of continuous combat, was to act on instinct and intuition. It was a complex and extremely busy airspace out there, with Harriers going in, US fast jets on standby and other Apaches providing close air support. And it was a constantly shifting battlefield, as enemy forces tried to outflank the British forces and infiltrate their lines.

At the same time as they were hunting down and hitting an elusive enemy, the flight *Ugly* airmen were being tasked to break off engagements and intercept Chinooks inbound to the battle field, so as to escort them in on casevac missions or resupply drops. On the ground it was equally noisy, with mortar teams in action and 105mm artillery units firing barrages in support of British troops.

'At one point we were having this stand-off with a mortar team commander,' remarks Steve. 'He's telling us: "You've got to move out of the area as we want to fire our mortars – we've been waiting all day for this." "Negative," we told him. "We can see the enemy and surrounding terrain: just tell us what you want us to take out and we'll do it." As much as the mortar teams were keen to get firing, we could see so much more.'

By now British intelligence assessments of the battle for Haydarabad reflected what was obvious to the troops on the ground – that the enemy were putting up a tactically astute and diehard resistance. Reports of a collapse in the morale of the enemy post Rahim Kalay and Op Tufaan appeared premature, to put it mildly. And as for the assumption that the battle for Haydarabad would be over in three hours, that had proven wildly optimistic.

British forces were well into day two of the battle for Haydarabad. They had pushed into the northern edge of the town but enemy forces in the centre were holding firm. The town was being fought for street by bloody street and each building was being contested in brutal close-quarter combat.

In the claustrophobic confines of the urban battlespace air power was unable to offer decisive, battle-winning support. The danger of friendly fire incidents – of hitting one's own troops by accident – was often too great to put down 30mm rounds, rockets or Hellfires on to enemy positions. It was sheer, brute soldiering that would win the day on the streets of Haydarabad.

'The enemy forces on the ground were putting up a massive fight,' remarks Steve. 'They were mining areas and putting in booby traps as they retreated – and our forces were meeting fierce resistance as they moved into Haydarabad. There was also a growing fear of SAMs for the aircrew as intelligence was reporting a large number being deployed into the area. Over the next forty-eight hours the enemy were expected to put up stiff resistance, and they were sending in more fighters, in groups of 150 at a time.'

Running low on avtur once more, flight *Ugly* broke off their engagement and headed north for Bastion. But they would soon be in the air once more, for the battle of their lives.

18

FOUR MEN DOWN

Day 70

By mid morning on day two of Op Chakush the flight was in the air again, doing a relief in place for *Geek Flight*. The location of the contact was five kilometres to the north-east of Haydarabad, just south of a settlement called Shorakyan. When the Apaches rocked up over the battlefield *Geek Flight* did a quick handover, passing the aircrew the call-sign of the *Widow* with whom they had been liaising.

Widow Seven Five briefed the four airmen on his situation. Earlier that morning he and his unit had advanced across a canal bridge, following the cover of a tree line across open fields towards two compounds. Some fifty metres short of the compounds they had been engaged by a far larger enemy force and pinned down. To either side of the tree line were rutted, ploughed fields that provided little or no cover.

Geek Flight had been repulsing repeated enemy attacks as their fighters tried to force a way through the tree line on to *Widow Seven Five*'s position. It went without saying that as the enemy were so close to him there was a serious risk of friendly fire. The *Widow*'s situation didn't sound very pretty, and from the Apache's vantage point the aircrew could see the predicament he was in.

Enemy forces were well dug in at the two compounds, with visible trenches and bunkers. The tree line in which *Widow Seven Five* was sheltering ran up to both compounds, providing the enemy forces with continuous cover under which to advance on his position. It was difficult for the aircrew to see the enemy on the move so they would have to rely on *Widow Seven Five* detecting their advance – by which time they'd be pretty much on top of him.

To the east of *Widow Seven Five*'s position a column of Mastiffs – the British Army's version of the US Cougar armoured car – were moving into position on the far side of the canal. The six-wheeled Mastiffs were operated by 2nd Royal Tank Regiment. They were being used to do exactly what the Mastiff is designed for: moving troops into battle in an IED- and mine-safe vehicle and then providing fire to support those troops.

Each Mastiff was fitted with a .50-calibre Browning heavy machine gun. The convoy could potentially put down accurate fire on to the enemy forces that were keeping *Widow Seven Five* and his men pinned down. The trouble was that the Mastiffs were a kilometre and a half back from the *Widow*'s position and they would face a ferocious battle to fight their way through to him. In the meantime, the flight *Ugly* Apaches would have to keep *Widow Seven Five* and his men alive and safe from capture.

After the briefing from the *Widow*, flight *Ugly* put in a couple of probing attacks against the enemy positions just to get a feel for how much clearance there was between friendly and enemy forces. Coming in from the east and firing over *Widow Seven Five*'s head, it was possible to hit the enemy compounds with bursts of 30mm cannon fire. Baz could see the rounds exploding in the tree line just to the south of the larger enemy compound. The trouble was that it would need something more substantial – flechette rockets or Hellfires – to hit the enemy hard in their dug-in positions.

As Baz considered their options there was an urgent call from the Bastion Ops Room.

'*Ugly*, this is *Zero Bravo*. We've lost all contact with a *Widow*. They're cut off, down to a handful of men and we haven't heard from them for some time. We think they've been captured or are in imminent danger of capture. This is now your priority mission.'

'Roger that, *Zero Bravo*. What's his call-sign?'

'We're not sure, *Ugly*. Try them all. *Find them*. Out.'

Flight *Ugly* contacted the Widow Tactical Operations Centre and requested all *Widow* call-signs from the battlefield. One by one they called each *Widow*, asking for a sitrep (situation report). None was in the type of situation outlined by the Ops Room, or in comparable danger.

Finally *Ugly* called the Bastion Ops Room, explaining that they had been in contact with every *Widow* and all were accounted for. But Bastion were having none of it: there was definitely a lost *Widow* and time was running out to find him and his men.

As they finished speaking with Bastion it suddenly occurred to the Apache aircrew that perhaps the 'lost' *Widow* was the very one with whom they had been working – *Widow Seven Five*. So far his laconic Suffolk tones hadn't communicated anything like that sort of danger or threat, but you never knew.

It was time to put a call through and ask. '*Widow Seven Five*, this is *Ugly*. Tell us again, just how bad is your sit?'

'Well, you could say we're in a spot of bother, *Ugly* . . . There's four guys down here, including me; the ANA have all run away; the enemy have us surrounded on three sides; they're fifty metres close in all buildings and the tree line; we're running short on ammo and up to our bollocks in water. Other'n that, the sun's shining and it's a great day.'

Flight *Ugly* put a call through to the Bastion Ops Room.

'*Zero Bravo*, this is *Ugly*. We've found the missing *Widow*. We're with him and on station, and we'll see how we can help.'

'Thank God for that. Good work, *Ugly*. Whatever it takes, stay with them. Out.'

As *Widow Seven Five* elaborated on his position in a calm and unhurried way, it transpired that he and his three fellow British soldiers had been co-located with a unit of twenty Afghan National Army (ANA) troops. Earlier that morning they had advanced across the canal bridge and walked into the enemy ambush. One of the ANA soldiers had taken a flesh wound and his nineteen buddies had promptly volunteered to escort him back across the bridge to safety. In other words, they had run away, leaving the four British soldiers to face a far larger dug-in enemy force.

The four men were hunkered down in an irrigation ditch full of water, which had doubtless saved them from getting killed or overrun. But they were down to their last few magazines of ammo and any movement attracted a murderous barrage of fire. In fact, the enemy were getting more confident as time wore on, and none of the air attacks seemed able to dislodge or kill them.

Widow Seven Five and his three fellow soldiers were so close to the enemy positions that they could hear them cat-calling and making crazed monkey noises during lulls in the fighting. They were clearly trying to intimidate the British soldiers, hoping that they might frighten them into showing themselves or making a fatal mistake.

Widow Seven Five came up on the radio net again: 'The bastards are coming for us, *Ugly*. I can hear them moving down through the tree line. I need fire on the tree line now, *Ugly*! *Now*!'

'Roger that. Engaging now, 30mm. Keep your bloody heads down.'

As *Ugly Five Zero* opened up with the 30mm cannon the fear for both pilots was of hitting their own troops. They watched as the first rounds chewed up the northern end of the tree line, wood splintering and spinning off in all directions. The 30mm was landing murderously close to *Widow Seven Five*'s position. As that twenty-round burst ceased, Baz felt his stomach knotted up with the tension of it all. The danger-close distance for 30mm high-explosive rounds is 150 metres: these were going in at a fraction of that range.

As the last rounds struck, *Widow Seven Five* came up over the net. 'I need more fire, *Ugly*, they're still coming . . . I need you to cover us. And closer, *Ugly*, get your fire in closer! They're trying to get to us through the wood line.'

'Roger, engaging now.'

Depressing the cannon in the Apache's chin turret just a fraction, the aircrew of *Ugly Five Zero* let loose with another twenty-round burst.

'Yeah! Just there! That's the right place. Hit 'em again, *Ugly*, put more rounds into that position.'

The airmen did as they had been asked, all the while praying that a stray round didn't fall short.

Having driven back that first enemy assault, the pair of Apaches set up in tight wheel formation directly over *Widow Seven Five*'s position. With each orbit *Ugly Five Zero* and *Ugly Five One* put a twenty-round burst onto the enemy positions in and around the two compounds. But it didn't appear to be having much effect. Hitting them while advancing through the woods was one thing, but 30mm cannon fire against trenches and bunkers was all but ineffective. And there was only so long that the pair of Apaches could do this before they ran out of ammunition.

There had to be something that the column of Mastiffs, with their turret-mounted heavy machine guns, could do to help. The Mastiffs held the high ground beyond the canal that overlooked the friendly and enemy positions. Putting a call through to the *Widow* embedded with the Mastiffs, *Ugly Five Zero* offered to talk their weapons onto target. From the one-and-a-half kilometres' distance the Mastiffs opened up with their heavy machine guns. But as flight *Ugly* tried to correct their fire there was an urgent call from *Widow Seven Five*.

'*Ugly*, *Widow Seven Five*. Where the hell is that fire coming from? I've got enemy on my back and my eastern flank! There's a heavy machine gun putting rounds onto my right flank . . .'

Widow Seven Five had mistaken the Mastiff's covering fire for an enemy attack, so close were the rounds falling to his own position. The Mastiffs were having to fire across *Widow Seven Five*'s location in order to hit the enemy and the trajectory was just too difficult. At flight *Ugly*'s behest the Mastiff's .50-cals ceased firing. As they did so, *Widow Seven Five* came up on the radio net once more. Another group of enemy fighters were creeping forwards through the tree line, making whooping monkey noises as they came for him and his men.

Ugly Five Zero came round on its orbit and fired off a twenty-round burst, its wing aircraft doing likewise, and driving the enemy fighters back into cover. Baz glanced down and to his left to check his computerised display: they were down to just 140 rounds of 30mm, but were nowhere near to neutralising the enemy force.

There was only one option left to them, Baz decided. They would have to try flying directly on to the enemy guns as the only possible way to deliver some serious punch. In theory, if attacking in a steep dive from directly above they could fire their 2.7-inch rockets and Hellfires right into the enemy trenches.

In normal circumstance the danger-close range for the 2.7-inch rockets is five hundred metres. But that was when firing them in a standard flat trajectory and from two kilometres' distance. If the pair of Apaches 'shotgunned' the enemy positions, firing into the ground at close range from above, it should significantly reduce that equation. The force of the rockets or missiles should bury them in the earth prior to explosion, further reducing the danger to *Widow Seven Five* and his men.

At least that was the theory. In the time that Baz had taken to consider the idea, *Ugly Five Zero* had already laid down another twenty rounds of 30mm, as had his wing aircraft. It was time to act. Baz and Tim shared the idea with *Ugly Five One*. Little discussion was required as the need to conserve the 30mm ammo was relentless and all-consuming. *Ugly Five Zero* radioed the men on the ground and explained what they had in mind.

'*Widow Seven Five, Ugly*. We're running low on ammo. We're still here for you, but we've got to decide what's best to use. We're going to go in danger-close, first with HEISAP rockets, then with flechette rockets. You happy with that?'

'Roger, danger-close with HEISAP and flechette rockets, happy with that . . . It's like the bloody Haydarabad Zoo down here: they're making animal noises again.'

'What's your best target?'

'We're taking sustained incoming from the tree line directly to the south of the main compound. See if you can hit that.'

'Visual, tree line south of the main compound. We're attacking on a heading of 190, four HEISAP rockets. Take cover.'

'Roger. Ground commander's initials are DG.'

Whenever requesting an airstrike that is danger-close a *Widow* has to pass up his initials to the aircraft to indicate that he's taking responsibility for the risk of doing so. Anticipating the Apache aircrew requesting his initials, *Widow Seven Five* had passed them up without being asked.

'Roger. Commander's initials are DG. Tipping in now. Engaging in thirty seconds. Out.'

'Roger. Cleared to engage.'

Baz took the lead aircraft in towards target at three thousand feet. A half-kilometre out, he put the Apache into a steep dive that grew steeper by the second. In no time the aircrew were staring at the hard Afghan earth as it rushed towards them. The view out the front of the Apache was directly onto the enemy position. Baz and Tim could see the enemy fighters glancing upwards in surprise . . . and an instant later they were bringing their weapons to bear on the aircraft that was screaming towards them.

Muzzles flashed fire as the enemy's machine guns loosed off on automatic, pumping rounds at the diving aircraft. Baz held a steady course through the streams of tracer as Tim stroked the cursor on his pistol grip column, bringing the crosshair sight on his computer screen directly over the tree line at the compound's southern border. They had a split second to get this right; a split second in which to get the dive, range and trajectory right, and fire.

With one hand he pressed the button to fire the laser, and with the other he pulled the trigger. There was a sudden burst of flame and smoke at the nose of the Apache and the four rockets streaked away, impacting an instant later in a blinding flash, the explosion throwing up a massive cloud of smoke and dust directly below the diving Apache.

'Pull up! Pull up!' Tim started yelling as the aircraft thundered earthwards. 'PULL UUUUP!'

Baz hauled hard on the cyclic, the G-force of slowing the diving aircraft putting a horrible strain on the airframe. Shaking and juddering, the Apache started to come out of the descent. Baz pumped hard on the pedals and threw the aircraft into a tight, swingeing right-hand turn, the rotors sweeping past the enemy positions just below, mud walls and trees flashing past the side of the aircraft.

Ugly Five Zero powered low and fast into the open ground to the north-west and for a second Baz felt the ecstatic relief of having pulled off the attack and survived. Then he remembered *Widow Seven Five*: had he and his men survived the rocket strike?

'*Widow Seven Five, Ugly*. Sitrep.'

'*Ugly, Widow Seven Five*. Nice shooting. Nice flying. I'm deaf as a bloody post though. Any chance you can do that again for us?'

'Roger. Coming in on a heading of 190, four flechette rockets – we have no more HEISAP. Make sure you're well in cover.'

'Happy with that. Clear to engage.'

As he brought the aircraft around for a second attack, Baz knew that this time the enemy would be forewarned and better prepared to engage. There was nothing he could do about that. There was a burst of static on the radio and the Bastion Ops Room came on the air. Baz was so engrossed in what he was doing that he barely registered what they were saying.

'*Ugly*, this is *Zero Bravo*. Sitrep.'

'*Zero Bravo, Ugly*. Wait out.'

Bastion were requesting an update on the situation. It wasn't the first time that they'd called for one, and as with the last they'd have to wait for an answer – wait out. The demands of the battle were just too intense right now.

'We were so fixated on what we were doing that we couldn't respond to that right away,' Baz remarks. 'You could throw the Apache around and it's a truly awesome aircraft to fly. We dived down vertically and fired off a rocket salvo into the enemy tree line. We'd formed up as a pair of aircraft in a "race track" pattern: we went in and fired, and as we came out our wing went in and fired. And you can hear the *Widow* going wild down there: "That's it! Bang on target! Keep it coming! Keep it coming! Come east fifty metres, nearer to our position . . ."'

Employing repeated diving attack profiles, *Ugly Five Zero* and *Ugly Five One* proceeded to Hellfire every building and tree line in the enemy's position. Once they'd run out of Hellfires they kept hitting them with salvos of flechette-armed rockets, but still the enemy kept on fighting.

'We'd hit them with everything we could, but it's unbelievable what they could live through and keep on coming back at us,' Steve remarks. 'We'd fired eleven Hellfires, so many rockets, hundreds of rounds of 30mm . . . You'd think there was no way the enemy could put up with that level of fire, but somehow they did.'

As flight *Ugly* prosecuted their attack, dive-bombing the enemy positions time after time after time, the Mastiff column attempted to push forwards to relieve the British soldiers on the ground. Their OC was in constant contact with the Apaches, but once the column neared the canal they ran into ferocious resistance. Enemy fighters were well dug in and entrenched all along the far side of the waterway. Eventually the convoy of Mastiffs was halted a kilometre or so out from *Widow Seven Five*'s position. For now, at least, the ground convoy's attempt to break through had failed.

By now the Apaches had been in the air for pushing two hours and their fuel supplies were approaching critical. They were all out of Hellfires and rockets. Baz wondered what on earth they were to do about it, for they couldn't desert the troops on the ground. All of a sudden *Widow Seven Five* put through a call. The enemy were counter-attacking, charging down the tree line in a human wave. Above the noise of *Widow Seven Five*'s shouted radio call, Baz could hear the cracking and whine of incoming rounds.

With barely a pause for thought Baz piled on the power to come round more tightly, throwing *Ugly Five Zero* into another dive. This time he centred the aircraft on the tree line just to the west of the friendly position. The chin turret on *Ugly Five Zero* spurted fire and Tim fired off its last twenty-round burst of 30mm, the rounds tearing into the woods directly below. *Ugly Five Zero* was now Winchester – completely out of ammo – and *Ugly Five One* would soon be likewise.

'We knew that Bastion was trying to get another flight out to replace us,' remarks Steve. 'We held off from some of the diving attacks to try to conserve some 30mm and rockets just in case – but we were going through ammo like it was going out of fashion.'

As they came around for another attacking run Tim leaned over and flicked the flares to manual operation mode. *Ugly Five Zero* was about to use the last 'weapon' it had left – its air-defence countermeasures. Baz dived the aircraft vertically onto the enemy positions and pressed the flare release button on the cyclic as he did so. A massive spray of white light trailed in its wake and drifted down onto the enemy.

Pray that that might keep the bastard's heads down, Baz told himself as they came around again.

Baz and Tim had heard from American pilots that flares could be used to set alight a tree line, flushing out enemy fighters. That's what they were hoping to achieve by sending their flares into the woods on the southern border of the enemy compound. The fire would drive the enemy out of cover, allowing their wing aircraft to nail them – if *Ugly Five One* had enough ammo left.

Back at Camp Bastion one of the Apaches of Charlie Hudson's *Greenpeace Flight* had been refuelled and rearmed on the flight line, ready for a relief in place (RIP) of flight *Ugly*. And one of the *Super Six* flight Apaches had been pulled off gun checks on the ranges in order to join them. Some thirty-six hours into Op Chakush and missions were so frenetic that flights were being thrown together as the need arose, based upon which aircraft – and pilots – were still serviceable.

'We knew we were out of ammo, and we were firing off flares into the tree line,' Baz remarks. 'We put a call through to base alerting them to the fact that we were out of ammo and that our wing was pretty much the same as us. The relief we felt when we heard that a flight was inbound to do a relief in place was just awesome.'

The two relief Apaches arrived over *Widow Seven Five*'s position just as flight *Ugly*'s fuel situation went critical. Baz, Tim, Steve and Alex did a very rapid handover and turned for home.

As they peeled away from the battlespace, flight *Ugly* put a final call through to *Widow Seven Five*, wishing him luck as they were going off-station. *Widow Seven Five* just had time enough to thank them for their efforts when the next group of enemy fighters were spotted moving forwards through the tree line.

The two Apaches set a course for Bastion, the four airmen sinking into an exhausted silence. Their minds were still wholly focused on the battlefield as the last chapter in what had been the fight of their lives unfolded for *Widow Seven Five* and his three fellow soldiers.

The aircrew listened in as *Widow Seven Five* outlined his escape plan to the newly arrived Apaches, plus a Harrier that was inbound to his location. He wanted the Harrier to drop a five-hundred-pound airburst bomb on the enemy position. In the shock and confusion of the explosion he reckoned that they would have a chance to make a getaway. He and his three men would head westwards, then south to link up with the Mastiff convoy. The role of the Apaches was to cover their escape as they ran hell-for-leather across the open fields that surrounded their position.

As the flight *Ugly* aircrew put down on the flight line back at Bastion they remained seated in their aircraft and fixated on the radio traffic. *Widow Seven Five* was coordinating the action between the Apaches of *Greenpeace/Super Six* flight and the Harrier, call-sign *Recoil*.

'*Recoil Three Four*, this is *Widow Seven Five*. My location: wood line south-east of two EF compounds. Mission grid is 14728596. Repeat, 14728596. EF located one hundred metres west, so danger close. Repeat, danger close.'

'*Widow Seven Five, Recoil Three Four*. Roger, good copy. Danger close, mission grid ref is 14728596, elevation 2880 feet, attack heading east to west, friendly forces one hundred metres west of attack point. I need your initials.'

'My initials are DG. Call when two minutes out.'

The next two minutes were filled with a tense silence. At the Camp Bastion flight line, the ground crew were running around like mad things, refuelling and rearming the aircraft in case flight *Ugly* had to do an RIP for *Greenpeace/Super Six* flight over *Widow Seven Five*'s position.

The groundies had been told that there were four British soldiers surrounded on the ground, and all that was keeping them alive was the Apaches. They were determined to get the pair of aircraft fuelled and bombed-up in record time. At some stage a bag of rock-hard sausage rolls was handed up to each of the pilots but they were left unopened.

Three minutes after the Harrier's call, the pilot came up over the air again.

'*Widow Seven Five, Recoil*. Two minutes out. I have a tree line oriented east to south with two smaller tree lines at either end, forming a U-shape; a compound to the north of that with a hole in the roof of one building. I can see plumes of smoke from there and what appear to be muzzle flashes. A canal lies two hundred metres to the east of that. Confirm this is the target.'

'Confirmed. We're in the tree line on the bottom of the U-shape.'

'Roger. Tipping in now, engaging in ten seconds. Keep your heads down.'

'Roger. Clear to engage.'

'Bombs gone.'

Seconds after release the five hundred-pound airburst exploded in a massive ball of flame, spitting jagged shrapnel into the enemy positions below. The moment that it did so *Widow Seven Five* and his three men were up and sprinting across the freshly ploughed fields. Hardly had they moved fifty metres when the enemy were up and in the aim, putting fire on them with their AK-47s and heavy machine guns.

Widow Seven Five and his three fellow soldiers were forced to fire-and-manoeuvre across the open fields – two running while the others took cover behind ruts, firing back at the enemy, then swapping roles. Finally the exhausted men reached the cover of some far buildings. They headed for the nearest, only to find themselves caught in the sights of a second bunch of Taliban, who were armed with machine guns and RPGs.

As the first RPG streaked towards their position *Widow Seven Five* gave a live commentary to the orbiting Apaches. The pair of aircraft moved in and began pounding the enemy position with 30mm cannon fire.

'Keep firing! Keep firing!' *Widow Seven Five* cried. 'You're bang on target, bang on target. The enemy are running and diving into the canal to escape. They're in the water now . . .'

The *Super Six* Apache was piloted by Susan Rachels, the lone woman pilot in 662 Squadron, together with the squadron's Weapons Officer, Ben Moore. Susan radioed *Widow Seven Five* for confirmation that they were okay down there but all she got in reply was an ominous, echoing silence. She kept speaking into the radio, repeatedly asking for a sitrep from *Widow Seven Five*.

Finally, the *Widow's* voice came up over the net.

'Sorry, we're having difficulties concentrating right now . . . It's been a long time since we heard a woman's voice and, well, we're gathered around the radio just listening to you talk. So keep it coming . . .'

With that, the men of flight *Ugly* felt a wave of relief wash over them – relief tinged with not a small degree of amusement. *Widow Seven Five* and his three buddies had made it out of there alive and were clearly turning their minds to more pleasant matters. The four soldiers would shortly be able to link up with the column of Mastiffs that was moving forwards to their position.

'This was the end of an epic firefight that had lasted some six hours,' Baz remarks. 'It had involved three RIPs by Apaches, a Harrier attack, Mastiffs firing in support and countless munitions. Collectively, we probably saved the *Widow* and his men who had been in a hopeless position – cut off and outnumbered and out-gunned. But it was, above all, his calm, brave actions that saved him, coupled with his great sense of humour.'

As the four flight *Ugly* airmen dismounted from their aircraft the exhaustion was acute. The adrenalin was flooding out of their systems, to be replaced by a leaden weight of tiredness such as they had never felt before.

'It was like we were at the end of the Rahim Kalay engagement, but worse,' remarks Steve. 'We emerged from the aircraft like the walking dead: zombies; shuffling walk; heads lolling on shoulders; monosyllabic grunts. And once again there'd been great teamwork with the groundies: anyone of any rank or qualification knew that if he worked for it he had a chance at becoming an Apache pilot, of graduating to be aircrew.'

The aircrew had put in some fifteen hours flying time over the last forty-eight hours, most of it in intense combat. They stumbled for their tent, finally getting their heads down at five o'clock in the evening. As soon as they hit their bunks they fell into the sleep of the dead. But it was not to last.

Some twenty minutes later they were dragged back to consciousness by the ringing of the field telephone. The four men pulled on their boots and made their way over to the Ops Room, trying to focus on the mission briefing. There was no point in whinging or complaining. They wouldn't have got the call unless it was necessary.

'I know you're knackered,' Ian McIvor, the Chief of Staff, began, 'but there's a big TIC on at Haydarabad, and we need to get a Chinook in to do a casevac and a resupply. I know you're over your hours. If you don't want to you can refuse. You've done your hours and more.'

The four aircrew told their Chief of Staff that they were fine and headed for the flight line. On the run in towards Haydarabad – how they were beginning to hate the name of that place – *Ugly Five Zero*'s HIDAS system crashed. As *Ugly Five One* pushed ahead with the Chinook *Ugly Five Zero* flew out into the open desert to try to reboot the system. As luck would have it, the reboot worked and with the radar turning *Ugly Five Zero* headed for Haydarabad to rejoin its wing.

They arrived over the battlefield just as *Ugly Five One* was shepherding the Chinook in to land. Steve and Alex kept eyes on the Chinook as it descended onto a hot LZ. Suddenly Steve noticed something that made his blood run cold. On his pilot night vision screen the blinding heat blob of an aircraft was bearing down on them fast. He grabbed the collective and threw the power on, and felt the Apache lift, the burning white silhouette of a helicopter flashing past right below his aircraft.

Fucking hell, that was a near miss like death. What the hell was that other aircraft?

'Any aviation call signs in our ROZ – come up on this frequency!' Steve screamed as he searched the skies around his cockpit for the rogue aircraft. 'Any other aircraft! Any other aircraft! Any other aircraft in the Haydarabad area!'

The only response was silence. The aircrew radioed air traffic control in Camp Bastion, demanding to know what the hell was going on. Was it a Chinook on a top-secret Special Forces flight? Was it the Yanks or something? Was that why no one seemed to know about the rogue aircraft?

As the recriminations flew and tempers flared Steve was hit by a blinding flash of realisation: that helicopter silhouette had been one of their own aircraft. It was an Apache. It was their flight leader's machine. *It was Ugly Five Zero.*

'I suddenly knew it was Baz and Tim's aircraft. I'd descended at a hundred feet per orbit and Baz had climbed two hundred feet or more. There was less than a hundred feet separating us when we passed . . . And that's how we almost allowed ourselves to wipe each other out. We pulled away with the Chinook in tow and I decided it wasn't the right forum – to discuss it on the open air. We'd both had a lapse of concentration and I said to Alex that we'd talk about it on the ground. In any case, we still had a job to do out there.'

A call came in from a *Widow* on the ground that he was under heavy fire. Acting almost as automatons the airmen headed for his position and asked for a talk-on to the enemy target. From their vantage point the enemy could clearly be seen firing sustained bursts of tracer from the cover of a building.

Slaving the gun sight to the hot point of the tracer – the enemy muzzle flashes – *Ugly Five One* fired a Hellfire right down the enemy's barrel. They followed up with a salvo of flechette rockets, by which time the enemy guns had fallen silent. It was high time the two aircraft headed for Camp Bastion.

Back on the flight line Steve decided to get the near-miss out in the open.

'Fucking hell, guys, we almost died out there tonight. That other aircraft – that was you, Baz . . .'

'Mate, we didn't even see you.'

The four airmen headed for the debrief in stunned silence, knowing that this time death really had been just a hair's breadth away. It was neither aircrew's fault. Each aircraft had been losing or gaining height by a hundred feet or so with every orbit, hence the near-collision course that they'd ended up on.

'It was the closest call ever,' Steve remarks. 'We'd turned our thoughts to the successes of the day and had become complacent. Alex just seemed to be asleep at this point, but as for Tim, he seemed really shaken by it. We got back to the tent and didn't sleep right away, even though we were exhausted. Baz and I had to tell Tim some stories of other near misses we were aware of, just to show him that it was life, and in life shit happened.'

'This time we did go for a debrief,' remarks Baz. 'The first thing that was asked of us was: were there any flight safety issues? There was no point beating about the bush, so I got it out plain and simple that it was us that had nearly crashed into each other. We discussed how we'd ended up doing it and what we could learn from it. At the end of the day the Chief of Staff had said: "Are you happy to go?" "Yes we are," had been our reply. We only had ourselves to blame. We misjudged it, and it almost cost us our lives.'

19

AFTERMATH

Days 71–100

During Op Chakush each of the men of the flight had completed nineteen hours in the air without a significant break. This equated to some thirty hours sitting in the aircraft, as a lot of time was spent bombing up and waiting for the 'go' on the flight line. *Ugly Five Zero* had fired off a total of 11 Hellfires, 74 rockets, and 1050 rounds of 30mm. *Ugly Five One* had fired 9 Hellfires, 49 rockets and 730 rounds of 30mm. *Ugly Five Zero* had also fired off 34 decoy flares, while trying to stop the enemy from overrunning *Widow Seven Five*'s position.

After three days' intense fighting Haydarabad finally lay in British hands and Op Chakush could be declared complete. An operation initially scheduled to last for three hours had taken slightly longer than planned. A new Forwards Operating Base, FOB Arnhem, was being constructed on the outskirts of Hyderabad in order to dominate the area. One of the compounds seized in the town had turned up a remarkable find. Hidden in a building was a Desert Hawk UAV that had been captured by the enemy, and a phonebook listing all the numbers of the Taliban's top commanders.

A few days after Op Chakush, *Widow Seven Five* came to visit the Apache base at Bastion. *Widow Seven Five* was Sergeant Dave Greenland of the Royal Artillery. The aircrew played their gun tapes so he could see what the battle had looked like from their end. Then Sergeant Greenland told the Apache crew about the most frightening moment of the whole battle. It had come when the Apaches had dived down and fired their flechettes.

The express-train scream of their inrush had ended with the darts peppering the end of the irrigation ditch in which he and his men were hiding. The Sergeant and his men could see them hitting the water – that's how close it had been.

By day seventy-four of 662 Squadron's deployment, intelligence was flooding in to the Apache Ops Room regarding the impact of Op Chakush. The defeat at Haydarabad was already being seen as a crushing blow for the enemy. Reports cited enemy forces remaining out of contact at all times.

'Their posture is now reactive and defensive,' one such report concluded.

Apart from their stronghold at Musa Qaleh in the far north of Helmand, all the enemy had remaining in the area were small mobile units disguised as civvies. The enemy's key objective was now to defend Musa Qaleh following a string of losses up and down the Helmand River valley.

Less than a week after the battle for Haydarabad, there were no further reports of hostilities in the area. The atmosphere in the town had improved markedly. Locals were turning up at British Army camps and offering to show them where the remaining minefields and the IEDs might be so that they might be disarmed and the town made safe.

With women and children moving back into the town, British forces held a *shura* with the tribal elders. It was a good, positive meeting, although the elders made it clear that they preferred the Taliban over the Afghan Police Force as the authority in their area. The Afghan police were famously corrupt, venal and inefficient. Time and time again the same thing was being said by the tribal elders: better even the Taliban than the Afghan Police Force.

The loss of Haydarabad had been a crushing blow for the enemy. The roots of the battle lay in Rahim Kalay but they had been very different battles. In Rahim Kalay, a probing patrol had stumbled upon a major enemy headquarters position complete with arms and weapons dumps and fortified strongholds. It was also a major resupply route for new fighters entering the jihad. Rahim Kalay had led in turn to Op Tufaan, and finally to the deliberate assault on the last enemy stronghold in the Upper Gereshk Valley – Haydarabad. In all of this, flight *Ugly* – plus their fellow Apache aircrews – had played their part.

For the flight *Ugly* aircrew the war really was over now. The men of 662 Squadron were scheduled to pull out of Camp Bastion at the beginning of August for one final rotation through Kandahar then back to the UK. Just prior to departure, one of the pilots, Dean Attril, made an informal kind of presentation to the four airmen. It was an X-ray picture that had been retrieved from an enemy trench system after the battle for Rahim Kalay.

The X-ray had been taken in one of the Taliban's makeshift field hospitals. It showed a man's body with the unmistakeable silhouette of a flechette dart embedded within in.

Back at Kandahar Airfield the aircrew met up with the replacement Apache pilots coming into theatre. Part of their final duty was to take the new boys around, show them the ropes and help get them settled in – and that involved a lot of squaddie story-telling and drinking (non-alcoholic) beer. There was also a degree of panic tanning so that the four men didn't end up going home with a 'squaddie tan' – lily-white all over, but brown above the neck. All four men were more than ready to get back to the UK. In fact, they had been gearing up to it for some time.

On their last evening in Afghanistan some old friends popped over from the Joint Helicopter Force headquarters to share a few beers. The aircrew sat around in the bar in the PX Mini Mall, reliving the story of the battle for Rahim Kalay. Once they'd finished talking one of the visitors turned to Steve and Baz and stared at them hard.

'You know something, you guys need a holiday bad,' he remarked. 'You seen yourselves recently? You're so old and knackered-looking.'

'He was dead right,' remarks Steve. 'I can see it in the photos of me and the other aircrew: we all looked a lot older. The long hours, the Apache programme – it really had taken it out of us.'

The flight back to the UK was on an RAF Tristar packed with troops going home. Baz and Steve looked around at the flashes on the uniforms: most were Royal Anglians, the soldiers with whom they had fought so many decisive battles. There was a general nodding between the ground soldiers and the Apache airmen, a real sense of warrior bonding. Both aircrew and ground troops had been through the mixer out there, either on or over the battlefields of Afghanistan.

Baz turned to one of the nearest Royal Anglians: 'Tell you one thing, I wouldn't like to be on the ground like you blokes. It's a bloody nightmare.'

The soldier shrugged. 'Suit yourself, mate. Far as I'm concerned, you've got the worst job in the world. Whenever you lot pitch up all guns turn on you.'

Fair enough, thought Baz. That's what we're there for. *Always outnumbered, never outgunned.*

After touching down at Brize Norton the men of the flight headed up the motorway in the minibus towards their Wattisham base. En route they stopped off at a MacDonald's to grab a burger and a brew. Standing in line in the queue, in full uniform and with a desert tan, nobody seemed inclined to let the airmen move up the line or to offer them any sign of appreciation or respect – not that they expected any, exactly.

On the contrary, Baz reckoned they were getting some very odd looks. It was almost as if people were thinking: where the hell have you lot come from? Wasn't it obvious, Baz reasoned? It was Afghanistan. Didn't they know there was a war on?

On arrival at Wattisham the minibus pulled up at the guardroom and the aircrew handed in their weapons. Then it was into the arms of waiting loved ones for a much longed-for reunion. It was two days before Baz felt he had truly started to relax, and then he just slept the sleep of the dead for a week. At the end of it he felt oddly dislocated. It was great to be back with his family but he was troubled by the fact that so few of the British public seemed aware that the country was at war.

In Afghanistan the British military was fighting its toughest war since Korea, yet it somehow felt as if it wasn't happening. British soldiers were giving their all for Queen and country, and in many cases sacrificing their health, if not their very lives. Young men were coming home horribly maimed and injured, or in flag-draped coffins. Yet what was it all for? No one seemed to know. No one seemed to give a shit. No one seemed to care.

At the end of that first week Baz found himself down his local Asda store, shopping with his wife. He was walking down an aisle when he came face to face with four Afghan men nattering away in Pashtun. He knew enough words by now to recognise the language, and in a flash he was back in theatre in Afghanistan. Two weeks ago I'd have been flying over your villages, he found himself thinking, shooting stuff up. He made a rapid exit from the store, feeling uncomfortable and ill.

That evening, Steve and his fiancée Tracey came round to Baz's house for dinner. Not big drinkers at the best of times, Steve and Baz imbibed a good deal of wine and started to relive some of their more testing Afghan moments. It wasn't something they normally would do in front of the ladies, and by the time Steve left he was half cut.

After that dinner Baz's wife Tracy asked him why he never talked to her about what had happened out in Afghanistan. Why was it only ever his soldier mates that he spoke to? Baz told her that he didn't think that she'd understand. Try me, was Tracy's response. So Baz stared telling her about his second day on operations, blowing away the Afghan boatmen on the Helmand River. He was relieved to be speaking to someone about it. The incident was starting to haunt his sleep, the bloody images replaying in his dreams.

Steve shared in Baz's disappointment, especially the sense that many in the UK seemed not to give a damn. Was the sacrifice all for nothing? Did it mean anything if no one knew or even seemed bothered? He also felt the loss of the *Ugly* fellowship keenly. After their Afghan deployment it was highly unlikely that the four of them – Baz, Tim, Steve and Alex – would get to fly together again. Next time around crewing needs would be different and crewing make-ups would be dictated by constraints in theatre.

'I was gutted that we would never fly and fight together again as a flight,' Steve remarks. 'We'd formed this bond that we'd never experienced before, and we will never experience that again. This flight was the best and we'll none of us ever have that same bond, and I know that. In fact, the squadron overall was great: we would all have given our lives to protect the others, and that's what the bonding of warriors is all about.'

Each of the airmen was offered a 'decompression briefing' at Wattisham once they were back on duty. This was an opportunity to talk about feeling down or depressed, or about any of the actions that might be troubling them. But the culture of the Corps meant that the take-up wasn't overly high. Mostly those that felt the need went and had a quiet chat with Nicola, the Regimental Padre – she who had handed out sweets as the aircrews had boarded the buses at the start of the tour.

'At the end, the Padre got us all together and talked to us about what we'd done,' Baz remarks. 'She talked us through our doubts and our weepy moments, and about some of the more vicious stuff that we'd been involved in . . . It was just a quiet chat about the whole mission, with no God stuff thrown in. And it was good; it was what we needed.'

A few weeks after returning to the UK the Corps was asked to send soldiers to attend the Remembrance Day Parade. Baz and Steve volunteered to go. They turned up in their full dress uniform. They marched to the Cenotaph and the oration and wreath-laying was all about the veterans of the First and Second World Wars. In the Royal British Legion club afterwards the speeches began in earnest, and again it was all about the two World Wars.

Baz felt himself shifting uneasily inside his starched uniform: was anyone even going to mention Afghanistan or Iraq?

Finally, in among the speeches about Gill providing the ham for the lunch and Bob's uncle having donated the white wine, there was a brief 'thanks to the lads for turning up in uniform'. Hold on a minute, thought Baz, is that a reference to us?

This was an ideal opportunity for him and Steve to remind those gathered of the continuing sacrifices that have and are being made on the battlefields of Iraq and Afghanistan.

'I got to my feet and politely took the microphone,' Baz remarks.

'I said: "Before we eat this fine spread I'd like to ask you all to be upstanding." The function room had fallen largely silent, and slowly they all stood. "Today there are soldiers all over the country that would love to have attended this and other parades, but unfortunately they can't. They are recovering in Selly Oak Hospital, or being rehabilitated in Hedley Court, after the injuries they have sustained in Iraq or Afghanistan.

'"It is important to honour the sacrifices of our young men and women serving today," Baz continued. '"So please take a glass in hand and join me in toasting our brave and wounded servicemen and women and wish them good health. To the wounded . . ." It was that sort of thing, anyway . . . After saying it Steve and I shook hands, hoping that a statement had been made that would be appreciated and remembered.'

Air Chief Marshal Sir Jock Stirrup would have the following to say when welcoming the Apache Attack Regiments home from their 2007 Afghan operations:

'They have earned their spurs in the heat, dust and fire of combat, in the face of challenging and complex operations and often in the face of great danger . . . You need only ask those on the ground who depended on them, day after day, to provide the crucial edge over the enemy. They will leave you in no doubt about what the Apache achieved.'

It was a fitting tribute to the men of flight *Ugly*, 662 Squadron as a whole, and the entire Corps.

At the end of January 2008, 662 Squadron would be heading to Afghanistan for a further tour of duty. During their flight out of Kandahar, Steve James had come up with the following, slightly altered rendering of Winston Churchill's famous remark about the pilots who fought the Battle of Britain. It was a phrase that had first come to mind after their actions during Op Chakush, but it summed up the deployment as a whole:

'Never in the field of human conflict has so much been fired at so many by so few.'

It was as good a motto as any for their mission in Afghanistan.

Epilogue

Operation Glacier

Lance Corporal Mathew Ford, the Royal Marine rescued from the Jugroom Fort, was pronounced dead on arrival at Camp Bastion. He had been shot and killed instantly in the initial assault, just as the men of the Commando breached the fort walls and advanced to contact with the enemy. He was the only fatality of Operation Glacier: the four other Royal Marines wounded during the assault survived their wounds.

Lance Corporal Ford was the oldest of three brothers brought up in Immingham, Lincolnshire, where his family still live. He had recently moved to Dundee with his fiancée, Ina. Fellow marines described him as a 'gentle giant'. He had joined the Royal Marines in 2001, but at the time of his death had begun to think about leaving the forces to start a family.

His mother Joan said of the loss of her son: 'We are all devastated by the news of Mathew's death. He was a larger-than-life character who lived life to the full. He was a wonderful son to me and a wonderful brother to Thomas and Scott, and he was looking forwards to his future with Ina. His love for life and his ability to make people laugh will always be with us.'

UK Task Force spokesperson Lieutenant Colonel Rory Bruce commented of the rescue mission: 'It was an extraordinary tale of the heroism and bravery of our airmen, soldiers and marines who were all prepared to put themselves back into the line of fire to rescue a fallen comrade.'

Lieutenant-Colonel Rob MaGowan RM, the commander of the Jugroom Fort operation, had the following to say: 'This was a deliberate, pre-planned operation to disrupt the insurgents' freedom of movement in southern Helmand, a vital area for insurgents to equip and move fighters into the centre of the province.'

The Apache pilot who flew his aircraft into the centre of the Jugroom Fort, Captain Tom Owen, received the Distinguished Flying Cross for his actions that day. Co-pilots Staff Sergeant Keith Arthur and Warrant Officer Mark Rawlings were each awarded the Military Cross for their role in leaving the aircraft and joining the rescue effort on the ground. Staff Sergeant Karl Bruce was also awarded the Joint Commander's Commendation for piloting his aircraft that day. Captain Dave Rigg, the commando-trained Royal Engineer who rode the aircraft into the rescue, also received the Military Cross.

Captain Nick Born, the pilot of the Apache providing covering fire during the Jugroom rescue mission, also received a Distinguished Flying Cross for his actions during his tour of Afghanistan. All the above aircrew were from 656 Squadron, Army Air Corps. There was some controversy that the Royal Marines – Warrant Officer Class One Colin Hearn, Marine Gary Robinson and Marine Chris Fraser-Perry – received no decorations for the part they played in the heroic rescue mission at Jugroom Fort.

Operation Kulang

The British solider killed when the US Chinook was shot down over Kajaki Sofle was twenty-eight-year-old Corporal Mike 'Gilly' Gilyeat of the Royal Military Police. Corporal Gilyeat was attached to the Media Operations team based in Kandahar and was filming the insertion of the US 82nd Airborne troops as part of a wider report he was producing on operations around Kajaki. His Canadian colleague, Master Corporal Darrell Priede, aged thirty, was killed alongside him. Corporal Gilyeat had served in Iraq and Northern Ireland and had volunteered for Afghanistan.

'Corporal Gilyeat was a gifted and enthusiastic member of the team, who had made a real difference in theatre,' commented his

Commanding Officer, Lieutenant Colonel Mike Smith. 'In his six weeks he had struck up a close relationship with his fellow photographer, Master Corporal Priede . . . The tragic loss of both of them is something that had been keenly felt by everyone in the team. We miss their infectious enthusiasm, consummate professionalism, and unwavering good humour.'

Rahim Kalay

662 Squadron's Apaches alone cannot take all the credit for the battle for Rahim Kalay. Prior to the flight's arrival over the battlefield, mortar rounds had started to land some seventy-five feet away from the British soldiers' positions. At that stage a *Dude* callsign – a pair of US F-15 fast jets – had checked in with the *Widow* on the ground. They were briefed with coordinates to seek and destroy enemy mortar teams. Within minutes *Dude One Six* had identified three males picking up and repositioning a hot barrel south of the river. He had engaged them with one GBU38 five-hundred-pound bomb, killing two instantly. The third man got away.

To the north of the river, *Dude One Five* had then identified four males hurriedly covering something up approximately ten metres from the grid given by the mortar-locating radar. One male was clearly armed, and all four proceeded to run into the cover of a mud-walled building. *Dude One Five* set up for an attack run and dropped a bomb on that building. It was at this stage of the battle that the Worcesters and Foresters reported having a man down. Attacks from enemy small-arms fire and RPGs had become intense, resulting in the one British soldier killed in action at Rahim Kalay.

That soldier's name was Lance Corporal Paul 'Sandy' Sandford, of 1st Battalion, Worcestershire and Sherwood Foresters. It was around 0645 hours local time when he was shot by small-arms fire. He was casevac'd out of the battlefield but was pronounced dead on arrival at Camp Bastion Field Hospital. Lance Corporal Sandford was twenty-three years old at the time of his death. He was an excellent soldier selected for promotion. He had just celebrated his first wedding anniversary. He had spoken recently to his friends about starting a family.

Major Simon Butt, Officer Commanding B Company, said of his death: 'It is a tragedy to his family and to B Company. Lance Corporal "Sandy" Sandford was enormously popular among the Company and our loss will be keenest felt among his Section and his Platoon, where he stood tall and was full of life. Our thoughts are with his wife Gaynor and his family at this difficult time. All who met him knew him to be a brave and highly professional soldier who had earned the respect of those who fought alongside him.'

Operation Wasir

As a result of lessons learned during Op Wasir, the importance of realistic simulation prior to deployment became clear. The Apache simulators run by Aviation Training International (ATIL) at Wattisham are extremely lifelike and realistic, employing state-of-the-art technologies to recreate the experience of flying, and fighting, an Apache. Each consists of an entirely lifelike mock-up of an Apache cockpit, enclosed by a domed screen onto which 'real life' missions are projected.

With a hydraulic seat that mimics the recoil of the aircraft's weapon firing and video effects modelled on real combat missions, the simulators are a world apart from the average video game. At times, a 'downed' aircrew would emerge from the simulator actually feeling the fear and shock of having been shot down for real. However, the absence of intense battle noise meant that pilots were not used to flying and fighting under such conditions in the field. Upon 662 Squadron's return to the UK, ATIL added battle noise to the simulations for Afghanistan sorties.

Operation Chakush

During Operation Chakush, and the battle for Haydarabad, Guardsman David 'Jaffa' Atherton, of 1st Battalion, Grenadier Guards, was killed. He was serving in the anti-tank section, in 3 Company, and lost his life on the third day of Op Chakush during a fierce firefight around the village of Mirmandab, south-east of Haydarabad. He had just engaged a Taliban position with a Javelin anti-tank missile when he was shot. His actions helped to neutralise the enemy, enabling his company to advance safely.

Guardsman Atherton was twenty-five years old and had already served in Bosnia and Iraq. Lieutenant Colonel Angus Watson, Commanding Officer of the Battle Group, said of his death: 'The tragic death of Guardsman Atherton this morning in Op Chakush has been keenly felt across the battle group. He died as his company was going forwards, bravely taking the fight to a tenacious and determined enemy.'

Captain Rupert King-Evans, his Company Commander, said of him: 'He was an excellent soldier and was someone who could be relied upon, both at home in England and on operations. I am privileged to have known him and my thoughts and those of the entire company go out to his family, especially his girlfriend and young daughter.'

His family said of their son's death: 'David was a professional and dedicated soldier. He loved the Army and it is hard to imagine him doing anything else. A kind, caring, loving father, son, brother and boyfriend, he was considerate, thoughtful and the light of our life, and the world will be a duller place without him.'

On the fourth day of Op Chakush a second British solider was killed in the area of Mirmandab. Sergeant Barry Keen, of 245 Signal Squadron, Royal Corps of Signals, was operating in conjunction with the Afghan National Army forces when a single mortar round hit his position. He was given emergency first aid but his injuries were too severe. Sergeant Keen was thirty-four years old, and had spent eighteen years in the Army, including tours in Bosnia and Northern Ireland.

Lieutenant Dave Phillips, his Troop Commander, said of Sergeant Keen: 'He was the epitome of the Royal Signals Senior Non-Commissioned Officer. An inspiration within the troop, he was widely respected and well liked by all. The soldiers he worked with looked up to him, and would willingly deploy alongside him. As his Troop Commander I relied upon his knowledge and experience on an almost daily basis, and not once did he let me down.'

Staff Sergeant Daz Edge, his friend and colleague, said of Sergeant Keen: 'An excellent team commander and operator, Barry led his team from the front and died carrying out his duty while under fire. The squadron will be so much the less without him, and all those who knew him will undoubtedly feel his loss greatly.'

His family said of their son: 'The devastating news of Barry's death has come as a shock to our family. Our only comfort is that he died doing a job that he loved and that he believed in.'

Since the start of military operations in Afghanistan, in November 2001, there have been over one hundred British military fatalities. The casualty figures in Afghanistan would doubtless be higher were it not for the role that the Apache Attack Regiments have played in providing close air support to the ground troops and escorting in Chinooks on casevac missions to extract wounded soldiers.

The arrival of the Apache Attack Regiments in Afghanistan has had a force multiplier effect on British operations. It has enabled more mobile offensive operations and has provided punch on the battlefield. Lieutenant Colonel Jon Bryant, the CO of 3 Regiment, Army Air Corps, had the following to say about the Squadron's summer 2007 deployment:

'The Apache played a key role in the offensive operations of the summer of 2007. Plus I believe it saved lives because there were fewer casualties from those offensive operations than there would have been without Apache support. It is a machine designed to kill people in the most efficient way possible, but the irony is it saved lives. As well as killing the enemy, the aircraft itself acted as a significant deterrent. It lived up to my expectations in theatre one hundred per cent, but it is only ever as effective as the aircrew who fly it.'

At the time of writing, any honours that may accrue to 662 Squadron for its summer 2007 deployment to Afghanistan have yet to be announced.

Author's Endnote

Many people have been curious as to how this book came about.

In 2006 I published a book called *Bloody Heroes*, which tells the true story of a small unit of British (and American) Special Forces soldiers on operations in Afghanistan. After several dramatic missions in the mountains and wildlands of the country, the unit of soldiers ended up in the ancient, mud-walled fortress at Qala Janghi, putting down an uprising by six hundred battle-hardened Taliban and al-Qaeda fighters. Eight days of extreme combat, tragedy and heroics ensued.

Bloody Heroes was read by several of the pilots of the British Apache Attack Squadrons. Recognising in themselves some of the same, maverick daring they felt a strong connection to the stories told. I was subsequently approached by Steve, the rear-seater of *Ugly Five One*. Having read *Bloody Heroes* he felt that the Apache pilots of the Corps had a similar story to tell. Steve asked me whether I would like to write the story of their first combat operations in Afghanistan.

I was invited up to their Wattisham base and persuaded to spend an hour in the Apache flight simulator. Once I had done so I realised what an incredibly challenging aircraft this was to fly and fight, and how doing so was an unrivalled experience of man meshed into machine. With the 30mm cannon locked to one's eye line, this was the closest one could get to being a cyborg, I reckoned. And that was where the book was born.

With the backing of the Army Air Corps, interviews with pilots followed, although most were epic sessions in the bar of the local hotel where war stories could be facilitated by a few pints of excellent ale. From first approach to final manuscript took a lightning five months, during which time I lived, breathed, ate and slept the British Apache Attack Regiment's story. I was blessed with fantastic teamwork from the Apache pilots featured in this book, who read and commented on successive drafts of the manuscript in double-quick time, even as they were back in Afghanistan doing a second, or third, tour of operations, and once again taking the fight to the enemy in the skies over Afghanistan. As such it was a team effort, from the first word to the final draft.

Glossary

2RTR – 2nd Royal Tank Regiment

AAA – heavy-calibre anti-aircraft artillery

AAC – Army Air Corps

ALPC – Arming Loading Point Commander

Avtur – aviation turbine fuel

BFBS – British Forces Broadcasting Services

bone – slang for boring and uneventful

BRF – Brigade Recce Force, a highly mobile group of elite soldiers trained to operate behind enemy lines

casevac – casualty evacuation

chin-strapped – slang for exhausted

cook off – Army slang for ammunition combusting due to extreme heat or sun

EF – enemy forces

FIBUA – fighting in built-up areas, strategies for urban combat

FLIR – forward-looking infrared, a target acquisition system that detects a target by its heat emissions

GPMG – general purpose machine gun, a 7.62mm belt-fed weapon that is a mainstay of British forces

HEAT – high-explosive anti-tank, an armour-piercing round or warhead

HEISAP – high-explosive incendiary semi-armour piercing, a 2.7 inch rocket used by Apache attack helicopters

HLS – helicopter landing site

HQ – headquarters

IAT – image auto tracker, an automatic system on Apaches that isolates a target and tracks it regardless of movement by the aircraft or the target

IED – improvised explosive device, most commonly a remotely detonated roadside bomb

ISAF – International Security Assistance Force, the NATO-led forty-strong coalition of countries providing troops in Afghanistan

JHF – Joint Helicopter Force, the tri-service command HQ for helicopters in Afghanistan

JHF (A) Fwd – Joint Helicopter Force Afghanistan Forward, the helicopter operational headquarters in Camp Bastion

HEISAP – high-explosive incendiary semi-armour piercing: a 2.7 inch rocket variant

JTAC – Joint Terminal Attack Commander, a soldier on the ground responsible for calling in air strikes

KAF – Kandahar Airfield

KIA – killed in action

LAW – light anti-tank weapon, a recoil-less rifle used by British, US and Allied forces

LRDG – Long Range Desert Group

LZ – landing zone

MOD – Ministry of Defence

MOG – Mobile Operations Group, Danish military mobile ground forces

NOE – nap-of-the-earth, a technique for flying at a very low level, hugging the contours

NVG – night vision goggles, equipment that enables a soldier to see in the dark

OC – Officer Commanding

PNVS – pilot night vision sensor, the Apache's nigh vision equipment that allows the aircraft to fly and fight in the dark

RC-South – Regional Command – South

RES – a real emotional shit: relieving oneself in a less than relaxing environment

RIP – relief in place, one aircraft relieving another over the battle-field

R & R – rest and recuperation

ROZ – restricted operating zone, an area of airspace generally over a battlefield where flight is restricted

RTU'd – returned to unit; a soldier being sent back from theatre to his parent unit in the UK

SA-7 – a Soviet-designed, shoulder-launched heat-seeking surface-to-air missile

SAM – surface-to-air missile

sitrep – a situation report

TA – Territorial Army, Britain's Army reservists

TADS – target acquisition and designation system, the Apache's targeting apparatus

TIC – troops in contact

UAV – unmanned aerial vehicle, a pilotless aircraft used for surveillance over the battlefield, sometimes armed

VBIED – vehicle-borne improvised explosive device, a mobile or stationary car bomb

VATPV – Viking All-Terrain Protected Vehicle, a tracked armoured vehicle used by British and allied forces

WLR – weapons-locating radar, a portable system carried by troops to identify enemy firing points

WMIK – weapons-mounted installation kit, a weapons configuration for the Land Rover

WTOC – Widow Tactical Operations Centre, a ground-based central command element for close air support

Roll of Honour, May–August 2007, Afghanistan

Guardsman Simon Davison: 1st Battalion Grenadier Guards

Lance Corporal George Russel Davey: 1st Battalion The Royal Anglian Regiment

Guardsman Daniel Probyn: 1st Battalion Grenadier Guards

Corporal Bonner: 1st Battalion The Royal Anglian Regiment

Corporal Mike Gilyeat: Royal Military Police

Corporal Paul 'Sandy' Sandford: 1st Battalion Worcestershire and Sherwood Foresters

Guardsman Neil 'Tony' Downes: 1st Battalion Grenadier Guards

Drummer Thomas Wright: 1st Battalion Worcestershire and Sherwood Foresters

Captain Sean Dolan: 1st Battalion Worcestershire and Sherwood Foresters

Sergeant Dave 'Pidge' Wilkinson: 19th Regiment Royal Artillery attached to the Grenadier Guards

Guardsman Daryl Hickey: The Queen's Company

Westfield Memorial Library
Westfield, New Jersey

Lance Corporal Alex Hawkins: 1st Battalion The Royal Anglian Regiment

Guardsman David Atherton: 1st Battalion Grenadier Guards

Sergeant Barry Keen: 245 Signal Squadron Corps of Royal Signals

Lance Corporal Michael Jones: Royal Marines

Private Tony Rawson: 1st Battalion The Royal Anglian Regiment

Captain David Hicks: 1st Battalion The Royal Anglian Regiment

Westfield Memorial Library
Westfield, New Jersey

662 Squadron, AAC: Munitions Fired, May–August 2007

As a squadron during the tour
18,500 30mm
550 rockets
72 Hellfire
34 flares in anger

Ugly Five Zero
2450 30mm
128 rockets
17 Hellfire

Ugly Five One
2536 30mm
137 rockets
15 Hellfire

Westfield Memorial Library
Westfield, New Jersey